Ancient History

2nd Edition

Michael Cheilik, Ph.D.

Anthony Inguanzo

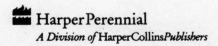
HarperPerennial
A Division of HarperCollins*Publishers*

An American BookWorks Corporation Production
Project Manager: Jonathon E. Brodman
Editor: Norman Neuerburg, Ph.D.

Library of Congress Cataloging-in-Publication Data

Cheilik, Michael.
   Ancient history / Michael Cheilik, Anthony Inguanzo. — 2nd ed.
     p.   cm.
   Includes bibliographical references and index.
   ISBN 0-06-467119-4 (pbk.)
    1. History, Ancient—Outlines, syllabi, etc.   I. Inguanzo,
Anthony.   II. Title
D59,C47   1991
930—dc20   90-56012

91 92 93 94 95 ABW/RRD 10 9 8 7 6 5 4 3 2 1

Contents

Preface vii

1 Prehistoric Man 1

2 Early Civilizations of Mesopotamia 10

3 Early Civilization in Egypt 21

4 Changing Dominions in the Near East 31

5 The Minoan and Mycenaean World 50

6 The Rise and Expansion of Hellenic Civilization 58

7 Greece in the Fifth Century B.C. 81

8 The Greek World in the Fourth Century B.C. 106

9 The Conquests of Alexander and the Hellenistic Period 120

10 The Emergence and Expansion of the Roman Republic 139

11 Stresses on the Roman Republic 165

12 The Final Stage of the Roman Republic 176

13 The Principate and the Early Empire 192

14 The Height of Roman Expansion 205

15 The Beginning of the Empire's Dissolution 218

16 Reconstruction and Fall of the Empire 227

Index 241

Preface

Civilization began in a number of places, including the river valleys of Egypt, Mesopotamia, India, and China, as well as regions in the New World. Because of limitations on the size of this work, only the ancient Near Eastern and Classical societies will be considered here in detail. The civilizations of Greece and Rome were the direct ancestors of most modern European and American cultures. The kernel of civilization, developed in the Near East and cultivated in the Greek and Roman world, was transmitted to western Europe at the beginning of the Middle Ages and survived despite the ravages of barbarian invasions and the contracting medieval world.

In the study of archaeology and history, time has a relative, not an absolute basis. Thus, in the early phases of the study of man (prehistory), thousands of years are a relatively short period, since cultural status changed slowly. However, with the growing role of invention in the development of civilization, the margin of allowable error in setting dates is necessarily reduced to hundreds of years. With the advent of written records, the study of man is called *history*, and dates must be established that are accurate to within decades. To do so is not always easy.

Until recently, it was extremely difficult to get even an approximate date for prehistoric sites, and earlier texts differ wildly as to relative chronology. The earliest archaeologists dug for artifacts (objects made and used by men) and ignored other aspects of a site. By the beginning of this century, excavation had become a science. The habitations of early men, such as caves, were now recognized to contain layer upon layer of refuse, each smoothed over and tamped down to make room for a new generation. A knowledge of the growing strata of a site was thus achieved, as remains and artifacts of the various layers of earth were placed in a chronological sequence relative to other sites. However, there was as yet little basis for a chronology of prehistoric periods. This was partially acheived by the carbon-14 test. Every living plant or animal absorbs radioactive carbon-14. When the organism dies, this process ceases and the radioactivity begins to disintegrate. With the aid of a variety of instruments, the age of traces of wood, plant life, and bone can be calculated approximately, but only within the last fifty thousand years or so. For earlier dates, the latest geological scholarship is necessary, while, for historical periods, written documents generally prove more accurate. Since even the dates reached by use of carbon-14 are approximate, this book generally makes use of that chronology that has been most widely accepted. The earliest date used in this book for manlike beings is that of Professor Louis B. Leakey in his investigations in Olduvai Gorge in Africa. The later Stone Age and Chalcolithic dates used are those of Professor James Mellart. Dates for pre-Roman rulers refer to their reigns, since their birth dates are uncertain. Dates for Roman emperors are those of birth and death unless otherwise specified. Until the discussion on Greece and Rome, most emphasis in this volume will be placed on the Nile Valley, Tigris-Euphrates, and eastern Mediterranean regions where Western man first settled. The chronology used in this connection refers only to the Near East, for the later Stone Age periods arrived much more slowly in Europe. The farther to the north or west an area lay, the more primitive its state of civilization.

1

Prehistoric Man

2,000,000 B.C.	Most primitive manlike apes—Australopithecines
750,000	Earliest apelike man—Pithecanthropus erectus
500,000–10,000	Paleolithic Age (Old Stone Age)
100,000–50,000	Neanderthal man (Homo sapiens neanderthalensis)
30,000–10,000	Appearance of modern man (Homo sapiens)—Cro-Magnon man
10,000–7000	Mesolithic Age (Middle Stone Age)
8000	Natufians—beginnings of agriculture
7000–6500	"Neolithic Revolution"—beginnings of settled life
5600–3500	Chalcolithic Period (Copper–Stone Age)—first metalwork
4250–3750	Sumerian Al-Ubaid culture—well-developed urban life

Ancient history is traditionally considered to begin with the invention of writing and the consequent recording of events. But many ages preceded this development. The tenure on earth of manlike apes goes back perhaps several million years, that of modern man tens of millennia. The cultures of the Paleolithic (Old Stone) Age, ca. 500,000–10,000 B.C., were characterized by a nomadic way of life and the use of chipped tools. (The Lower Paleolithic or earliest Old Stone Age strata have been given an arbitrary beginning at 500,000 B.C., but as will be seen even the most primitive man-like ape [ca. 2,000,000 B.C.] made some use of tolls.) During the Mesolithic (Middle Stone) Age, ca. 10,000 B.C.–7000 B.C., tools were improved and the dog was domesticated. In the Neolithic (New Stone) Age, ca. 7000–ca. 5600 B.C., a revolution took place that brought about the introduction of agriculture and the start of community life. The Chalcolithic (Copper-Stone) phase of cultural development occurred in the Near East about 5600 to 3500 B.C., when copper was first worked. The Bronze Age began about 3500 B.C., when tools were made of bronze—an alloy of copper and tin. This is the period of the first great Mesopotamian cities.

THE EVOLUTION OF MAN

About two million years ago, the earth was a very different place from what it is today. At that time, glaciers covered much of northern Europe and the area that is now the Sahara Desert was a region of abundant rainfall. In zoological terms, this was the Age of Mammals. Of the various groups of these animals, one of the primate order was destined to evolve into man. Primates had the great advantages of having developed very flexible digits and binocular vision, giving a continuous stereoscopic view instead of a separate field for each eye. The highest family of primates was the ape. It has recently been discovered that manlike apes *(Australopithecines)* had evolved in Africa about two million years ago. They made use of stones in a tool-like way and are to be distinguished from apelike men, whose remains date from about 750,000 to 200,000 B.C. The first men (species *Pithecanthropus erectus*) were different from their ancestors and cousins in having an erect, not stooped, posture and a completely opposable thumb. They were thus able to make tools and build fires.

THE FIRST MODERN MEN

The Pleistocene was characterized by periods of glaciation followed by periods of relative warmth. It is thought that, during the so-called Riss-Wurm interglacial period (100,000–50,000 B.C.), a highly developed type of man appeared. His form was not quite that of modern man, and his brow was beetling, but his brain capacity was about the same. He has been called *Homo neanderthalensis* by those who distinguish him from modern man and *Homo sapiens (neanderthalensis)* by many scholars who believe him to be only an extinct subspecies of modern man.

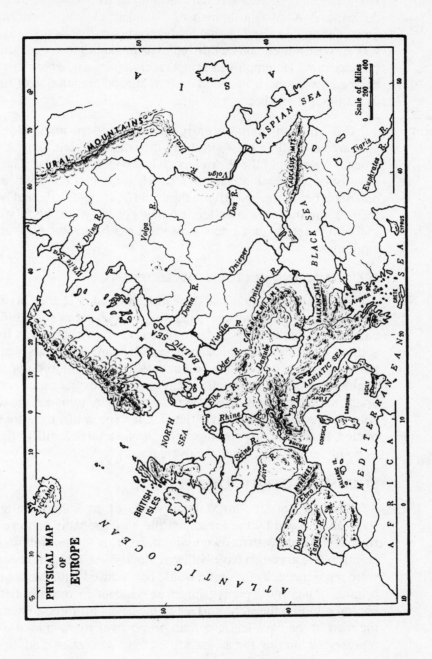

PHYSICAL MAP
OF
EUROPE

Neanderthal Man

The habitat of Neanderthal man ranged over Europe, the Middle East, Africa, and Asia. One branch of Neanderthal man developed a culture, known as the Mousterian, much advanced over that of his predecessors. He was a cave dweller, and he utilized tools to much greater advantage than did his ancestors. He employed scrapers, choppers, and spear tips of skillfully chipped flint, bone, or wood in the hunting and preparation of such big game as mammoths and bears.

Cro-Magnon Man

Cro-Magnon man, an early race of modern man *(Homo sapiens)*, appeared sometime between thirty thousand and ten thousand years ago, when the glacier of the Wurm epoch had begun to retreat. The most highly developed cultural phase of Cro-Magnon man, known as the Magdalenian, began around fifteen thousand years ago. Life had become more refined for the cave dwellers of this epoch. More sophisticated tools, including such diverse items as needles and harpoons, were added to their equipment.

ECONOMIC AND CULTURAL DEVELOPMENT

Up to this point, man had done little to mold or change his environment; bare survival was his all-encompassing concern. However, during the Magdalenian period, there is evidence of temporary shelters away from caves, as well as of a beginning of labor specialization. It appears that the women gathered food while the men hunted. What is even more remarkable is the beginning of art. On the walls of caves at Lascaux in France and Altamira in Spain, superb paintings have been found. Bison, reindeer, ibexes, and other animals are portrayed in vivid detail. On some walls, they are shown being hunted. In addition to paintings, sculptured female "fertility" figures, as well as bodily ornaments, were discovered.

BEGINNINGS OF RELIGION

Some, if not all, Cro-Magnon works of art indicate religious beliefs. Early man, awed by the forces around him, probably endowed every tree, rock, and stream with its own living spirit. This form of religion is known as animism. He may also have believed that if a desirable and necessary object were reproduced, its facsimile would be endowed with the same spirit as the original. Thus by depicting bison or reindeer in realistic detail, utilizing natural relief on the stone surface of the caves for three-dimensional effect, the man in the cave had a certain power over these animals. If men were represented hunting the animals, the effect was intensified. Some scholars, however, think that the paintings are narrative rather than religious representations. The female fertility ("Venus") figures are thought by many anthropologists to have been religious statues through whose magic fertility for the next generation was guaranteed.

MESOLITHIC MAN

All of the modern races of man were in existence during the Mesolithic period, lasting roughly from 10,000 to 7000 B.C. At this time, life changed radically, for the ice cap from the last glaciation withdrew to more or less its present Arctic position, resulting in a much warmer climate in the present temperate regions. Game, once extremely plentiful, was reduced in number, and if man were to survive he would have to adapt himself to his new environment of spreading forests. Tools were now more finely executed, and woodworking became common. Many scholars put the beginnings of animal domestication and primitive agriculture in this period.

Wild grasses such as wheat and barley grew in abundance in the fertile areas of the Near East. In addition to his hunting activities, man supplemented his diet by gathering these grains, but he suffered from droughts. The Palestinian Natufians (ca. 8000 B.C.), who lived in caves around Mount Carmel, appear to have been a link between the primitive past and sedentary life. They built outlying huts, perhaps for easy access to the game that they hunted and the wild grasses that they harvested. It is believed that women, who took charge of gathering food, first stuck blades of grass, then seeds, in the ground, hoping to reproduce the plants. Thus planting was discovered, and eventually utilized for security from the vagaries of nature. The dog, a former scavenger of cave sites, was domesticated and used as an aid in hunting.

THE NEOLITHIC REVOLUTION

A new age dawned when man truly settled down, domesticated animals, and planted crops regularly. In the Near East, this "Neolithic Revolution" appears to have taken place between 7000 and 6500 B.C.

Economic and Social Change

Implements used by man in his various activities, instead of being chipped, were now highly polished. It is thought that the goat, which lives off wild grass, was the first farm animal tamed, followed by sheep and pigs. Last were cattle, which take more care. Men no longer lived in communal caves or scattered huts, but in organized communities, numbering at first approximately one to two hundred inhabitants, then rising to about a thousand. Woolen garments were woven, replacing clothing made of skins.

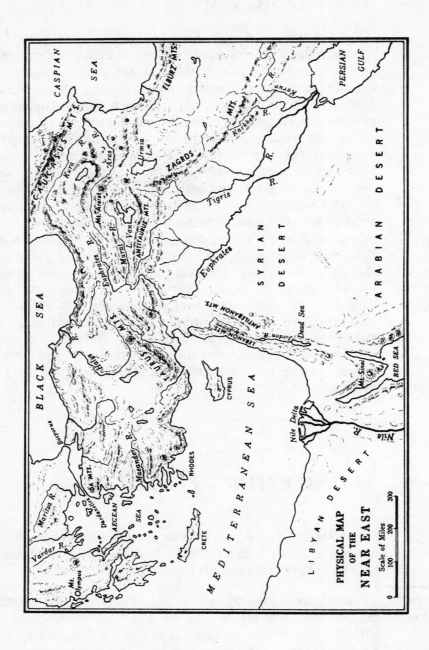

PHYSICAL MAP
OF THE
NEAR EAST

Scale of Miles

0   100   200   300

In addition, there is evidence of early trade in obsidian, a vitreous volcanic substance ideal for tools. This early stage and subsequent development of civilization can be seen clearly in the lower strata of such sites as Jarmo in northern Mesopotamia and Jericho in Palestine.

Pottery

It seems that baskets and wooden, as well as stone, vessels had been invented before the sixth millennium B.C. Clay, a very plentiful plastic substance, was probably first used in its sun-dried state for carrying dry objects. Perhaps, as is often imagined, in a fit of pique a Neolithic woman hurled such a vessel onto the fire, and its accidental baking thus resulted. Henceforth pottery became a hallmark of civilization, for it can be broken, but not destroyed. In the strata of debris for different periods, potsherds decorated in a variety of ways have been found—another aid in establishing relative chronology. At first baked pottery was buffed to a shining surface decorated with incised designs. Later vessels were often covered with painted designs. An important site of this period is Hassuna in northern Mesopotamia.

THE CHALCOLITHIC PERIOD

Beginning with the fifth millennium B.C., copper was used for tools. It was utilized only sporadically, by no means supplanting stone. Thus the period (ca. 5600–3500 B.C.) received its name (Greek *chalcos,* "copper," + *lithos,* "stone").

Economic and Social Development

During the Chalcolithic period, there appears to have been a great population increase, and Chalcolithic cultures flourished. Notable centers were the Halafian settlements (ca. 5000 B.C. in the Tigris-Euphrates region) and Hacilar in Asia Minor (beginning about 5500 B.C.) Following the domestication of draft animals, the wheeled vehicle was invented, and transportation over long distances became possible. A higher stage of development was achieved in southern Mesopotamia at Al-Ubaid (ca. 4250–3750 B.C.), where temples were included in the architectural complexes of towns.

Religion

As man began to settle down, and society became complex, simple animism and fertility cults developed into a higher form of religion. To Chalcolithic man, the forces of the universe were no longer undefined, but had become quite personal. This stage of intellectual development, known as *mythopoeic* (myth-making), persisted for many centuries in the ancient Near East. Indeed, it was supplanted by philosophical and scientific speculation only in Greece, and there only among the intellectual elite. Since all of the mythological forces were personal, they behaved like people—eating, sleeping, loving, and hating. Cycles of stories, taken as fact, grew up explaining all natural phenomena. For example, to early man the sun—be it called Re, Shamash, or Utu—was a living being, and so were the earth, the seas, and even the air.

At first, it appears, the elders of a village served as priests, but as time went on and religious needs became more specialized, a priestly class grew up. Temples were built where the gods resided and could be reached—at least in some of their aspects. In areas where nature was unpredictable, the priests, because of their supposed status as intermediaries between man and the gods, became the most powerful element in society.

COMMUNICATION

It is apparent from the behavior of animals that a measure of communication is achieved by mere sounds. Precisely when sounds were first shaped into coherent languages is not known, but this more advanced sort of communication must have been present in some form in the latter Paleolithic period. Early languages lack the elements of abstraction, so that their relative vocabularies are larger and more specific than those of modern tongues. There might be words for *bison, reindeer,* and *mammoths,* but no word for the concept *animal.* Also there might be words for *small reindeer, female reindeer,* and *strong reindeer,* but there would be no term abstracting the concept of *reindeer* as such. According to some scholars, early words might have had a mimetic quality. It appears that nouns were the first words; when verbs were created, the forming of sentences was achieved.

In order to communicate with a person who was not present, some forerunner of writing evolved. Wall paintings of the Paleolithic period may have served this as well as other functions. The development of picture communication into writing belongs to the historical age.

The primitive Stone Age settlements eventually developed into the first urban centers. Man was on the threshold of a whole new way of life.

Selected Readings

Braidwood, R. J. *Prehistoric Men* (1963)
Clark, G. *The Stone Age Hunters* (1967)
Coon, C. S. *The Races of Europe* (1939)
Glyn, Daniel. *The Idea of Prehistory* (1964)
Levy, G. R. *Religious Conceptions of the Stone Age and Their Influence upon European Thought* (1963)
Streuver, S. (ed.). *Prehistoric Agriculture* (1971)
Von Koenigswald, G. H. R. *Meeting Prehistoric Man* (1956)
Wenke, R. J. *Patterns in Prehistory* (1980)

2

Early Civilizations of Mesopotamia

7000–5600 B.C.	Neolithic Age (New Stone Age) begins in Near East
7000–6500	Neolithic Revolution—beginnings of settled life
5600–3500	Chalcolithic Period (Copper-Stone Age)—first metalwork
4250–3750	Sumerian Al-Ubaid culture—well-developed urban life
3500–1300	Bronze Age
3500	Sumerians arrive in Mesopotamia
3500	Beginning of pictogram writing
3200	Beginning of ideogram writing
3200–3100	Beginning of phonogram writing (syllables)
2800	Rise of kingship in Sumer
2750–2650	Royal Burials at Ur
2700	Kingship becomes hereditary in Sumer
2300	Akkadian dominance—Sargon I
2150	Revival of Sumer under Third Dynasty of Ur (Ur-Nammu)
2000	Invasion of Amorites and Elamites—end of Sumerian rule
1800	Hammurabi king of Babylonians—law code
1600	Kassites destroy Babylon

Civilization began in two Near Eastern regions, in the Fertile Crescent and in the Nile Valley. When people had settled down in communities and begun to develop complex societies based mainly on agriculture, it was in those areas that they found the richest soil. At an early date, the Sumerians migrated to the southern part of Mesopotamia, laying the basis for much of the future civilization of the Near East. Their city-states were conquered by the Ak-kadians, but then revived. The history of this area was one of continual migrations and invasions, with the newcomers first seeming to destroy, but actually absorbing and adding to, the kernel of Sumerian civilization. (The Nile Valley civilization will be discussed in the next chapter.)

THE GEOGRAPHY OF THE FERTILE CRESCENT

The Fertile Crescent—the traditional term for the area bounded by the Mediterranean to the west, the Arabian Desert to the south, the Taurus Mountains to the north, and the Zagros Mountains to the east—is the focus of the Near East. In ancient times, the lands around the Mediterranean, especially those between the Tigris and Euphrates rivers, were extremely fertile. If a semiagricultural people sought new lands, the river valleys provided them with near-ideal conditions. The Greeks called this region the "Land between the Rivers," or Mesopotamia (*mesos,* "between," + *potamos,* "river").

The Tigris and Euphrates rivers flooded annually, leaving a layer of fertile silt washed down from the uplands. This provided a constant reenrichment of the soil. However, there were several obstacles to easy agriculture in Mesopotamia. The flooding times were unpredictable and varied in nature. If a community was established, it might survive several years, but then be obliterated by an unforeseen, large flood accompanied by violent storms. There was another problem in the most fertile areas. After flood the lands were marshy and, if they were to be utilized to advantage, they had to be drained. On the other hand, the area was desiccated during the summer droughts and some form of irrigation was essential for successful agriculture. This knowledge was grasped by the early inhabitants of Sumer, in the southernmost part of the valley, and those of Akkad farther to the north. Their canals and reservoirs were the source of wealth to the region until they were destroyed by the Turks in modern times.

MESOPOTAMIA
SHOWING MOST IMPORTANT CITIES
CONSTRUCTED BY THE SUMERIANS,
THE BABYLONIANS, THE ASSYRIANS,
AND THE PERSIANS
Scale of Miles
0   100   200   300

THE ADVENT OF THE SUMERIANS

The location of the Tigris-Euphrates Valley exposed it to continual invasions. One group of immigrants from the mountains to the east, perhaps from Elam, were known as the Sumerians. They possessed elements of civilization, and they arrived in a land not wholly uncivilized, for goodly-sized Chalcolithic settlements were already present at such sites as Al-Ubaid and Warka (Uruk, Erech). The advent of the Sumerians has been put at about 3500 B.C. and the beginning of their civilization at about 3200 B.C.

The Development of Writing

Writing was evidently invented by the early Sumerians. Yet, as was the case with the discovery of copper, so with writing: it took several hundred years for the innovation to make a profound impact on civilization.

The first stage (ca. 3500 B.C.) in the written word was a stylized picture of an object, known as the *pictogram*. As a form of communication, pictograms had the disadvantage of slow execution and were limited in what they could represent. In order to add verbs to the repertoire of written communication, symbols were devised indicating action (for example, a recumbent man for the concept, "to sleep"). These characters (invented ca. 3200 B.C.) are called *ideograms*.

The range of human communication was by no means complete with these forms of writing since they could not represent a large repertoire of abstract ideas. For example, it would be very difficult to render the concept, *belief,* with pictograms, or even ideograms. The clever method of utilizing homonyms for such purposes was eventually discovered. This might best be illustrated by a hypothetical example from the English language. In the repertoire of pictograms, there would surely be characters representing a bee and a leaf. If English had no alphabet and the abstract concept, *belief,* were to be committed to writing, the two pictograms, *bee* and *leaf*, would be combined. The resulting sound would represent the abstract word. After losing its original connection with fauna or flora, these two characters have only a sound value. Characters used in this type of writing (ca. 3200–3100 B.C.) are known as *phonograms*. With the simplification of symbols for speed and convenience, they were developed into a syllabary. The Sumerians utilized syllables impressed by wedge-shaped styli on clay tablets, subsequently baked. This form of writing was known as *cuneiform* (from Latin, *cuneus,* "wedge") script.

Social and Economic Life

The early settlements in the Tigris-Euphrates Valley were built of sun-dried brick, since stone was very scarce in the region. The Sumerians adopted this means of construction and built an extensive system of canals for drainage and irrigation. Within a relatively short time, a series of Sumerian city-states had begun to spread out along the valley at such sites as Ur, Uruk, and Jemdet-Nasr, with populations numbering in the tens of thousands. Each of the cities was independent and protected by a moat and a wall. The population consisted of farmers who worked the fields surrounding each city and artisans such as carpenters and potters. In addition, there appears to have been a well-developed priestly class who controlled the state. Since money was nonexistent, a system of barter between farmers and craftsmen evolved.

THE FIRST HIGH POINT OF SUMERIAN CIVILIZATION

As the population increased, so did the size and number of city-states in the lower Tigris-Euphrates Valley. The Sumerians not only developed the religious and cultural bases for future civilizations, but also continued the advances in technology that had begun in the Neolithic period. The wheel, now fully utilized, was a solid, clumsy affair but convenient for the transport of goods on Sumerian roads. By the middle of the third millennium, wheeled chariots drawn by onagers (wild asses) were used in warfare. Early in the third millennium, it was discovered that, by smelting copper and tin, bronze—a metal harder and more durable than either—was created.

Among the important cities during the Sumerians' rise to greatness were Ur, Uruk, Larsa, Eridu, and Kish. Population estimates of each city range from about 15,000 to 25,000, although the latter figure is probably a bit high. Beginning about 2800 B.C., highly developed monarchies grew up in the major Sumerian city-states.

Government of the City-State

The character of the river-valley civilizations was determined by the Sumerian cities. Since the area was open and always subject to invasions, the basic form of government remained the city-state. Empires grew and fell, but the region's strength lay in its urban units. According to many scholars, at first there was little class distinction among the citizens. To be sure, there was a variety of economic functions among the inhabitants, but there is little indication of aristocracy or monarchy before 2800 B.C. It seems to some scholars that all citizens met in an assembly to select a leader. Slavery began at a very early period, as it occurred to conquerors that killing one's adversaries was wasteful. Why not take them alive and use their labor? But the number of slaves was quite small.

THE RELIGIOUS BASIS OF GOVERNMENT

Mesopotamia's unpredictable climate imbued its inhabitants with many apprehensions and fears. Hence, the world-view of the Sumerians took on an extremely religious cast. Indeed, the real world was in every detail regarded as only an imperfect copy of the primal cosmos. Consequently, everything that existed on earth was thought to have its divine prototype. Each city-state had its heavenly original. Every urban institution was already present at the time of creation and the early assembly of citizens reflected the gathering of the gods. As time went on and institutions developed, they, too, were assigned divine origins. This process was quite easy, for every city-state was in theory the private property of a god who ruled it as he saw fit.

THE ORIGIN OF KINGSHIP

The early, undifferentiated citizen body was soon put under a highly centralized form of government. Because the religious aspect of life was essential, the priests of the god of a given city were its most important body. Their claim to supreme power appeared quite logical to most Sumerians: since the god owned all of the lands of a city-state, and the priests were intermediaries between the gods and men, the priests were in charge of all lands. (Later, private property "rented" from the god became an important institution.) Thus, in many Sumerian cities, the religious leaders made all major decisions concerning agriculture, trade, and war. The temples were the chief storehouses and centers of writing. Toward the middle of the third millennium, the conditions of peace and war required firm leadership. The cities were often at war with one another, and there was a continuous threat of invasions. Thus kingship arose in the major Sumerian cities. Characteristically, its origin was attributed to the gods, for if a god possessed a city, he could pick his representative to rule it. The line of demarcation between a priest-ruler (sometimes called *patesi* and more often *ensi* or *en*) and a divinely appointed king-priest *(lugal)* is far from clear. As the representative of the god on earth, the king had the major religious position in the state, and there was potential conflict between him and the priest. Still, the emphasis of priest rule was likely religious and domestic, while that of the king tended more toward the secular with an emphasis on war. Kingship probably originated as a temporary expedient at times of emergency, with the king elected by the assembly. But by 2700 B.C. it had become an hereditary institution.

Social and Economic Life in the City-States

With the advent of kingship, a noble class of royal assistants also came into being. Their life centered on the palace, which, together with the temple, formed the major architectural complex in a city. The houses of rich and poor alike were made of sun-dried brick which, because of its low resistance to water, had to be frequently replaced. With the increase of trade there arose a commercial class, who formed a middle group between the exalted nobility and the mass of the population. Trade became widespread, for the Sumerian cities were far from self-sufficient. Stones, metals, and other minerals were imported from the mountains of the east or from Egypt. In exchange, the cities sent grain to the east and finished products westward.

Cultural Development

Works of art were highly developed at this time, as the treasures from the Royal Burials at Ur (2750–2650 B.C.) attest. The characteristic cylinder seals, used to roll out identifying devices, had a widespread vogue and have been found also in Egyptian tombs.

A class of scribes took charge of records, imprinting on rectilinear tablets documents, letters, and laws in cuneiform script. Confidential documents were put in envelopes of clay fastened with a seal. To ensure permanence, tablets and envelopes were baked. Laws were established to provide for the smooth running of the community, and it appears that people within each class were judged in the same way,

The Dominance of Lagash

Conquest of many regions of Mesopotamia seems to have been accomplished by the city of Kish, but its hegemony was quite temporary. By the middle of the third millennium, the city-state of Lagash had succeeded in conquering its surrounding areas. Under the enlightened rule of King Urukagina, who reformed the state from within, Lagash reached its zenith. But neighboring Umma, under Lugalzaggesi, much of whose territory Lagash had invaded, put an end to its rival's hegemony.

THE AKKADIAN INTERLUDE

A Semitic people inhabited the portion adjoining Sumer to the north, known as Akkad. They participated in the developments of early Mesopotamian civilization, and by the last third of the third millennium, they were in a position to conquer the entire valley.

The Akkadian king, Sargon (Sharru-kin) I, who lived about 2300 B.C., was the first great imperialist of the Near East. (Legends of his great deeds became so deeply engrained that, about fifteen hundred years later, an Assyrian conqueror named himself Sargon II.) Sargon defeated Lugalzaggesi and took over total control of Sumer. The basic form of the city-state was retained, but policy was directed by the Akkadian king through troops and representatives in the conquered areas. The Akkadians wrote their Semitic tongue in the cuneiform characters of Sumer. The high-point of the Akkadian Empire was reached under the grandson of Sargon, Naram-sin, but as was often the case in Mesopotamia, an invasion, this time of the Guti from the east, broke up the empire.

THE HEIGHT OF SUMERIAN CIVILIZATION

Lagash had remained an important commercial city under the Guti, and under the *ensi,* Gudea (ca. 2100 B.C.), it recovered some of its high position, However, the dominant city-state of the period was Ur. Under Ur-Nammu, the Third Dynasty of the city was founded (ca. 2150 B.C.) and the Guti were defeated. Ur-Nammu's successor, Shulgi, was able to establish hegemony over much of the Mesopotamian region, ruling an empire with an efficiently organized administration and a standard law code. Time was running out for the Sumerians, however, and by 2000 B.C. new invaders, the Semitic Amorites from the west and the Elamites from the east, destroyed the Third Dynasty of Ur. They also took over the corpus of Sumero-Akkadian culture. Cuneiform writing lasted in some places into the modern era, but the Sumerian language, like Latin during the Middle Ages, became a dead, literary and religious tongue.

Sumerian Religion

As noted previously, the Sumerians conceived of the universe as a complete body created at the beginning of time. Everything, including the gods and their instiutions, had its place and order. Myths, by means of which reality was explained, were codified and standardized from stories and legends of an early period. An was the supreme god of the universe, the sky divinity who presided over the Council of the Gods. His son, Enlil, was lord of the air, storms, and floods. Because of his control of those natural phenomena that the Sumerians feared but also needed, Enlil became the most powerful god and acquired the status of lord of war. Natural forces were also represented by Ninhursag, goddess of earth; Enki, god of water; and Inanna (the Semitic Ishtar), goddess of love. Some of these gods ruled cities as their private property. For example, Enlil controlled Nippur (the most important religious center, even during the supremacy of Ur), and Inanna possessed Uruk. Since man was created by the gods to serve them, and he and his civilization were regarded as imperfect copies of heavenly prototypes, there was little feeling of joy or optimism. At a moment's notice, Enlil might destroy an entire city with his flood. Indeed, one flood in the early history of Mesopotamia was so traumatic that it became the prototype of future inundation myths.

The great festival of the Sumerians was that of the New Year in April. It was closely connected with fertility and with the goddess Inanna, who went to the underworld in search of her consort, Dumuzi. The basic myths, the rituals, and the gods themselves (with different names) were taken over by the successors of the Sumerians and transmitted, essentially intact, to future civilizations.

Sumerian Literature and Science

The literature of ancient Sumer was closely tied to its myths. Cycles and legends were created concerning early founders and kings of cities and their relations with the gods. These stories were written down in epic form during the Third Dynasty of Ur. The most famous is the story of Gilgamesh, King of Uruk. The entire Gilgamesh epic survives only in later versions, but its basic story never changed: the king tries unsuccessfully to bring his friend, Enkidu, back to life and to achieve immortality for himself.

Also allied with religion was science. Since observation of the forces of nature was essential to the well-being of the community, and since each of the gods had a number allotted to him, there was an early investigation of astrological and mathematical phenomena. The year was of lunar derivation and was geared to religious festivities. The basic number of calculation was sixty (that of the god, An), and its legacy can be seen even today in the minutes of an hour and the degrees of a circle.

Sumerian Art

The Sumerians created a new architectural form, the ziggurat. From early times temples had been located on raised platforms, perhaps from a racial memory of the period when the Sumerians were dwellers of the mountains of Elam. The ziggurat was in itself an artificial mountain tapering in form with setbacks and ascending staircases. This expressed very well the closeness of the priesthood to the gods. The core of the building was of sun-dried brick and the facade of baked brick. Its walls were decorated with paintings and mosaics.

Minor arts in gold and bronze were extremely well done, as were reliefs representing religious and historical events. Especially characteristic of Sumerian art were figurines of people praying, wide-eyed and seemingly afraid of the divine forces of nature. High skill was employed in the engraving of cylinder seals on imported hard stone. When rolled out on clay, the jewellike execution of the surfaces produced clear, finely detailed rectangular reliefs.

THE BABYLONIANS

The invasions of the Amorites and Elamites totally disrupted the political order in southern Mesopotamia. The city-states survived, but central authority had been eclipsed. The fulcrum of power then shifted northward, as such cities as Mari on the Euphrates River and Ashur on the Tigris grew in importance. The Semitic Amorites settled in the as yet historically insignificant town of Babylon, and easily absorbed the Sumero-Akkadian civilization of the region, henceforth to be known as Babylonia.

Under King Hammurabi (ca. 1800 B.C.), Babylonian domination reached a high-point and included the entire valley. The empire was well organized and a comprehensive code of laws was written down. The capital Babylon—the center of gravity between north and south—became the most magnificent city of the Near East. However, as in ages past in Mesopotamia, the life span of the empire was not long. Invaders were pressing from the north, among whom were Indo-Europeans. Members of this group (Aryans), perhaps originating in the steppes of central Asia, conquered India; others included the Hellenic, Italic, Germanic, Celtic, and Slavic invaders of Europe. Among them were also the Hittites, who, together with the Kassites, conquered and destroyed Babylon (ca. 1600 B.C.) . (The origin of the Kassites is unknown. Some scholars believe that they also were Indo-Europeans.) Civilization was not destroyed, for eventually the newcomers were absorbed into the nexus of Mesopotamia. The Kassite kingdom lasted until the twelfth century B.C., when it was overthrown by Elamite invaders from the east.

Babylonian Culture

The literary tradition of the Sumerians was continued and augmented. Certain stories were altered, for Marduk, the god who possessed Babylon, had to achieve a very prominent position in the pantheon. Construction and the arts continued in traditional fashion.

The Code of Hammurabi

The greatest legacy of the Babylonian era was the Code of Hammurabi. This law code delineated a society divided among nobles, both religious and secular; merchants and farmers grouped together; and slaves, whose relative number had greatly increased since Sumerian times. Three types of justice applied to the three groups, and within each group all individuals were equal before the law. Aspects of the code appear to us unduly harsh, especially regarding the noble class. If a noble put out an eye of one of his fellows, law required that his eye be removed, too. But if he put out the eye of a member of a lower class, he would only have to pay a specified fine in silver. Women held a high place in society. They could, for example, hold property. Slaves were able to buy their freedom, and their treatment was regulated by law.

*T*he ancient Near East was one of the two crucibles of civilization of the West. Many of the characteristics of subsequent cultures such as those of Greece and Rome can be traced back to this region. The other crucible was Egypt, which in its early phases developed independently of Mesopotamia, if at about the same time. In later times, there would be much interaction between the two.

Selected Readings

Bermant, C., and Weitzman, M. *Ebla: A Revelation in Archaeology* (1979)
Burney, C. *The Ancient Near East* (1977)
Chiera, Edward. *They Wrote on Clay* (1938)
Contenau, G. *Everyday Life in Babylon and Assyria* (1966)
Frankfort, Henri. *Kingship and the Gods* (1949)
Kramer, S. N. *The Sumerians* (1963)
Lloyd, Seton. *From the Tablets of Sumer* (1978)
Moscati, Sabatino. *Ancient Semitic Civilizations* (1957)
Pritchard, J. B. *Ancient Near Eastern Texts* (1954)
Roux, Georges. *Ancient Iraq* (1980)
Weiss, Harvey., ed. *Ebla to Damascus* (1985)

3

Early Civilization in Egypt

3500 B.C. Nile Valley fully utilized for agriculture

3200 Upper and Lower Egypt united by Menes

3200–2700 Protodynastic Period (Dynasties I–II)

2700–2185 Old Kindom (Dynasties III–VI)—Memphis capital

2700 Imhotep invents stepped pyramid

2600 Pyramid of Khufu (Cheops)

2200–2050 First Intermediate Period

2050–1800 Middle Kingdom (Dynasty XI–XII)—Thebes capital

1878–1840 Height of Middle Kingdom under Senusert (Sesotris) III

1800–1570 Second Intermediate Period

1730 Hyksos conquest

The Egyptians belong to the group of people called Hamites who were closely related to the Semites. The history of human habitation in Egypt goes back at least two hundred thousand years. Civilization, however, began at about the same time as in Sumer. In uniting the two parts of his country, Menes created what developed into the Old Kingdom. In contrast to Mesopotamia, the geography of Egypt insulated it from outside invasions. The result was a uniform, conservative civilization which lasted with little change for at least two thousand years. The Old Kingdom fell apart not from external invasions, but from inner weakness. Its successor, the Middle Kingdom, was ended by the Hyksos invasions, but so strong were Egyptian tendencies to centralization that the New Kingdom, or Empire, was established on the same pattern as its predecessors. Indeed, the same traditions were still common as late as the conquest of Egypt by Alexander the Great in the fourth century B.C.

THE GEOGRAPHY AND CLIMATE OF THE NILE REGION

After the Sahara region became a desert, a strip of extremely fertile soil remained on either side of the Nile River in eastern Africa. The Nile begins its course in the uplands of central Africa and flows northward. Consequently, the land flanking it from the first cataracts to its delta was known as Upper Egypt. The fertile portion of the valley in this region was very narrow, sometimes only about three miles across on each side of the river, for it was hemmed in by granite cliffs. The flat Delta area, where fertile soil was lost in the multiple waterways and the horizon was very low, was known as Lower Egypt. While sections of the valley appeared different, they formed a continuous unit, bordered on the east by the Sahara Desert and the Red Sea, on the south by the cataracts, on the west by the Libyan Desert, and on the north by the Mediterranean Sea and the labyrinthine channels of the delta. Since the line of north-south communication was very narrow, the country had to be united if it was to prosper.

In contrast to the Tigris and the Euphrates, the Nile often flooded in a regular, predictable way, inundating the Delta by October of each year. No significant rain fell on the land, although the strip bordering the sea had a typical Mediterranean climate, including a rainy season. Indeed, rather than a turbulent summer and winter, as in Mesopotamia, there were in Egypt three regularly spaced seasons: floodtime (June to December), during which fertile soil was placed on the valley floor; the receding flood period (December to February), which was ideal for planting; and the dry season (March to April), when the crops were gathered. This almost mechanical regularity molded the Egyptians' belief that the universe was run on the principles of justice and kept them from the fearful apprehensions that characterized the Mesopotamians.

UNIFICATION OF EGYPT

Civilization developed in Egypt in the same way as it did in Mesopotamia and for the same reasons. Beginning with the middle of the fifth millennium, agriculture became an established institution in both Upper and Lower Egypt but its methods were limited. By 4000 B.C., farming techniques had improved

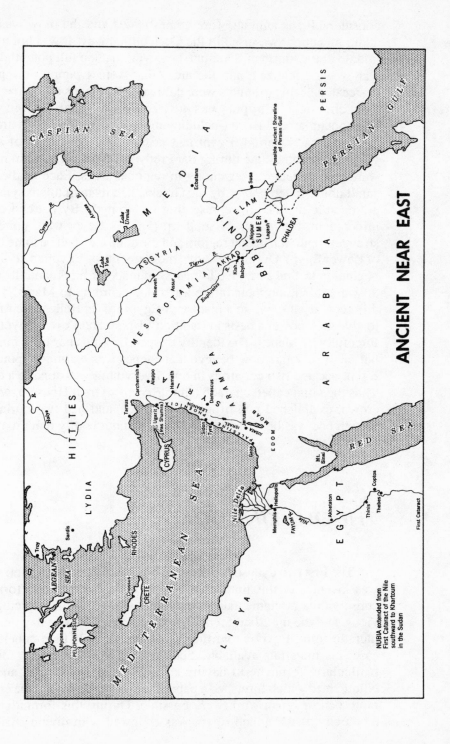

ANCIENT NEAR EAST

NUBIA extended from
First Cataract of the Nile
southward to Khartoum
in the Sudan

considerably, as animals were domesticated and the plow was utilized. In addition, copper was used in the Chalcolithic way. It was not until after the middle of the fourth millennium, however, that the full potentials of the Nile Valley were realized, and the areas that were swampy during floods and desiccated during droughts were cultivated by means of drainage and irrigation channels. Copper was utilized to a great degree, and much Mesopotamian influence (including cylinder seals) has been uncovered.

In its early period, Egypt had been a land consisting of a number of villages. At some time during the Predynastic period, certain noble leaders were able to achieve hegemony in regional areas. Each of these relatively small units, called *nomes* by the Greeks, had its own totem symbol (such as a crocodile or falcon), representing its strength. By the end of the fourth millennium, the nomes of southern (Upper) Egypt were united under the strongest nomarch in that region, and the delta area had become the Kingdom of Lower Egypt. During this time, the elements of Egyptian civilization were beginning to find form. Buildings were made of brick, and the essentials of art were taking on their future aspects. According to Manetho (who in the third century B.C. wrote a history of Egypt for its Hellenistic rulers in order to give their power a basis in tradition), Upper and Lower Egypt were united forcefully by Menes. The identity of specific kings has been much disputed, but many scholars now believe that Menes was Narmer. Upon unification, Egypt became two countries in one. Everything was done in a dual fashion. Thus the king, called pharaoh (from *Per Ao,* "Great House"), wore a double crown, established two official residences, and had two burial places (although one was obviously a cenotaph, without bodily remains).

THE OLD KINGDOM

The first two dynasties began the historical period in Egypt, since writing was invented at this time. Henceforth, it appeared in two forms: the very conservative monumental hieroglyphic, whose origin in pictograms is obvious, and the modified hieratic, a script used for everyday purposes. In its hieratic form, Egyptian writing was more flexible than cuneiform. In any case, the materials available dictated the form of writing, for Egypt was particularly fortunate in having an ample supply of stone and papyrus, a Nilotic reed which furnished a paperlike substance. Thus, fine engraving and rapid pen or brush work were possible. During this formative period, the monarchy of the united Egypt was endowed with divine attributes. Some scholars call the period of the first two dynasties (ca. 3200–2700 B.C.) "Protodynastic."

Centralization and advances in civilization occurred relatively rapidly in the first years of the Old Kingdom, which began about 2700 B.C. The government under the king-god was able to control the entire country with no visible opposition. The Egyptians believed that this system of government had been created at the beginning of time, together with the seas, mountains, and sky. It was characterized not by an arbitrary, hopeless permanence as was Mesopotamian government, but by a steady, benevolent absolutism. Pyramids, houses of the dead kings, joined earth with heaven by their great height.

The Pharaoh

The divinity of Mesopotamian kings, perhaps because of the evanescent quality of their kingdoms, had never been fully achieved. Rulers remained, at best, representatives of the gods on earth. In Egypt, it was different. Each king was believed to be a god. His place in Egypt and Egypt's place in the center of the universe were immutable facts to the ruler and his subjects. The Egyptians, like other early peoples, explained all natural phenomena by means of myths, and to them each living pharaoh was a son of Re, the sun-god. When he died, the pharaoh became one and indivisible with the god, Osiris. Through his benefices, the Nile rose and receded, children were born and prospered, and crops grew to fruition. Since he was the living god, all of the lands in Egypt belonged to him, and he could treat them as his private property. Every aspect of life, from agriculture to commerce to the mining of such minerals as turquoise and copper in the Sinai Peninsula, was controlled by the monarch. He ruled from Memphis, an ideal capital located at the juncture of Upper and Lower Egypt. To keep divinity within the family, the pharaoh married his sister.

The Concept of Ma'at

It might appear that this system of government would have given rise to a bloody tyranny, but such was not the case. The term, Ma'at, is nebulous to modern ears. One of its meanings is divine justice or, in other words, the king's will. While this was somewhat arbitrary, it must not be forgotten that the divinely ordained scheme of things in Egypt lacked the aspect of capriciousness associated with the gods of Mesopotamia. Ma'at surrounded and infused both gods and men, and thus it was not only incumbent upon, but instinctive to, the monarch, as father of his country, to act within the bounds of reason. Of course, this was sometimes not the case, but it was a general rule during the height of the Old Kingdom.

Political and Social Life

It is obvious that the king could not rule the entire country single-handedly. A hierarchy of officials was established with the hope, not always fulfilled, that their activities would be guided by Ma'at. Under the pharaoh were viziers, two in number in the early phases of Egyptian government, who controlled a bureaucracy managing agriculture, commerce, and industry. The members of this ever-growing body, which also had religious functions, were referred to as scribes. The commercial class, centering on the scribes, was free but directed by the government. During this time, it was possible for a man of humble origins to advance to the position of scribe, if he had great skills. The provincial nobility, who considered themselves descended from the chieftains of the once independent nomes, were called nomarchs. They ruled local governments as subordinates of the pharaoh and his viziers. Nobles also surrounded the royal household, and they were prominent in government and the army. On their country estates their word, in reality, was law. The lowest class was that of the peasants who toiled ceaselessly, with little variety and no improvement in their lot. Their labor belonged to the pharaoh, who might use them for mining or building public works such as pyramids.

THE DECLINE OF CENTRAL AUTHORITY

As with all human institutions, change was inevitable for those of Egypt. Although the divinity and omnipotence of the pharaoh were part of the cosmic scheme of things, central authority began to decline. As time went on, the officials and bureaucracy began to take on a life of their own. A dynasty ended either when there was no heir or when a usurper succeeded in claiming divine descent. The Third Dynasty, founded by the magnificent King Djoser (Zoser), lasted from about 2700 to 2650 B.C. and, together with the Fourth Dynasty (ca. 2650–2500 B.C.) founded by King Snefru, formed the height of the Old Kingdom. After this, decline set in and was accelerated during the reign of King Pepi II (ca. 2275–2185 B.C.), which ended the Sixth Dynasty and the Old Kingdom. At this time, authority broke down and nomarchs became supreme in their areas, but none was strong enough to restore central rule. This epoch has been called the First Intermediate Period (2200–2050 B.C.). It was a time of chaos and, hence, of great agony. For the Mesopotamians, this state of affairs was to be expected, because of continual invasions and displacements, but for Egyptians it ran contrary to the laws of the universe and the rhythms of the Nile. When the nomarchs of Thebes succeeded in once more reuniting the country, it was with great relief that the people saw the pharaoh reestablished as the god incarnate of Upper and Lower Egypt.

THE MIDDLE KINGDOM

The Middle Kingdom (ca. 2050–1800 B.C.) is identified with the Eleventh and the Twelfth dynasties, established under Amenemhat I (Amenemes) of Thebes. Evidently, it took both force and cajolery to reestablish central rule. The new capital, Thebes, now became the center of Egyptian life; and its god, Amon, identified with Re, became known as Amon-Re. Although the new pharaohs claimed divinity, this was no longer the basis of their rule. The nobles had tasted autonomy and in the Middle Kingdom were able to retain some of their acquired rights and benefits, including a percentage of taxes collected in their nomes. It is significant that they now claimed a certain connection to the divine order, for it was thought that they, as well as the pharaohs, could join Osiris in the hereafter.

Administration

The antagonism between king and nobles was reflected in the fact that few if any of the nomarchs were appointed as royal advisers. Indeed, even members of the pharaoh's family were passed over in favor of unequivocally loyal officials from the scribe class, thus giving rise to a middle class. The independence of the nobles can further be seen from the fact that they did not even wish to be courtiers, preferring to live in their own regions and to be buried there, rather than in necropolises centering on a deceased pharaoh. In this sense, the pharaoh was less powerful than before. In addition, the fact that public works on the scale of the pyramids were no longer built indicates a diminution of central authority.

Trade

At the same time that the pharaoh's power was lessening in Egypt, trade and contacts with other countries spread pharaonic influence to the corners of the Near East. The port of Byblos on the Phoenician coast was a large emporium for Egyptian products. So great was the influence of Egypt that its artifacts were in demand in such widespread places as Minoan Crete and Mesopotamia, sometimes affecting the local products of these regions. With the conquest of Nubia (Sudan), a vast source of gold was acquired. This high-point of prosperity was reached under Senusert (Sesostris) III (1878–1840 B.C.).

HYKSOS DOMINATION

Two factors brought about the fall of the Middle Kingdom: internal weakness under Amenemhat III and the invasions of a people from Palestine called the Hyksos. Thus began the Second Intermediate Period (1800–1570 B.C.), in which local rulers controlled the south (Upper Egypt) and the nomarchs of the Delta area were vassals of the invaders (Dynasties Thirteen through Seventeen). In certain respects, the presence of the Hyksos in Egypt was more traumatic than the chaos of the First Intermediate Period, for the land of the Nile had always felt protected from foreign invasion. The Egyptians' primordial sense of security had now been shattered.

The newcomers, although greatly hated by the natives, brought with them improved military techniques, which included the spoke-wheeled chariot, and bronze-working. The urgency with which the Egyptians finally expelled the Hyksos (ca. 1570 B.C.) created once more a unified country ruled by a Theban dynasty. (The New Kingdom is discussed in the next chapter.)

RELIGION AND CULTURE

The religious and cultural life of Egypt was truly a unique phenomenon and remained constant, except for certain details, from the Old Kingdom to the Hyksos invasions. Since everything had its place in the preordained scheme of things, change was considered to be against divine laws. The pyramids symbolized this desire for permanence. With greater autonomy of nobles and the rise of a middle class in the Middle Kingdom, there was increasing emphasis on literature.

Religion

In a polytheistic society, a multiplicity of myths explaining natural phenomena was regarded not as a hindrance but as an aid to true understanding. The several myths explaining Creation were considered different facets in the total comprehension of the beginning of the cosmos. The number of gods was potentially limitless, for was it not possible to worship the sun in a variety of guises? Thus, it was not considered a breach of dogma to meld Re of Lower Egypt with Amon of Upper Egypt or, at a later period, to identify Amon-Re with Zeus. The ways to the truth were many. This world-view explains the great variety of Egyptian gods and the many forms, including regional variations, which they took.

The Gods

As the sun shone on earth while gliding along his path during the day, so he passed through the nether regions at night. Thus, there was a total unity of day and night, life and death, gods and men. Hathor, goddess of earth, was often represented in the shape of a cow or with bovine characteristics. Osiris, who became the major fertility god, was married to his sister, Isis. His brother, Set, dismembered him and scattered his limbs throughout Egypt, but Isis was able to collect them and to resurrect her consort. Their son, Horus, the falcon god, avenged his father by overthrowing Set. He was identified with the living pharaoh, Osiris, who became, with the dead king, ruler of the underworld.

The Cult of the Dead

In the Old Kingdom, when a king died, he returned to Osiris. It was essential, however, that first all funerary preparations take place. Because of an accretion of beliefs, the Egyptians thought that the deceased had several lives after death. One such concept was that the tomb was a house of the *ka,* or that part of the being related to the body, which was mummified to preserve it. Therefore, all material advantages of life were placed, with the embalmed body, in magnificent tombs, such as pyramids. In early times, the pharaoh's attendants were also killed when he died, but later this practice was given up in favor of representing them by statuettes (*ushabtis*). Another aspect of the spirit was the *ba,* which left the body in the form of a bird and penetrated the world of the living. The *akh* appears to have been the divine aspect of the soul. Barks were provided for passage of the dead over water to the beyond.

At first, only the pharaoh was thought to return to Osiris, but by the Middle Kingdom nobles and others who could afford it were also considered able to accomplish this. Texts indicating the essential steps were written; if one lived by the precepts of Ma'at and followed all the necessary religious formulas, his soul would be lighter than a feather and he would have a proper afterlife.

Art

Since the monarchy was an important element in the immutable universe, representations of pharaohs had to have a permanence, and not depict only transient features. Hence wooden and stone representations in the round and in relief were highly stylized. Painted figures and those in relief represented characteristic angles of the body, but did not aim to represent reality with photographic accuracy. Thus, the face was in profile but the eye frontal. The chest was frontally represented, but the legs and eyes were in profile. A variety of scenes of everyday life appeared in tombs as aids to a full life in the hereafter. Statues of the pharaohs and their wives also represented their eternal aspects. In the Old Kingdom, royal expressions were free of earthly concern, but in the Middle Kingdom they were careworn. Nobles were represented in quite a realistic fashion. The minor arts, especially metalwork, work in semiprecious stones, and in faience, were prized at home and abroad.

The Pyramids

Until the Third Dynasty, the tombs of pharaohs were simple brick structures in the shape of solid rhomboids called mastabahs. Imhotep, who is credited by tradition with having been an Egyptian version of the Renaissance "Universal Man," invented the stepped pyramid, the first major stone building in history, built as a sumptuous tomb for Djoser (ca. 2700 B.C.) at Sakkarah. It was 204 feet high. During the Fourth Dynasty, the greatest pyramids were built at Gizeh. Stone replaced brick, and instead of having the appearance of ever-diminishing mastabahs on top of one another, the sides were fitted to become smooth plane surfaces. The greatest of these structures was the pyramid of Khufu (Cheops) (ca. 2600 B.C.), pointed in the cardinal directions and 481 feet high; others were built for Khafre (Chephren) and Menkaure (Mycerinus). The massive levies of men and materials required to build these tombs could not be duplicated in later dynasties.

Literature

At first, Egyptian writing was not especially literary in content, but during the First Intermediate Period and the Middle Kingdom, an introspective literature arose. As an unaccustomed chaos prevailed, Egyptians tried to explain why this had happened. An ethical literature concerning how to live had much of a vogue because of the spread of admissions to the underworld. A magical literature on how to die, including the Coffin Texts, grew up alongside of this. In addition, stories of adventures, such as those of Sinuhe, were now written down.

Egypt was a most stable society, and its forms of culture remained much the same throughout its history. Its pyramids, literature, and science had an enormous effect first on the Aegean Bronze Age civilizations and later on the Iron Age Greeks.

Selected Readings

Aldred, Cyril. *Egypt to the End of the Old Kingdom* (1973)
———. *The Development of Egyptian Art* (1962)
Edwards, I. E. S. *The Pyramids of Egypt* (1961)
Emery, W. B. *Archaic Egypt* (1961)
Fairservis, W. *The Ancient Kingdoms of the Nile* (1962)
Frankfor, Henri. *Ancient Egyptian Religion* (1948)
Gardiner, A. H. *Egypt of the Pharaohs* (1961)
Hayes, W. C. *The Scepter of Egypt* (1953)
Van Setters, J. *The Hyksos* (1966)

4

Changing Dominions in the Near East

2000 B.C.	Settlements of Hittites in Anatolia
1600–1200	First blossoming of Phoenician cities
1570	Hyksos expelled from Egypt
1570–1090	New Kingdom (Empire) Egypt (Dynasties XVIII–XX)—Thebes capital
1528–1495	Thutmose I—Egypt penetrates to Euphrates Valley
1490–1456	Thutmose III—imperial expansion of Egypt
1398–1361	Amenhotep III—Egyptian Empire at its height
1361–1353	Akhnaton—worship of Aton the sun disk; decline of the Egyptian Empire
1350	Height of Hittite expansion
1290–1224	Ramses II—revival of Egyptian Empire
1287	Battle of Kadesh—Hittites and Egyptians
1200	Destruction of the Hittites and other Near Eastern civilizations by invaders
1200	Iron Age begins
1200	Hebrews arrive in Palestine
1180	Philistines pushed back from Egypt
1090	Upper and Lower Egypt once more separate
1000–961	David king of Hebrews
970–940	Hiram king of Tyre
961–922	Solomon king of the Hebrews
883–859	Assyrians under Ashurbanipal conquer Phoenicia
722	Assyrians under Sargon II destroy Samaria
704–669	Height of Assyrian expansion
700	Phrygia destroyed by Cimmerians

655–610	Psammeticus I breaks with Assyria and establishes Dynasty XXVI in Egypt
625	Medes under Cyaxeres establish independent kingdom
612	Chaldean state established by Nabopolassar of Babylon
612	Nineveh falls to Chaldeans and Medes
586	Chaldeans destroy Judah
560–547	Croesus king of Lydia
550	Cyrus the Persian overthrows Median dynasty
547	Cyrus conquers Lydia
534	Cyrus conquers Greek cities of Asia Minor
539	Cyrus conquers Chaldeans and enters Babylon
530–525	Cambyses conquers Egypt
522–486	Darius brings the Persian Empire to its greatest territorial extent

The years immediately following 1600 B.C. saw a series of invasions that radically changed the civilized world. As the new invaders settled down and absorbed the elements of civilization, other barbarian incursions took place. After 1200 B.C., important new cultures arose, including those of the Hebrews, the Phoenicians, the Aramaeans, and the Assyrians. By the sixth century B.C., Persia had conquered the Near East and had designs on the Greek world.

THE NEW KINGDOM OF EGYPT

The Hyksos were expelled under Ahmose I (ca. 1575–1550 B.C.) of the Eighteenth Dynasty of Thebes. Not only were the Egyptians more consciously nationalistic than ever before, but they embarked on a venture of foreign conquest. It was no longer considered sufficient for Egypt to be united, but it was now regarded as essential to carry on a program of expansion. No matter how low the fortunes of the Egyptian Empire, the boundaries during the New Kingdom, ca. 1570–1090 B.C., were always more extensive than they had been in earlier periods.

Early Conquests   Under Thutmose I (ca. 1528–1495 B.C.) and his immediate successors, Egypt continued to expand in the northeasterly direction begun when Ahmose had driven the Hyksos into Palestine. The pharaohs penetrated as far as the Euphrates Valley, but during the initial excitement of conquest they did not organize their empire. Hatshepsut, a very determined woman, took

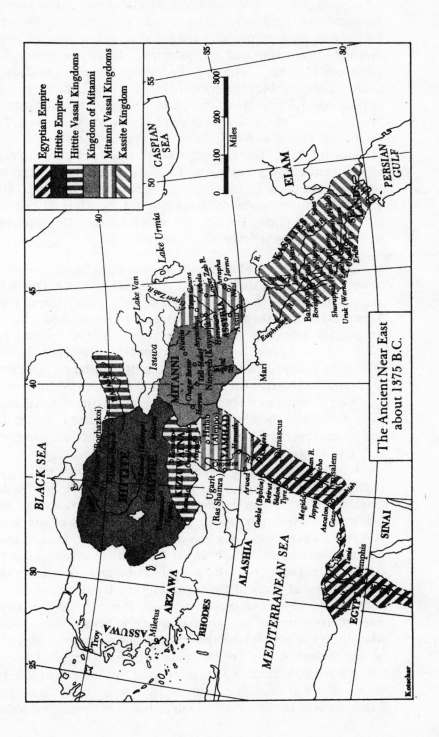

The Ancient Near East
about 1375 B.C.

the unprecedented step of becoming a female pharaoh (ca. 1486–1468 B.C.). To members of her family and the military establishment, she was anathema, for her policies were peaceful and her attitude toward large-scale construction and the arts appeared to them retrograde. Her successor, Thutmose III (ca. 1490–1456 B.C.), whom she had usurped when he was still a boy, tried to erase every visible memory of her. As a break from the peaceful policies of Hatshepsut, Thutmose embarked on a vast program of imperial expansion. The Egyptian Empire now stretched from Libya on the west, Nubia on the south, and Palestine and Syria on the northeast, making such a nation as Mitanni tributary. The empire, however, did not have a centralized administration, but was comprised of a series of vassal states kept in subjection by Egyptian troops. By the reign of Amenhotep (Amenophis) III (ca. 1398–1361 B.C.), the domains of Egypt reached their largest extent. Under his successor, Amenhotep IV, the tide was reversed and Egypt fell into a decline from which it would never quite emerge.

Akhnaton

One phenomenon of the New Kingdom was a tremendous increase in the power of the priests of the god Amon. During the Old Kingdom, the sacerdotal class of the sun-god Re of Heliopolis (across the Nile from Memphis) had great power, but this had been counterbalanced by belief in the pharaoh's divinity. When the dynasties of Thebes reunited Egypt during the Middle and New Kingdoms, the priests of the god Amon (who was eventually coalesced with Re) grew steadily in influence. One reason for this may have been that, since the otherworld had been "democratized," proper guidance of religious leaders was now more important than ever. In addition, from the time of the Middle Kingdom, the king had begun to depend more and more on scribes for his bureaucracy, and these were in turn controlled by the priesthood.

When Amenhotep IV came to the throne (about 1361 B.C.), he wanted to change the situation and restore power to the monarchy. No doubt he was genuinely interested in reforming religion, but it must be realized that his major motive was to break the power of the priests of Amon. A new god, Aton the Sun Disk, was proclaimed the only divinity in the universe. With a gesture, Amenhotep, who changed his name to Akhnaton and moved his capital from Thebes to Akhetaton (Tell el Amarna), tried to abolish more than a thousand years of Egyptian religion. By some, Akhnaton has been considered a sage, a precursor of monotheism. This is partially true, but it must not be forgotten that, whereas in a monotheistic religion the worshipers have direct contact with their god, Aton could not be venerated directly. Only his son, Akhnaton, could receive prayers of the Egyptians. Quite predictably, the new religion failed and the priesthood was more than able to recoup its losses after the pharaoh's death in 1353 B.C. To add another god to the pantheon was not only conceivable, but sometimes desirable. What the

Egyptians recoiled from was the abolition of any part of their inherited religion.

Under Akhnaton, the empire fell apart, but a brilliant intellectual life grew up at Tell el Amarna. In addition, the perennial official art of Egypt, which had become sapped of strength, was given a refreshing injection of naturalism; this did not, however, continue long after Akhnaton.

The Successors of Akhnaton

The priesthood of Amon appears to have been in full control when the young Tutankhaton (who shortly changed his name to Tutankhamon) (ca. 1352–1344 B.C.) returned the capital to Thebes. Meanwhile, the Hittites, whose presence had been felt as early as the seventeenth century B.C., were in control of an important empire in Asia Minor and expanding steadily. Under King Suppiluliumas, it overran Egyptian domains in the Fertile Crescent. Tutankhamon was dominated by Ay, a priest of Amon, who eventually became pharaoh for a few years. It seemed that anarchy would win the day, but a general, Harmhab, reestablished strong central rule and organized the Nineteenth Dynasty (ca. 1340–1309 B.C.).

THE END OF THE EMPIRE

Not only had Egypt lost much of its empire, but the presence of new powers throughout the Near East had made recovery of all the lost domains impossible. However, under Seti I (ca. 1309–1291 B.C.) and especially under Ramses II (ca. 1290–1224 B.C.), Egypt witnessed a new revival. The empire was temporarily restored, and vast architectural schemes, such as the colossal Colonnade Hall of the great temple at Karnak, were executed. The Hittites were the major power standing in the way of Egyptian expansionist plans. Conflict resulted, and the Egyptians, although fighting valiantly, lost a major battle to the Hittites at Kadesh in 1287 B.C. Eventually, both powers signed a peace treaty delineating their respective spheres of influence. Hattusilis (Khatushilish) II was the Hittite monarch at that time. This peaceful scheme of things did not last long, for by the end of the thirteenth century B.C. the Near East was disrupted by massive invasions of peoples with iron weapons. The fearful Hittite Empire vanished and Egypt itself was threatened. Under Merneptah (ca. 1224–1214 B.C.), the Land of the Pharaohs was saved. But in the next century all possessions outside of the Nile Valley were lost. The New Kingdom came to an end about 1090 B.C., when once again Upper and Lower Egypt split into two kingdoms. The Upper Kingdom was ruled by the priests of Thebes, now become pharaohs, and the Lower Kingdom was ruled by pharaohs of the Delta.

THE HITTITES

The land of Asia Minor, or Anatolia (modern Turkey), played an important role in the development of civilization in the Near East. The peninsula was not a self-contained unit as was the Nile Valley. Instead, it fell into several geographic regions including the Aegean coast, a fertile area with an indented coastline similar to that of the Greek mainland; a central plateau ringed by mountains; and the heavily forested Black Sea coast. Evidence for civilization in the region goes back to at least the fourth millennium, but no unified political organization took place until the advent of the Indo-European Hittites.

By 2000 B.C., the Hittites had settled in the Anatolian peninsula, occupying that part of the central plateau called Hatti, which was drained by the Halys River. The Hittites subdued the native people of the region and ruled over them. They quickly acquired the elements of civilization, from a variety of sources, especially from the Hurrians, who controlled northern Syria. Thus, the cultural benefits of Mesopotamia filtered through to the Indo-Europeans of Asia Minor. Hittite history is divided between the Old Kingdom, when political and cultural institutions were still in a state of flux and central authority was far from settled, and the empire, when the Hittites became the supreme power in the Near East.

The Old Kingdom

The culture of the Hittites combined indigenous elements embedded in accretions from conquered and neighboring peoples. As in other early Indo-European cultures, the rulers of the state were the chiefs of the nobles who in council elected one of themselves as king. This system led to weak decentralized rule, and under it the Hittites were unable to accomplish great imperialistic ventures. When Hattusas (Khattusha, modern Boghazköy) was made the capital city, power became more centralized, and the monarchy was strengthened. The king now had some Near Eastern characteristics and was referred to as "The Sun." At death he was deified. Although much of Asia Minor fell under Hittite influence, expansion southward into the Fertile Crescent was not yet feasible.

The Height of Hittite Power

By the fourteenth century B.C., Mitanni (which included a large Hurrian element) was not able to oppose Hittite conquest, and the force of the Egyptian Empire had lessened, for Akhnaton was now on the throne and his vassal states in Syria were breaking away. The Hittite king Suppiluliumas (ca. 1380–1335 B.C.) took advantage of the situation and was able to penetrate into southern Syria. After the defeat of Ramses II at Kadesh and the subsequent peace treaty dictated by the Hittite king Hattusilis III, the Hittite Empire reached its pinnacle. It is ironic that Egypt, which had preceded the Hittites and was humbled by them, managed to survive the barbarian onslaughts of 1200 B.C., while the Hittite Empire left few traces.

Hittite Culture

The capital of the Hittites, Hattusas, was built on a virtually impregnable outcropping of rock and fortified with enormous walls and towers. Their art was a heavy-handed pastiche of Near Eastern elements, as can be seen in their surviving reliefs, and it reflected their bellicose nature. Their literature also manifested their syncretistic tendencies; they adopted cuneiform and sometimes hieroglyphics for their own writing, while using also the Sumerian and Akkadian tongues. Religious and mythological, as well as historical, events were put into literary form. The religion of the Hittites combined various Near Eastern concepts. The fertility god, Telepinu, whose absence brought life on earth to the brink of chaos and whose return produced a revival, was the mythical explanation of seasonal change. He can be equated with the Sumerian Dumuzi and even the Egyptian Osiris. Sharsha embodied the vital functions of love as had Inanna or Ishtar. The Hittites also took over the Hurrian weather gods such as Teshub and his mate Hebat, the sun goddess.

THE NEW CIVILIZATIONS OF THE NEAR EAST

The invasions of iron-producing peoples, occurring around 1200 B.C., altered the course of civilization in the Near East as well as in the Aegean (see Chapters 5 and 6). Soon, however, the shocks of invasions had been overcome, and the new civilizations of the Hebrews, the Phoenicians, and the Aramaeans evolved in the western portion of the Fertile Crescent.

The Early History of the Western Fertile Crescent

The region of Palestine and Syria—bordered by the Euphrates and the Arabian Desert on the east, the Sinai Desert on the south, the Mediterranean Sea on the west, and the Lebanon and Anti-Lebanon ranges on the north— formed an early center of civilization. Its geographic location between the

Tigris-Euphrates and Nile valleys had great advantages, especially for trade, but made it extremely difficult to defend. The major river within the area, the Orontes, opened the inland to seaward trade. The coast was indented, providing good harbors and fertile lands for agriculture. Jericho and other early inland settlements have revealed in their progression of strata the beginnings of civilization. Another early site, Mari on the Euphrates, was ruled by a series of Semitic peoples, including the Amorites (ca. 2000 B.C.) and eventually (ca. 1550 B.C) by the Hurrians. The subsequent kingdom, Mitanni, served as a buffer between Hittites and Egyptians. Also on the Euphrates was the city of Carchemish. Between 1600 and 1200 B.C., several cities on that part of the coast known as Phoenicia reached their pinnacle of prosperity. Ugarit (Ras Shamra) was an international emporium and an eastern outlet for the Achaean Greeks. Byblos was a port that served as a trading center for Egyptian artifacts and local products such as purple dye and timber. Other cities were the inland Damascus and Kadesh on the Orontes River. The general Semitic culture of the area has been called Canaanite. About 1200 B.C., invaders destroyed Ugarit and crippled the rest of the region. But by the eleventh century, iron was used regularly.

The Phoenicians

Recovery was rapid for most of the Phoenician city-states, although Ugarit was never rebuilt and Tyre supplanted Byblos as the major power. By the eleventh century B.C., Phoenician ships were plying routes throughout the Mediterranean and organizing a series of important trading posts along the coasts. It was through the Phoenician traders that many of the benefits of Near Eastern culture reached the ends of the Mediterranean. Under King Hiram (ca. 970–940 B.C.), Tyre reached its high-point of prosperity and had close connections with such monarchs as King Solomon of the Hebrews. Tyre also founded Carthage—a colony that would outpace its mother city— on the African promontory of the Mediterranean, now part of Tunisia. The major contribution of the Phoenicians to civilization was the alphabet, which many scholars believe had its origin in Egyptian hieroglyphics. For practical purposes of commerce, cuneiform was much too awkward and hieroglyphics much too cumbersome. The system of syllable representation could be ambiguous, as can be seen by the Greek written during the Achaean period in the Minoan Linear B syllabary. Therefore, the alphabet, representing only one letter at a time, was devised. The Semitic language of the Phoenicians was based on consonant roots, making vowels not essential for comprehension. The Greeks, who acquired the alphabet about 800 B.C., invented vowels.

The Aramaeans and the Philistines

By the twelfth century B.C., the dominant people in Syria were the Aramaeans, although the remaining Syro-Hittite kingdoms in the north retained great prosperity until their conquest by Assyria in the eighth century B.C. The Aramaeans became the great traders of the inland regions of the

Near East, as the Phoenicians were the commercial leaders of the seas and coastal regions. The Aramaean capital of Damascus, at the end of the major caravan route across the desert, became the most important city of the region. Camels were essential in this overland trade between Babylonia and Syria. So pervasive was Aramaean influence that their language was the major commercial tongue of the Near East well into the time of the Roman Empire.

The Philistines were sea raiders who, pushed back by Ramses III of Egypt (ca. 1180 B.C.), settled on the coast of Palestine in such cities as Gaza and Askalon. Their origin is very obscure and has been variously identified with Minoan, Achaean, or Asia Minor civilizations. They came into frequent conflict with the early Hebrews who settled inland.

THE HEBREWS

The origins of the Hebrews are as much in doubt as those of other Semitic peoples of the ancient Near East. In recent times, scholars have given much credence to the Biblical stories of Abraham and Moses. Some place the advent of the Hebrews and their patriarch, Abraham, in the third millennium B.C., when the Amorites entered Mesopotamia. It appears very likely that, during this time of invasions and displacements, the Hebrews, a tribe related to the Amorites, also appeared in the region. Tradition states that the Hebrews then migrated to Palestine. According to some scholars, this may be shown by the fact that the Hurrians, an important people in the area at that time (1700–1600 B.C.), had a version of the Flood myth most similar to the Biblical tale of Noah and the Ark. The Hebrew sojourn in Egypt has been given substance by the fact that, in an inscription of Ramses II, the word *Habiru* is mentioned. However, some scholars say Habiru means any wanderers, not necessarily Hebrews. More widely believed is that a victory inscription of the pharaoh Merneptah (ca. 1224–1214 B.C.) mentions the Hebrews for the first time. It appears credible that Moses led the Hebrews from the delta region back to Palestine around the end of the thirteenth century B.C.

The Land of Milk and Honey   The Hebrews, finding that the "Promised Land" was already occupied by Canaanites, appear to have used the combined tactics of force and infiltration. It was an opportune time, for the Egyptians had lost Palestine to the Philistine sea raiders. The Hebrews were to a certain degree absorbed by the culture of Canaan, but they retained their tribal organization. The real distinction between the newcomers and the natives was one of religion, for the Hebrew god Yahweh was the only and exclusive deity recognized by his people, while the Canaanites worshiped many of the traditional Near Eastern gods, easily adding to their number. Still, the Hebrews found the temptation to worship the local Baalim, or agricultural deities, to be very great. At first, the Hebrews were far from unified; in each region judges, or military-religious leaders, ruled the tribes.

The Hebrew Kingdoms

In the eleventh century B.C., the judge Samuel anointed Saul as first king of a united Hebrew nation. Saul was unable to cope with his royal position and eventually (ca. 1000 B.C.) killed himself while fighting the Philistines.

Under David (ca. 1000–961 B.C.), not only were the tribes of the south united with those of the north, but the Philistines were defeated. The kingdom, with Jerusalem as its capital, was expanded to cover the lands east of the Jordan River and parts of Syria, including Damascus. The worship of Yahweh was centered in Jerusalem, and the government took on the trappings of a typical Near Eastern monarchy. Under Solomon (961–922 B.C.), son of David and Bathsheba, the kingdom displayed its greatest brilliance. Rich copper mines near the Red Sea added to royal revenue, and an alliance with King Hiram of Tyre extended commercial connections. A magnificent temple was built to Yahweh in Jerusalem, and dazzling public works were constructed. When Solomon died, his son Rehoboam (922–915 B.C.) could not keep the kingdom together, for he refused to reduce the inordinately high taxes. The ten northern tribes revolted and established a new nation called Israel, centered on the city Samaria. The two southern tribes, comprising the nation of Judah, remained loyal to Jerusalem.

The Destruction of the Hebrew Nations

The Assyrians, whose expansion began to reach alarming proportions in the ninth century B.C., were repelled by King Ahab of Israel in 853 B.C. at Qarqar. However, during the next century the Assyrians met with unqualified success, destroyed Samaria, and carried off the leaders of Israel (722 B.C.). The ten northern tribes, always more prone to assimilation with surrounding peoples than the inhabitants of Judah, vanished into the populace of northern Palestine. Judah did not officially lose its independence, although it was a vassal state of the Assyrians. Indeed, under Josiah (640–609 B.C.), it withstood Assyria, but only because that mercurial empire was on the brink of collapse. The Chaldeans, or Neo-Babylonians, who had participated in the conquest of Assyria, under King Nebuchadnezzar, finally destroyed Judah in 586 B.C. Its leaders and many other inhabitants were taken to exile in Babylon, whence they returned in 539 B.C. after Cyrus the Persian, conqueror of the Chaldeans, liberated them.

The Hebrew Religion

The Old Testament, the Holy Book of the Hebrews, incorporating legends, history, laws, and divine revelations, was written over a period of at least eight hundred years, beginning perhaps around 1200 B.C. In it the growth of the Hebrew religion is mirrored. Yahweh was the only god of the Chosen People, and disobedience to him could arouse him to the height of vengeance. The commandments said to have been given to Moses on Mount Sinai embodied Yahweh's moral requirements of his people. Obedience was rewarded by his care and protection. At first there was no definite place for his worship, but with the centralization of the kingdom under Solomon, the temple became the focal point of devotion.

With the schism of the two kingdoms, and the sliding of the people and kings of Israel toward paganism, there arose a series of seers or prophets who foretold doom if the Scriptures were not heeded and who called for morality and social justice. Elijah, living during the reign of Ahab in the mid-ninth century, spoke out against the construction of pagan shrines by the king's wife, Jezebel. Jeremiah (626–580 B.C.) foresaw the destruction of Jerusalem as punishment for his people's sin. The faith survived the destruction of the temple, as Jeremiah and others expounded the idea that every man could worship God individually while obeying his laws. By the same token, Yahweh was the Lord of the entire universe. During the Babylonian Exile, other prophets, including Ezekiel, continued to lead the Hebrew community. On the exiles' return to Jerusalem after their liberation, Ezra codified and expanded the law based on the Pentateuch, which was now strictly enforced upon the Hebrews.

ASSYRIA

The northern portion of the Fertile Crescent had major importance in the development of civilization from the earliest times, as can be seen in such archaeological sites as Tell Halaf and Hassuna. Of the various city-states which grew up in the region during the fourth and third millennia, Ashur (Assur) was destined to predominate. Its location in the middle Tigris Valley put it in the nexus of Mesopotamian communications. The sun-god Ashur, who owned the city, also gave it its name and that of its people, the Assyrians. The Assyrians were a Semitic people related to such groups as the Amorites and Babylonians, although some of their barbarism never died out. When the Hurrian-dominated Mitanni Kingdom began to decline in the fourteenth millennium, the Assyrians were able to fill the power vacuum. Under

Tikulti-Ninurta I (ca. 1242–1206 B.C.), the empire expanded and for a brief period even included Babylon. But the invasions of 1200 B.C. temporarily shattered Assyrian hegemony.

The Rise of Assyria

The invasions not only destroyed the Assyrian Empire, but they created a power realignment. Eventually this resulted in such newly revived states as those of Urartu, a people related to the Hurrians in the upper reaches of Mesopotamia, and the Phrygians, who had destroyed the Hittite Empire. Despite these obstacles, the Assyrians steadily gained in power. Adadnirari II (911–891 B.C.) began conquest in a westerly direction, while Ashurnasirpal II (883–859 B.C.) not only conquered the important city of Carchemish on the Euphrates River, but also reached the Mediterranean, making the cities of the Phoenician coast into tributaries. His new capital, Calah (Nimrud), had a magnificent palace. His son, Shalmaneser III (858–824 B.C.), took Damascus, and soon Babylon was conquered, although that kingdom was always a source of trouble for the Assyrians. Urartu, now a traditional adversary of the empire, continued to vex its forces. By the middle of the eighth century B.C., it appeared that the Assyrian Empire was going to fall apart, from external and internal pressures, but Tiglath-Pileser (745–727 B.C.) seized the throne just in the nick of time. Not only did he defeat the Urartians, but he recaptured Syria and became king of Babylon. Now the king of Assyria was the representative on earth both of Ashur and of Marduk (god of Babylon). Under Sargon II (722–705 B.C.), expansion included the destruction of Samaria, the capital of Israel, and near dissolution of Urartu. In addition, Sargon II contained the Phrygians and successfully fought off an invasion of Cimmerian raiders.

The Height and Decline of Assyrian Power

Sennacherib (704–681 B.C.) built a new capital, Nineveh, on the Euphrates. He subdued Judah, making it into a vassal state, and he destroyed Babylon after yet another revolt. His son, Esarhaddon (681–669 B.C.), conquered the Delta region of Egypt, but he was not successful in using local rulers as vassals, for they continually revolted. The end came rapidly for the Assyrian Empire. Under Ashurbanipal (669–627 B.C.), the Egyptians and Babylonians revolted, while the Lydians, successors to the Phrygian Empire, posed a grave danger. In 612 B.C. the new kingdoms of the Medes and the Chaldeans (Neo-Babylonians) pooled forces and obliterated Nineveh from the face of the earth. Within two years, all traces of the Assyrians had been extirpated.

Assyrian Administration

One cause for the rapid decline and almost total disappearance of the Assyrians was their great cruelty. Assyria entered all phases of conquest by attempting to destroy local autonomy. In order to break up regional loyalties, the Assyrians resettled whole peoples. The conquered areas were assimilated into provinces with legates appointed by the Assyrian king and bolstered by

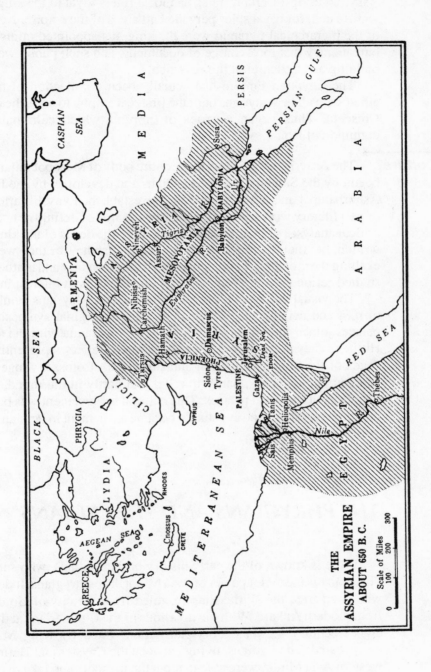

THE
ASSYRIAN EMPIRE
ABOUT 650 B.C.

Scale of Miles

0   100   200   300

Assyrian troops. Certain states had local rulers loyal to the king, but no one was trusted, for royal spies pervaded all areas of the empire. At the pinnacle of the hierarchical pyramid were the king, his appointed ministers, and the bureaucracy that took charge of documents and such public works as road-building and agricultural improvements.

The Egyptian Empire had actually been a collection of tributary and allied states. The Assyrians built the first real empire to unite the entire Fertile Crescent. Thus began a series of empires which culminated with the dominion of Rome.

Assyrian Culture   The Assyrians were heirs to the entire body of Mesopotamian civilization begun by the Sumerians and Akkadians and developed by the Babylonians. Ashurbanipal and other Assyrian kings established vast libraries consisting of past literary works, while their scribes compiled definitive texts and wrote critical analyses of them. Annals recounting the deeds of the kings were also written, but their historical truth is open to dispute, for they were geared to exalting the monarch. The sciences such as astronomy and mathematics were studied seriously, and even the kings displayed great interest in botany.

The visual arts were highly developed. The Assyrians combined motifs of past and neighboring civilizations into an original synthesis. The great palaces joined the bricks of traditional Mesopotamia with the stones of the Hittites. They were decorated with narrative reliefs representing the great deeds of the king, executed in amazing detail. Colossal winged bulls with bearded human heads, partly in relief and partly in the round, adorned the entrances of the royal palaces. This cultural achievement was bequeathed to the successor states and eventually became an element in Persian civilization.

THE PHRYGIANS AND THE LYDIANS

Little is known of the early history of the Lydians, who supplanted the Phrygians as the major power of Asia Minor. The Phrygians, Indo-Europeans who conquered the Hittite Empire, ruled from the city of Gordium not far from modern Ankara. With the invasions of the Cimmerians at the end of the eighth century B.C., the Phrygian nation, ruled by King Mita (Midas), disappeared. The Lydians, living between the Cayster and Hermus rivers in western Asia Minor, were able to repel the invaders and take over rule of the area. King Gyges (685–657 B.C.) established his capital at Sardis, a city that later became immensely wealthy. He was killed when the Cimmerians invaded again.

The kingdom continued to expand in the sixth and fifth centuries B.C., for it was rich in electrum, a natural alloy of gold and silver. Coinage was first invented in Lydia. Precious metals had a long history as a means of exchange in the ancient world, but at each transaction they had to be weighed. Coinage was first conceived of as standard measures of electrum with the king's imprint guaranteeing its weight. The Greeks and Persians spread the use of coined money. Under Croesus (560–547 B.C.), the Lydians were for all practical purposes in control of the neighboring Greek cities on the Asia Minor coast. However, in 547 B.C. Lydia fell to the conquering armies of the Persian king Cyrus.

THE SAITE KINGDOM OF EGYPT

King Esarhaddon of Assyria put Necho, the local prince of Sais, in control of the Delta region of Egypt. Necho's son, Psammeticus I (Psamtik) (ca. 655–610 B.C.), broke away from the Assyrians and reestablished an independent Egyptian kingdom (the Twenty-sixth Dynasty). The kingdom reached its high point of prosperity under Amasis (569–526 B.C.), who gave a franchise to the Greek trading city of Naucratis, founded under Psammeticus I, at the mouth of the Nile. Although Saite Egypt marked a nationalistic reaction to foreign domination and a conscious return to the past, especially to the glories of the Old Kingdom, it sought world trade. Commercial relations were especially close with the Greeks and the Lydians. Egypt fell to the Persian king Cambyses in 525 B.C. at which point the Twenty-seventh Dynasty began. Although Persians now controlled the land of the Nile, Egypt's age-old culture continued in the same time-honored way.

THE CHALDEANS OR NEO-BABYLONIANS

The state of the Chaldeans was established by Nabopolassar of Babylon in 612 B.C. after the coalition led by Babylon had destroyed Nineveh. Like Egypt, this kingdom considered itself heir to a glorious past. In 605 B.C., the Chaldeans won a smashing victory over the Egyptians at Carchemish and were then able to conquer the lands which the Assyrians had controlled in Syria and Palestine. Under King Nebuchadnezzar (605–562 B.C.), Judah was taken and Jerusalem destroyed (586 B.C.). The Chaldean Kingdom reached its height at this time, and Babylon became the fabled metropolis of the Near East. Its famed Hanging Gardens formed one of the Seven Wonders of the Ancient World. However, under the usurper Nabonidus (556–539 B.C.) and his son, Belshazzar, the kingdom declined rapidly. The alienation of the priests of Marduk from the monarchy hastened the process, and in 539 B.C. Cyrus the Persian became the king of Babylon.

THE PERSIANS

A group of Indo-European tribes collectively called Iranians seems to have appeared in central Asia during the second millennium B.C. During the next millennium, they followed a southwesterly route bringing them to Iran on the eastern fringes of the Fertile Crescent, where they remained, assimilating some of the elements of the ancient civilizations. The early organization of the Iranians appears to have been similar to that of other Indo-European peoples, with tribal chiefs bolstered by a council of elders.

The Median Kingdom

During the seventh century B.C., one of the Iranian groups, the Medes (under King Cyaxeres), was able to establish itself as a kingdom independent of Assyria (625 B.C.). The Medes had defeated the nebulous Scythians, whose habitat ranged from the Caspian Sea to the Danube region, and thereby had acquired control over large areas of central Asia. Indeed, the Median kingdom was the dominant power east of the Zagros Mountains, which formed the eastern boundary of the Fertile Crescent. It appears to have been not a highly centralized nation but a series of vassal states, sometimes tied to central authority by bonds of blood. One of these was the Achaemenid dynasty, which ruled in what is now the southern part of Iran. By 612 B.C., the Medes were prestigious enough to unite with the Chaldeans in the destruction of Assyria. Although the Chaldeans got the lion's share of the Assyrian domains, the Medes gained some sections of northern Mesopotamia. The Median Empire now stretched from central Asia to the Halys River in Asia Minor, where a truce line had been set with the Lydians. Astyages, who succeeded to the throne in 584 B.C., wanted to control the rich lands of the Fertile Crescent. But in a surprise move, the Chaldean king Nabonidus allied himself with the vassal and grandson of Astyages, Cyrus of the Achaemenid house.

The Growth of the Empire Under Cyrus

In 550 B.C., Cyrus overthrew the Mede Astyages, thus establishing the Persian Empire. Since the Persians and Medes were essentially the same people, although originally ruled over by different families, there was no real change in the ruling class. Cyrus now set out on a program of conquest that in his lifetime would unite central Asia with the entire Near East.

Lydia, besides being rich in precious metal and thus a coveted prize, threatened the borders of Persian domains in Asia Minor. Cyrus, after defeating the Lydian Croesus and taking over his kingdom (547 B.C.), seized the Greek coastal cities (by 540 B.C.). To complete his hegemony of the Near East, Cyrus entered Babylon in 539 B.C., deposing Nabonidus and his son, Belshazzar. Because of his own tolerant attitude, and perhaps from his observations of Assyrian shortcomings, Cyrus treated his newly conquered domains with extreme lenience. In Babylon he was made king, successor to Hammurabi and representative of Marduk on earth. To the Hebrews and other peoples, he was considered a liberator because he allowed them to return to their homelands. When Cyrus died in 530 B.C., he was succeeded by his son Cambyses.

The Rule of Darius

Cambyses (530–525 B.C.) added Egypt to the Persian Empire and became its pharaoh under the newly established Twenty-seventh Dynasty. While Cambyses was in Egypt, a pretender to the throne rose in Persia, and Cambyses is reputed to have committed suicide. Darius, a distant relation in the Achaemenid clan, became king after deposing the pretender (522–486 B.C.). Under him, the Persian Empire reached its height of territorial expansion, stretching from India to Thrace. Only in Greece were the Persians repelled.

Persian Administration

Darius completed the organization of the empire, which was divided into thirty satrapies, or provinces, each ruled by a satrap appointed by the king. In each satrapy, there were also a general and a financial officer responsible only to the king. To ensure honesty, the Persian monarchs followed the Assyrian model with a series of spies known as the "Eyes and Ears of the King." In general, local laws and customs were respected, and they were even codified in certain regions. To provide rapid communications, the "Great Royal Roads" were built, the longest link of which was from Sardis, capital of the satrapy of Lydia, to Persepolis, a stretch of sixteen hundred miles. A standard system of weights and measures was put into effect for the whole empire. *Darics* were the major gold coins, in which many of the provincial taxes were paid. All Persians were immune from taxes.

The commoners made up the army infantry as well as the "Ten Thousand Immortals," an elite royal bodyguard. The nobles supplied the cavalry and formed the official classes. The Persian king was considered a representative of Marduk on earth and of Amon-Re incarnate abroad. Darius was the first king to become the defender of Ahura-Mazda, the god of light. The major Persian capitals included the cities of Susa in Elam and Persepolis, east of the Zagros Mountains.

Persian Religion

The Persians were originally fire worshipers and later paid homage to Ahura-Mazda (Ormuzd). With exposure to Mesopotamian civilization, such local gods as Anahita (Inanna, Ishtar) were assimilated—all presided over by priests called Magi. During the sixth century B.C., under the prophet Zoroaster, Persian religion was reorganized to give it a theology and a cosmic view. The great god Ahura-Mazda presided over all that was good in the universe, but evil spirits, daevas, headed by the archvillain Ahriman, god of darkness and evil, threatened all good things. Man must not be tempted by evil, but should abide by the good. In a later period, the sun-god Mithra rose to help save mankind. At the end of the world, the forces of good and evil were to fight a battle which Ahura-Mazda would win. The damned were to suffer to the end of time and the good were to live in heavenly bliss. This religion was to have important effects on the development of Christianity.

Persian Culture

Although Persian written in cuneiform was used for monumental purposes, Aramaic written in alphabetic form was the lingua franca of the empire. As heir to the Mesopotamian past, Persian art incorporated Assyrian and Chaldean, as well as native, ideas. For example, the great palace at Persepolis was on a high platform reached by a monumental stairway, in the Assyrian tradition. The walls were covered with reliefs depicting the glories of the monarchy, but their finesse of execution and the slimness of the figures point to influences from outside Mesopotamia. The minor arts, especially metalwork, showed the native Persian genius, above all in the representation of animals.

*T*he period after 1200 was crucial in the Near East. Many aspects of modern culture were formed at that time. These included the development of the alphabet, and the formation of Judaism. The Persian religion, in its several forms, in turn influenced Judaism, and later both were instrumental in the formation of Christianity.

Selected Readings

Ahironi, Y. *The Archaeology of the Land of Israel* (1982)
Albright, W.F. *The Archaeology of Palestine* (1956)
Bright, J. *A History of Israel* (1981)
Contenau, G. *Everyday Life in Babylon and Assyria* (1966)
Cook, J. *The Persian Empire* (1983)
De Vaux, R. *Ancient Israel: its Life and Institutions.* 2 vols. (1965)
Gurney, O. *The Hittites* (1964)
Moscati, S. *The World of the Phoenicians* (1965)
Oates, J. *Babylon* (1972)
Olmstead, A. *A History of the Persian Empire* (1948)
Saggs, H. *The Greatness That Was Babylon* (1962)

5

The Minoan and Mycenaean World

2900–2000 B.C.	Early Minoan Period—beginnings of Cretan society
2000–1600	Middle Minoan Period—cities of Crete reach maximum expansion
1900	Arrival of Indo-European peoples on Greek mainland
1650–1500	Beginning of Achaen ascendancy—shaft graves
1600–1150	Late Minoan Period—decline sets in
1500	Beehive (tholos) tombs
1250	Troy VIIa destroyed
1200	Dorian invaders devastate Achaean cities
1184	Traditional date for destruction of Troy
1150	Dorian conquest

The Aegean world developed its own civilization, although it learned much from the ancient Near East. The culture of Crete, called Minoan, eventually spread over a large portion of the Aegean region. Indo-European newcomers settled on the Greek mainland around 1900 B.C. and eventually absorbed many Minoan elements. The result was the synthesis known as Mycenaean or Achaean civilization. About 1200 B.C., when the entire ancient world was suffering invasions, Dorians and other barbaric invaders of Greece attacked the Mycenaean citadels and destroyed them. Much was lost, but much lay dormant until three hundred years later, when the classic Greek civilization began to arise.

THE GEOGRAPHY OF THE AEGEAN BASIN

The Aegean Sea, which separates Asia Minor from the Greek peninsula, is filled with islands. The major island group, called the Cyclades, centers on Delos. To the south is the long island of Crete. The mainland has an extremely indented coastline and is cut by mountains into many small valleys. The area to the north of the Gulf of Corinth, known as Central Greece, includes the regions of Aetolia and Boeotia. Jutting southward from Boeotia is Attica. A land bridge, the Isthmus of Corinth, connects Central Greece and the Peloponnesus. The Peloponnesus has as its main regions the Argolid in the northeast, Laconia (Sparta) in the southeast, and Achaea in the north. The rivers of Greece are generally short and nonnavigable.

MINOAN CIVILIZATION

The Neolithic Age, which left such important settlements as Sesklo and Dimini on the Greek mainland, came later to the Aegean world than to the Near East. By the end of the fourth millennium B.C., agricultural communities were present on Crete, and by the third millennium towns were being established. The eastern and especially the central parts, including Cnossus (Knossos) near the north-central coast, seem to have had a dense population.

The Chronology of Crete

Since the turn of the century, when the English archaeologist Sir Arthur Evans began excavations at Cnossus, much has been learned about the ancient civilization of Crete, and a chronology based on pottery styles has been established. The Minoan world had extensive trade connections with the Near East, especially with Egypt, as indicated by the excavation of datable Egyptian artifacts from Minoan strata. The chronology of Crete has been divided into periods: Early, 2900–2000 B.C., when Minoan society was beginning to develop; Middle, 2000–1600 B.C., when the cities of Crete reached their maximum expansion and height of cultural achievement; and Late, 1600–1150 B.C., when decline began to set in and both commercial and military hegemony fell to the Achaean (Mycenaean) cities of the mainland.

There is much uncertainty concerning the eclipse of Cnossus, the chief Minoan city. The one sure fact is that the city was completely devastated and burnt around 1400 B.C. Some say that the Mycenaeans had conquered the

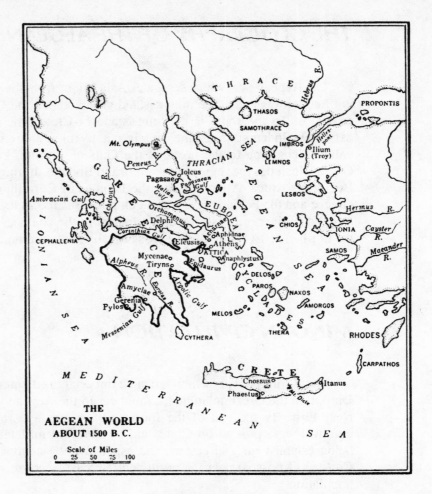

THE
AEGEAN WORLD
ABOUT 1500 B.C.

Scale of Miles
0   25   50   75   100

island previously (as evidenced by the fact that Linear B writing was in current use) and that the Cretans now revolted, or barbarians invaded, and destruction ensued. Others believe that it was actually the conquering Achaeans who destroyed Cnossus. At any rate, although civilization continued on Crete, there was a steady decline until around 1150 B.C., when catastrophic invasions befell the entire ancient world.

Minoan Cities

It is very difficult today to get an accurate picture of the Minoan cities, for the original Cretan language is undeciphered. However, to the Greeks of the period, as well as to subsequent generations, the great city and palace which grew up at Cnossus must have made a very strong impression. Indeed, the basis of the legend of Theseus and his slaying of the Minotaur is the labyrinth that can be identified with the complex floor plan of the palace of Minos (apparently, the generic name for the Cretan king).

Throughout the island, palaces similar to the one at Cnossus have been excavated, and it is now believed that they were a major component of an urban complex. They appear to have served their communities as economic and religious centers, political centers, and royal residences. The palace of Cnossus contained a throne room and cult areas with religious symbols such as the double ax and bulls' horns. The Cnossus palace, as well as other palaces on the island, had bathtubs and running water (water conduits, which were tiled with terra-cotta, have been discovered by archaeologists). Vast storerooms have also been uncovered.

None of these cities was fortified, an indication that, in addition to economic hegemony, Crete probably had physical mastery of the Aegean.

Minoan Culture

The artifacts and murals which have been found on Crete do not indicate an all-enveloping preoccupation with religion, although religious symbols are omnipresent. The attitude of Minoans appears to have lacked the fatalistic gloom of the Mesopotamians and the painful bureaucratic overlay of the Egyptians. Several of the wall paintings in the palace of Cnossus contain depictions of sea life, particularly dolphins. Some of the ceremonies represented in paintings, such as jumping over a bull's horns, appear secular because they are represented in a rather joyous way. Besides the emphasis on bulls, which can also be found in the Minotaur myth, a major female goddess is apparent. Statuettes of her and of her attendants show extended forearms intertwined with snakes. Some believe that this goes back to a matrilinear phase in Cretan society.

The Minoan language, Linear A, which was a syllabary developed from pictograms, is not understood. Perhaps like the Linear B documents of the Mycenaeans, which can now be read, it was used for commercial documents or inventories.

The vases of the Minoans, especially those from the high-point of Cretan culture (ca. 2000–1400 B.C.), are extremely beautiful. Often the shape of the vessel was ignored, and sea animals such as squids were painted on with wild abandon.

THE MYCENAEAN (ACHAEAN) WORLD

The geographic conformation of the Greek mainland with its easily fortified heights and isolated valleys, as well as the belligerent tendencies of the Indo-European Greeks, indicated that mainland civilization would take on a cast different from that of Crete. From the sixteenth century B.C. until about the year 1200 B.C., the Mycenaean culture was on the rise. In Homer's *Iliad,* Mycenae is represented as the most powerful of Achaean cities, with the result that the term Mycenaean is interchangeable with Achaean. Other cities, including Pylos, Tiryns, and Corinth, were also important.

As a result of the decipherment of the Linear B Achaean script by Michael Ventris and John Chadwick in the 1950s, tentative reconstruction of the earliest Greek civilization has become possible.

Mycenaean Cities

Many Mycenaean sites had such strategic importance that they formed the cores of classical cities, including Athens, Thebes, and Corinth. The ideal location was a defensible hilltop overlooking a valley not far from the sea. This hill was the site of the king's palace, as well as the place of refuge in time of war for inhabitants of the town below. The center of the palace was always the same: a vestibule led to a large room with a round hearth. This room, called a megaron, was derived from an early form of hut. It served as the king's throne room and council chamber. It was also perhaps the symbolic hearth of the city, whose symbolic father was the king.

Surrounding the palace complex was a series of fortifications with a monumental entrance through which the main road entered from the town. To the rear was a postern gate.

Mycenaean Religion and Art

The religion of the Mycenaeans seems to have resembled to a large extent that of the later Greeks. Names of Greek gods, including Zeus, Poseidon, and Apollo, have been found on Linear B tablets. Some scholars believe that Poseidon, in his capacity as horse-tamer and earth-shaker, was the major god. In the earliest times of Achaean ascendancy (1650–1500 B.C.), the dead (at least of the royal family) were buried in shaft graves in a flexed position; but by 1500 B.C., elaborate beehive-shaped tombs were being built.

The beehive, or tholos, tombs were underground chambers of remarkable construction, covered with corbel domes. The corbel is not a true dome but rather a series of ever-decreasing rings of stone, supported by the solid wall of which it is part; but it does show the engineering prowess of the Mycenaeans. Within these tombs were many chased gold cups, masks, and swords. Mycenaean masonry was of massive polygonal stones fitted together without mortar.

Mycenaean potters took over many of the elements of Cretan design, such as squid motifs, but made them more stylized and symmetrical so that they were in harmony with the vessel on which they appeared.

THE MYCENAEANS AND TROY

For more than two thousand years of Hellenic, Hellenistic, and Byzantine civilization, the *Iliad* and *Odyssey* of Homer were the first literary works presented to the growing child, and the most familiar ones to adults. The story of the *Iliad* deals with the consequences of the abduction of Helen (sister-in-law of Agamemnon, king of Mycenae) by Paris (Alexander), son of Priam, king of the Asia Minor coast city of Troy (Ilium). The resulting war lasted ten years and involved a massive coalition of Greek cities against the Asiatic foe.

THE TROJANS

According to Greek tradition, the date of the Trojan War was 1184 B.C. In the nineteenth century, the German archaeologist Heinrich Schliemann began excavation of the site of Troy, but it was not until recently that an accurate idea of strata of the various settlements of the town has evolved. The earliest settlement was made sometime after 3000 B.C. About 1900 B.C., after the destruction of Troy VI (the sixth stratum of civilization above bedrock), a new people came in. In artifacts and architecture, they resembled the Achaean peoples of Greece, although it is not known what language they spoke. It appears certain that Troy was not inhabited by Hittites, as were neighboring regions, although the Trojans may have been part of an Asian league dominated by the Hittites.

The War

Only recently has the scope of Mycenaean trade been realized. It expanded from Italy to Egypt to Mesopotamia to an extent not reached in later Greek civilization until the eighth century B.C. Since ships hugged the coast wherever possible, the strategic position of Troy near the Hellespont could be used to hinder eastward and northward shipping. It is thus entirely possible that the Trojans took advantage of their position and, exacting high tolls, harassed Greek ships. Several or many Mycenaean cities may have banded together for mutual defense to rid the seas of their opponent, either in a series of raids over a long period of time or in a protracted struggle. Troy VIIa was apparently destroyed by Mycenaeans about 1250 B.C., a date relatively close to the traditional date of the war, considering the usual inaccuracy of such chronology. Another fact supporting the theory that Troy VIIa was the Homeric Troy is that its much richer predecessor, Troy VI, appears to have declined without destruction as a result of invasion. However, Mycenaean hegemony did not last long. By 1200 B.C., invasions were sweeping away older civilizations throughout the Mediterranean area, and Greece was no exception.

THE CYCLADES ISLANDS

The Cyclades is a group of islands located in the Aegean Sea roughly southeast of Attica. Mountainous islands, whose climates are similar to that of Attica, they are perfect for the production of wine and olives, but not of grains. Naxos, Delos, Thera, and Siphnos are four of the Cyclades Islands.

The Neolithic period began in the Cyclades ca. 3600–3500 B.C., several thousand years after it began in Crete. During the Neolithic period, societies with a clearly defined social hierarchy developed in these islands. This social development continued despite the settlement of Bronze Age peoples in the Cyclades ca. 3100–2900 B.C. (Scholars know that these peoples came from Asia Minor because pieces of pottery found in the Cyclades dating to this time are similar to pieces found in Asia Minor.)

The Cyclades, due to their location near Crete, came under the influence of the Minoans. Through commerce, Minoan art styles as well as everyday items found their way into homes of the Cyclades. As proof of this, both Minoan-style wall frescoes and pottery have been discovered there.

A volcanic eruption on the island of Thera around 1500–1450 B.C. destroyed the settlements there and is reputed to have contributed to the decline of Minoan civilization. Crete is seventy-five miles south of Thera and tidal waves associated with the eruption would have quickly reached Crete, destroying coastal settlements on that island. The prevailing winds would have blown large amounts of ash toward Crete. The Minoans were, however, able to rebuild their settlements on Crete. (It is possible that the eruption on Thera gave rise to the legend of "Atlantis." This was a civilization that, according to mythology, existed under the sea—and, after the eruption, the center of Thera was underwater.)

THE DORIAN INVASIONS

Sometime before 1200 B.C. new tribes, called Dorians, broke into the Greek peninsula, seeking fertile lands and, perhaps, booty. Many of the Mycenaean cities fell immediately, but some held out awhile. Since Attica appears to have had less appeal than the Peloponnesus, or perhaps because Athens had an extremely strong defensive system, the invaders bypassed it. According to tradition, and many modern scholars, refugees from the Dorians fled to Athens, and the Ionians, of whom the Athenians were a branch, soon occupied the Cyclades Islands and the central part of the Asia Minor coast.

Because the Achaean cities perished by fire, there was little left of their civilization. Unfortunately, the invaders' level of civilization was quite low. Rather than mingle with the local inhabitants, the Dorians often enslaved them after executing their leaders. Cultural continuity was of course broken by these tactics. In other sections of Greece, such as the remote parts of the Peloponnesus where the Achaeans managed to flee, civilization was also eclipsed, as the struggle for existence became of paramount importance. Within decades, the art of writing was lost, and it was not regained until about 800 B.C.

However, the Greek world would recover rather quickly after 800 B.C., and by the fifth century B.C., Greeks were on the brink of their greatest cultural and political achievements, as well as failures.

Selected Readings

Blegen, C. W. *Troy and the Trojans* (1963)
Chadwick, J. *The Decipherment of Linear B* (1958)
Evans, A. J. *The Palace of Minos at Knossos*. 4 vols. (1921–35)
Finley, M. I. *The World of Odysseus* (2nd ed., 1977)
Graham, J. W. *The Palaces of Crete* (1962)
Higgins, R. A. *Minoan and Mycenaean Art* (1967)
Hood, M. S. *The Minoans* (1971)
Hutchinson, R. W. *Prehistoric Crete* (1963)
Marinatos, S. *Crete and Mycenae* (1960)
Ventris, M. and Chadwick, John. *Documents in Mycenaean Greek* (1956)
Willetts, R.F. *The Civilization of Ancient Crete* (1977)

6

The Rise and Expansion of Hellenic Civilization

1180–750 B.C.	Greek Middle Age (beginning of Iron Age)
850–750	Greeks adapt Phoenician alphabet
800–700	Homer's *Iliad* and *Odyssey*
776	First Olympiad
750–700	Hesiod, author of *Works and Days* and *Theogony*
750–500	Greek Archaic Period
750	Cumae—first Greek colony—founded by Chalcis
750	Sparta conquers Messenia (First Messenian War)
734	Syracuse founded by Corinth
700	Birth of Archilocus, first major lyric poet
700	Union of Attica
683	Transition from monarchy to aristocracy completed at Athens
655	Cypselus establishes tyranny at Corinth
650	Messenians revolt (Second Messenian War)
632	Cylon tries to establish tyranny at Athens
625–585	Tyranny of Periander at Corinth
626–546	Thales—natural philosopher
621	Draco promulgates law code in Athens
620	Birth of lyric poets Alcaeus and Sappho
610–545	Anaximander—natural philosopher
594	Solon becomes archon at Athens
585–525	Anaximenes—natural philosopher
570	Birth of lyric poet Anacreon

560–556	Peisistratus twice seizes power in Athens, but is exiled
546–527	Peisistratus returns to Athens and establishes a benevolent tyranny
540–520	Polycrates tyrant of Samos
540	Persians conquer Greek cities of Asia Minor
540	Xenophanes, natural philosopher, flourishes
531	Pythagoras, natural philosopher, emigrates to Croton
527	Hippias and Hipparchus, sons of Peisistratus, rule Athens
525–456	Aeschylus—writer of tragedies
518–438	Pindar—writer of odes
514	Hipparchus murdered
513	Persians cross Hellespont and conquer Thrace
510	Hippias exiled; aristocracy restored in Athens
508–505	Cleisthenes overthrows aristocracy and establishes democracy in Athens
505	Formation of Peloponnesian League
501	Athenian army reorganized according to tribe rather than wealth
500	Hecataeus of Miletus writes first geography
500	Heracleitus, natural philosopher, flourishes

The destruction of Mycenaean civilization brought to Greece only a temporary eclipse. By the seventh and sixth centuries B.C., the Hellenic world had more than recovered from the invasions and was well on its way to the Golden Age of the fifth century B.C. The uniquely Greek political unit, the polis, *rose to prominence and in Athens, at least, led to democracy. In other places, tyranny and oligarchy prevailed, while in conservative Sparta, the monarchy was maintained. After the middle of the sixth century B.C., the prosperous Ionian cities of the Asia Minor coast were engulfed by Persia, and Greece itself was threatened.*

THE GREEK MIDDLE AGE

The period known as the Middle, or Dark, Age in Greece began immediately after the twelfth-century Dorian invasions and lasted until about 750 B.C. Although the newcomers had iron, they had little else, and the state of

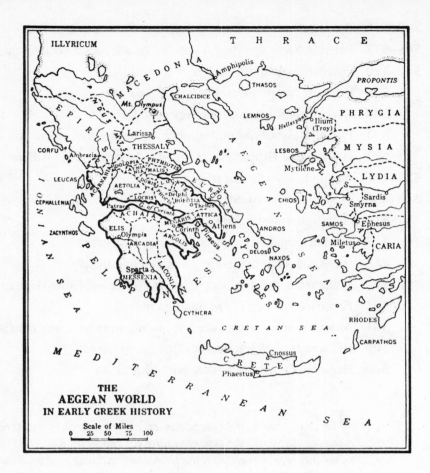

THE
AEGEAN WORLD
IN EARLY GREEK HISTORY

Scale of Miles
0   25   50   75   100

civilization in Greece retrogressed several hundred years. Even Athens, which had apparently held out against the invaders, sank to a low level of poverty.

The Works of Homer

The major source for our knowledge of Greek life during the Middle Age is Homer. Until the eighteenth century, his authority remained unquestioned, but from that point onward, the credentials of the "blind bard" have been disputed. What in the works of Homer refers to the Mycenaean period—which he was depicting—and what refers to his own age? Can the *Iliad* and the *Odyssey* have been written by the same person? The *Iliad* describes a warlike world whose chief virtues are personal courage and prowess, while the *Odyssey* describes a world of travel and commerce whose chief virtues are intellect and cunning. It appears that the great epics of the Trojan War and its aftermath were derived from Achaean heroic stories, but much of the detailed descriptions in the *Iliad* and the domestic scenes in the

Odyssey refer to Homer's own period. Homer, or the poets writing under that name, created the *Iliad* for a noble audience like that in the Middle Age. The *Odyssey,* on the other hand, seems to reflect a later time when geography was beginning to be understood and the wide world held much fascination. The literary composition of the epics must be dated after contact with the Phoenicians gave the Greeks the alphabet (ca. 850–750 B.C.). Nonetheless, the writings of Homer are the conclusion of a long tradition of epic, so that it is possible to glimpse early Greek life in his works.

Political Organization

The typical city-state could not have been very large, and those that resembled Odysseus' Ithaca were nothing more than estates. It appears that the king *(basileus),* who was considered the father of the community, did not have absolute power but was advised and limited by a council of noble chiefs. In early Greece, the citizens comprised a majority of a community and formed a popular assembly that served as a mandate for the king's actions. The cities, or rather towns, appear to have had fortifiable citadels, and they were not far from the sea.

THE REAWAKENING AND EVOLUTION OF GREECE

It will be recalled that, by the tenth century B.C., the western coast of the Fertile Crescent had recovered from the ravages of the thirteenth-century invasions, and that the Phoenician commercial cities, including Tyre, had been established or revived. These cities sent out settlements throughout the southern and western Mediterranean littoral. Most were only trading posts, where products and ideas were diffused, although Carthage was a full-fledged colony. The Greeks not only got the alphabet from the Phoenicians, but they were also drawn into the Phoenician orbit of trade. Greece's acute overpopulation and desire to expand its horizons led, in the eighth and seventh centuries B.C., to an intensive campaign of colonization. Soon southern Italy, as well as the Black Sea area, had more than a superficial layer of Hellenism.

Within each of the city-states *(poleis),* which had grown from modest Middle Age settlements, political changes were taking place. In most cases, the monarchy gave way to a rule by aristocrats, which in turn led to tyranny and a readjustment in power according to wealth, as befitted commercial cities. By the end of the sixth century B.C., this development had led to democracy in certain cities.

Colonization

The soil of Greece was never very rich, even in ancient times when forests provided a better ecological balance than exists today. As the population on the land increased but the ancestral estate remained indivisible, it became obvious that there was too little land for too many people. The aristocrats sought to increase their own holdings, and the impoverished farmers sought to get out of debt; thus a need arose for migration of excess population. At a time when trade was beginning to flourish, the idea of an akin city in the remote west and east appealed greatly to a Hellenic polis. In this way the "mother city" colonization movement began.

Early Colonies

According to tradition, Cumae (Cyme), founded by Chalcis (ca. 750 B.C.) was the first Greek colony. (During the Middle Age, the coasts and islands of Asia Minor had been populated from the mainland. Aeolians settled in the north center, Ionians—traditionally said to have come from Attica—in the center, and Dorians in the south.) Within decades, there were dozens of colonies in southern Italy, including Taras, founded by Sparta (ca. 710 B.C.). The local inhabitants were by no means absorbed; as late as the Roman period, the Lucanians and Samnites of southern Italy were powers to be reckoned with. The Etruscans also interacted with the Greeks, to their cultural advantage but eventually to their military detriment. In Sicily, the native peoples, including the Sicels, Sicans, and Elymians, retained their identity, although the east coast of the island became Hellenized at an early date. Syracuse was founded by Corinth about 734 B.C. The Carthaginians controlled the western part of Sicily and proved a continual source of friction to the Greeks.

In the east, the Greeks settled along the coast leading to the Black Sea, where Potidaea was founded by Corinth about 600 B.C. This area, a projecting three-pronged peninsula, was so thoroughly settled by Chalcidian colonists that it was known as the Chalcidice. Byzantium was founded by Megara (ca. 667 B.C.) on the eastern shore of the Bosporus, while Sinope on the south coast of the Black Sea was founded by Miletus at about the same time. Sinope in turn colonized neighboring Trapezus (Trebizond). In addition, the Greeks had a trading post on the coast of Syria by 750 B.C. and at Naucratis in Egypt sometime after 650 B.C. There was even a Greek colony, Cyrene, in Libya, which was founded by Thera around 630 B.C.

Organization of a Colony

A colony was organized by a founder known as an *oikistes*, who was usually from a noble family. After consultation with the oracle at Delphi, the founder and future citizens (sometimes coerced into joining) set sail for the new city, taking with them the cults of the mother city. On arrival, land was divided and the city constructed. Once a colony was founded, it was a fully

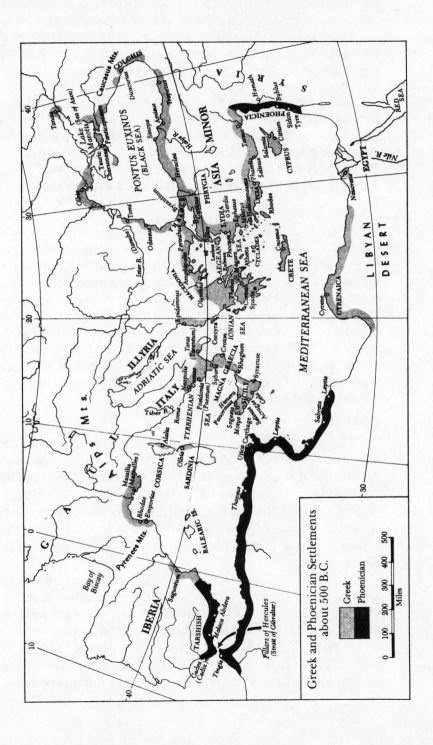

Greek and Phoenician Settlements
about 500 B.C.

Greek

Phoenician

Miles

0 100 200 300 400 500

independent, self-sufficient *polis,* capable of founding other colonies, thus spreading Hellenic civilization to an ever-expanding area.

Trade flourished in this environment. With the minting of the first coins by the Lydians and then, in the seventh century B.C., by all of the Greek states, commerce increased in scope and intensity.

The Passing of the Monarchy

The paternalistic city-state of the Middle Age seemed an anachronism in the eighth century B.C., and the noble clans chafed at the restrictions put upon them by the king. The transition from monarchy to aristocratic government appears to have been relatively rapid, although by no means sudden. When the nobles took over the state, the lot of the small farmer worsened. The supreme power of the king was divided among several officials elected by the clans for short terms.

The Coming of Tyranny

The rule of the aristocrats was most distasteful to the majority of the citizens of a *polis.* Not only did noble clans oppress other classes, but they warred among themselves as well. Consequently, it was often possible for one man to galvanize the mass of the people into overthrowing aristocratic rule and putting him in power, instead. Tyranny took a variety of forms in the various city-states. In some, it resulted in democracy, and in others oligarchy, which made wealth the determining factor of power. The new rulers were called tyrants, but the term must not be interpreted in its modern sense. The tyrants were originally defenders of the majority against the aristocracy, and under them important innovations took place in the political, economic, and cultural spheres.

CORINTH

The aristocratic family of the Bacchiads had governed Corinth from a very early date, but in 655 B.C. a new government was established by a semimythical figure, Cypselus. (His name comes from the Greek word for "chest" because, according to legend, as a child he was hidden in a chest to protect him from the wrath of the Bacchiads, whom an oracle had predicted he would destroy.) Cypselus broke the power of the aristocrats by violent means and made Corinth into one of the foremost commercial powers in the Greek world.

In 625 B.C., Cypselus was succeeded by his son, Periander, also a semilegendary figure. Under Periander's rule, Corinth reached the pinnacle of its prosperity. The arts flourished, and Corinthian influence spread to newly founded colonies, to Hellenic city-states in Greece, Asia Minor, and Sicily, and to Egypt. After the death of Periander in 585 B.C., the fortunes of Corinth began to decline, as Athens had begun to overtake its commercial hegemony and Sparta was infringing upon its internal policies.

OTHER TYRANNIES

The city of Sicyon lay to the west of Corinth. From a very early period, there was conflict in this city between the Dorian aristocracy connected with Argos and the descendants of the Achaeans. Under Orthagoras (ca. 650 B.C.), the nobles were eclipsed, and Sicyon's importance increased. Cleisthenes (ca. 600–560 B.C.), the son of Orthagoras, made his city virtually independent of Argos and raised it to its high-point of prosperity.

The island of Samos was taken over by the tyrant, Polycrates, around 540 B.C. Because Samos was in a crucial position off the coast of Asia Minor, Polycrates was able to achieve a stranglehold on trade. He built many public works on the island, but he proved a thorn in the side of the Persians, who had recently taken over command of Asia Minor. He was killed by Persian officials about 520 B.C. Samos then became subject to Persia.

THE RISE OF ATHENS

Athens, which was destined to be the greatest Greek city, had been a monarchy in its early period, but by the seventh century B.C., an aristocratic government had gained control. In the following century, reforms by Solon made Athens into a plutocracy (a government in which wealth was the criterion for holding office). Under the benevolent tyranny of Peisistratus, land was redistributed, and under the leadership of Cleisthenes, the grip of the aristocrats was finally broken and the bases for democracy were established.

The Union of Attica

According to tradition, Theseus was the last king of Athens and the founder of its commonwealth. In order to believe this, however, one would have to ignore much chronology. From the time of the Middle Age, the large Greek city-states found themselves in control of fair-sized land areas in which there were smaller settlements. As Thebes dominated Boeotia and Sparta controlled Laconia, so by 700 B.C. Athens had conquered Attica. In most places the large city continued to control adjacent areas by force. However, the *synoecism* (or union) of Attica, which was the basis of future Athenian strength, erased in every practical way the distinction between a citizen of Attica and one of Athens. Thus, the city and its surrounding region became one political unit.

Early Political Development

In the Middle Age, the population of Attica seems to have been divided into three classes: the *eupatrids* (nobles); the *georges* (free farmers); and the *demiurges* (artisans). The highest class was one of birth rather than of choice or of wealth. By the beginning of the seventh century B.C., the king's executive, military, and religious powers had been divided among three elected officials: the *archon eponymous,* who gave his name to the year (a calendar based on archon lists was established); the *polemarch,* who was the commander-in-chief of the army; and the *archon basileus,* or king archon, who took charge of the state religion. All ruled for only one year. (It is interesting to note that, since the kingship was somehow connected with divinity, the term *basileus* continued to be used in a religious context.) The shift from kingship to elected magistrate happened gradually. It appears that the *polemarch* was the first office created (perhaps in the eighth century B.C.). The first entry of *archon eponymous* on the list was in 683 B.C.

The aristocracy controlled the government through the Council of the Areopagus, a descendant of the Council of Elders of the Middle Age. This body elected the archons, who joined it after their tenure of office. The gulf between the upper and lower classes was wide indeed, for only the nobles *(eupatrids)* were members of the *gene* (singular, *genos*), or clans, which were quasi-religious bodies based on kinship.

Seventh-Century Changes

In the seventh century B.C., the political situation began to change because of new prosperity. The aristocrats, however, remained firmly in control. Every citizen of Athens was a member of one of four tribes *(phylae)*, each of which was now divided into twelve *naucraries,* or districts furnishing enough money for a fully equipped warship. Every Athenian also belonged to a *phratry,* a religious brotherhood based on kinship. This system recognized the divine origin of citizenship, as each *phratry* had its own ancestral cult. It did not, however, imply descent from gods for individual families as did the aristocratic *gene,* now more vital than ever. It is possible that, for purposes of military organization, society was already divided according to wealth rather than birth on the following basis: (1) *hippeis* (usually nobles), who were wealthy enough to supply a horse for the cavalry; (2) *zeugitae,* who owned oxen and hence could afford armor; and (3) *thetes,* the rest of the population. In reality, the new divisions, if they occurred at this time, were not overly different from the older classifications of *eupatrids, georges,* and *demiurges.*

Because of the growing complexity of the community, six minor archonships were created after 650 B.C. Each of these officers *(thesmothetes)* wrote down laws as they were passed. Their other function, which within decades would be their primary one, was that of judges.

A particularly severe case of the economic ills that had overtaken the rest of Greece befell Athens in the seventh century B.C. The aristocrats controlled vast estates that grew larger each year. The rural population was on the brink of starvation, and with every generation, per capita acreage got smaller through population increase, while the soil got poorer through misuse. Wheat was raised in large quantities for export, although Attica was singularly unsuited for that crop. In order to survive droughts and other adverse conditions, the small farmer could obtain grain from neighboring aristocrats, but the repayment was assessed at one-sixth of his crops each year. This was impossible during a hard year, and so it happened that, since the land itself was inalienable, small farmers fell into bondage to the aristocrats. At the same time, the aristocrats, constantly at odds with one another, did not present a responsible image as rulers of the state.

CYLON

The obvious solution at Athens, as in the rest of the Hellenic world, was tyranny. However, the first attempt was unsuccessful. In 632 B.C., Cylon, a good athlete who was connected by marriage to the neighboring city-state of Megara, tried to seize power. Megacles, the archon at the time, was a member of the Alcmaeonid family, one of the most powerful in Attica, and apparently had popular support. Cylon was trapped by Megacles on the Acropolis and sought sanctuary in a temple. In an excess of zeal, the forces of Megacles decimated those of Cylon. Because they had violated a sacred place, they brought such a stain on the whole family of the Alcmaeonidae that they were exiled. Strife among the clans was thus exacerbated, and blood feuds became frequent.

DRACO

About 621 B.C., Draco, as *thesmothete,* tried to remedy the situation by establishing a set of laws on homicide. It appears that, although a murder was considered a pollution to the state and the individual, certain types of killing such as that in self-defense could now be expiated. Thus, an attempt was made to end vendettas among the clans by putting punishment for homicide within the state's judicial power. The prestigious Council of the Areopagus traditionally had the responsibility of trying persons accused of homicide, but it had often been bypassed. Now it became the sole judge on such cases.

Sixth-Century Reforms

During the sixth century B.C., Athens had uniquely adept leaders who not only healed the wounds of the state, but also established the supremacy of Athens in the Hellenic world.

SOLON

The ills of Attica were not cured by Draco; in fact they worsened, in part because of continual war with Megara, which began after the destruction of Cylon's forces. Solon, a noble military leader (he had forced the Megarians to return Salamis to Athens) and poet, was considered the one person who could save Attica from chaos. Becoming archon in 594 B.C., he immediately set out to rectify the unbearable situation of his fellow citizens.

Agricultural and Economic Reforms. The first reform of Solon was the abolition of all debts and mortgages of the oppressed farmer class. Thus, at one stroke the small landholding class found itself in possession of its former lands. In order to prevent a reversion to bondage, Solon forbade enslavement for debt. Since Solon was a "reconciler" and not a revolutionary, he considered it sufficient punishment for the aristocrats to lose their indebted clients. Hence, the great estates remained intact, and the plight of the landless was not remedied. On the other hand, land was now made disposable by the individual.

In the economic sphere, Solon shifted the Athenian currency from the Aeginetan standard to the lighter coinage of Euboea, thus bringing it in line with that of the major commercial powers of the day. He forbade the exportation of wheat, and as a result Attica switched to the more suitable olive and vine crops. Grain, however, was now at a premium and had to be imported; this fact was to have far-reaching consequences for Athenian foreign policy in the area of the Chalcidice and the Hellespont. Solon also sought to increase trade and industry by offering Athenian citizenship to skilled artisans who would settle in Attica.

Political and Military Reforms. Solon clearly defined the financial status of citizens in regard to political rights and military obligations. Members of the highest class were those whose yearly income was equivalent in value to five hundred bushels of wheat; they were the chief officers of the army. The three-hundred-bushel men (*hippeis,* or knights) served as cavalry and officers. The bulk of the new army was made up of the third group, the two-hundred-bushel men *(zeugitae).* They were the *hoplites,* foot soldiers who formed armed lines in a phalanx, or wedge. The men in each line interlocked their shields so that the enemy was met with an invulnerable armored wall. (This was a far cry from older Greek methods of warfare in which horses had played a major role.) The remaining class were the propertyless *thetes.*

The *Ecclesia,* assembly of all citizens, had existed in Homeric times, but had been eclipsed or lay dormant during the ascendancy of the aristocracy. Solon revitalized this body so that in it all citizens, *thetes* included, voted on legislation and elected the magistrates, although only members of the first two classes were eligible to hold the nine archonships. A council, the *Boule,* consisting of four hundred members (one hundred from each tribe), was created to prepare legislation for the *Ecclesia.* In judicial matters, members of the *Ecclesia* served as the *Heliaea,* or court to which acts of magistrates considered unjust might be appealed by any citizen. The only powers left to the Council of the Areopagus were those of trying cases of homicide and impiety and review of magistrates in office. When his tenure in office was finished, Solon left Athens to go into voluntary exile.

PEISISTRATUS

The reforms of Solon had curtailed strife in Attica, but by no means eliminated it. Indeed, new factions arose, ranging from those who desired further reforms to those who wanted a return to aristocratic hegemony. The "Plain Party" was composed mostly of landed aristocrats. The "Coast Party" consisted of urban artisans who wished to retain the status quo. The "Hill Party," made up of landless rural poor, demanded redivision of land; the nobleman Peisistratus was their leader. By 560 B.C., Peisistratus was able to seize power, but he was subsequently exiled. On his return (556 B.C.), he utilized his dramatic flair by entering Athens under the aegis of Athena (actually an enormous, robust farm girl dressed up as the goddess). During yet another exile, he became involved in Thracian affairs and acquired vast amounts of silver. Following his final return (546 B.C.), he was able to carry out his policies.

Although Peisistratus was technically a tyrant, he achieved a redistribution of wealth that made democracy possible. Because many of the intransigent aristocracy had been killed in factional combat or were in exile, much land was available for redistribution among the poor. A small tax was exacted upon the land. Judges traveled on circuit throughout the countryside, tying farmers to the ways of the city. Peisistratus invited to Athens artists and scholars of Asia Minor who were fleeing the Persian onslaught, and offered them citizenship. The result was the greatest cultural flowering Greece had yet known. Magnificent public buildings were constructed, and Athenian works of art were prized on the world market. By now Athens had supplanted Corinth in commercial hegemony and was becoming a leader in international affairs and colonization.

The Sons of Peisistratus

In 527 B.C., after the death of Peisistratus, his sons, Hippias and Hipparchus, took command of Athens. They continued his policies, but were hated for private reasons by a faction headed by Harmodius and Aristogeiton. In 514 B.C., Hipparchus was murdered. Afterwards, Hippias became bitter and tyrannical. At this time, Sparta was headed by the aggressive King Cleomenes, who intervened to bring back the exiled Alcmaeonid clan. Hippias was exiled, and the aristocracy was restored (510 B.C.).

CLEISTHENES

The reactionary Isagoras became archon in 508 B.C. However, the people would not be deprived of their rights and joined with the Alcmaeonid Cleisthenes to overthrow Isagoras, despite the latter's support by Sparta.

Between 508 and 505 B.C., Cleisthenes reformed the Athenian state so thoroughly that the three geographic parties (the Shore, the Hill, and the Plain) lost all reason for existing. Furthermore, the hold of the noble clans, which had been based on geographical blocs, was decisively broken.

The New Basis of Citizenship. The basis of citizenship now became residence in Attica. Instead of being registered in a *phratry* or *naucrary,* citizens were enrolled in *demes,* or village units, each with a council and a *demarch.* If a citizen moved, he still was a member of the same *deme,* and so were his descendants. The *demes* were divided among thirty *trittyes* (or thirds). Cleisthenes created ten new tribes (in place of four), each consisting of three *trittyes*—one each from the Plain, the Shore, and the Hill. Thus, every tribe had a cross-section of *demes* from all over Attica. The revolutionary aspect of this move must not be underestimated, for the original tribes were hallowed by kinship, tradition, and cult. Athens had been most conservative in this respect. In order to make the reforms palatable, the *phratries* were retained for cult reasons, and ten eponymous ancestors were found for each of the new tribes.

New Organs of Government. A new *Boule,* consisting of five hundred members, fifty chosen by lot by each tribe, was established. This Council of Five Hundred served as a steering committee for the *Ecclesia,* which continued to include all citizens. Since five hundred was rather a large number for a steering committee, the calendar year was divided into ten parts, or *prytanies.* The fifty representatives of each tribe were given one-tenth of the year at the helm, and every day a new chairman of this subcommittee was selected by lot. After a measure had been introduced by the *Boule,* the *Ecclesia* voted upon it. This system gave all citizens a chance to participate directly in government. But democracy was not yet complete, for only the richest three classes could hold the archonships.

In 501 B.C., the army was reorganized according to tribe rather than, in the old manner, according to wealth. Each tribe now organized its own contribution to the military and elected a *strategos,* or general. In the next century, these generals would be the chief magistrates in the state. Democracy had become a flourishing institution in Attica.

THE RISE OF SPARTA

By the end of the sixth century B.C., Sparta (Lacedaemon) was the rival of Athens, and both were the undisputed leaders of Greece. According to the *Iliad,* Sparta had been one of the major cities of the Achaean world, and did not then differ radically from such places as Mycenae or Pylos. Luxury and the fine things in life were prized, and Sparta was neither more nor less militaristic than its neighbors. The Dorian invasions destroyed the old Lacedaemon, and an entirely new type of state eventually rose in its stead.

Early History

As noted previously, following their invasion of Greece, rather than commingle with the Achaeans, the Dorians enslaved them. In some areas, such as Corinth, this relationship was modified over time, but in Sparta it was exacerbated. Still, the situation was not bad during the eighth century and part of the seventh century B.C. Lands of Laconia in the southeastern Peloponnesus, well-watered by the Eurotas River, had been allotted to Dorian Spartans, who worked them with the aid of *helots,* descendants of the original Achaeans. Some pre-Dorians living in villages in the hills were free, and had rights in their own communities, but were not Spartan citizens. They were known as *perioikoi* ("those who reside around"). The Spartans were divided into five villages, which served as political units. During this period, the arts appear to have flourished, and there are signs of luxury items such as ivories.

In the eighth century B.C., the Spartans, like the Athenians, felt the pressures of population expansion. But rather than send out colonies, they conquered Messenia, which lay to the west of Laconia (the First Messenian War). Unfortunately, they converted the native population into *helots* and divided the land among themselves. This action further diluted the Spartan population in the state. Those dissatisfied with the situation were sent off (ca. 710 B.C.) to southern Italy, where they founded the colony of Taras (Tarentum).

The Messenian Revolt and Its Consequences

Sometime around 650 B.C., the Messenians revolted (the Second Messenian War), and the Spartans suddenly saw that if they were to continue in their superior position, they would have to build up a military machine capable not only of suppressing revolts but of nipping them in the bud. A tightly disciplined Spartan *hoplite* phalanx defeated the Messenians after twenty years of warfare. Within one hundred years, the Spartan state had become a military machine, and the Spartans apparently lived only to fight. Lycurgus (thought by some scholars to be a mythical figure and by others to have been an actual leader) is traditionally credited with the militaristic changes in the Spartan constitution, but his ninth-century date appears to have been too early.

SPARTAN POLITICAL LIFE

The trend in Spartan politics in the sixth century B.C. was toward an equalization of rights among the Spartans themselves. The state's traditional dual monarchy, which consisted of one member each from the more prestigious Agiad and the junior Eurypontid families, was undercut by the introduction of five magistrates, *ephors,* elected from each of the five villages. They began with supervising the two kings, but as time went on they superseded them in the executive and judicial branches of government, although not in the military or religious spheres. The kings, together with twenty-eight men over the age of sixty, formed the *Gerousia,* or council of elders, and all held this office for life. (The *Gerousia* was probably a descendant of the Homeric council.) Besides acting as a law court, the *Gerousia* prepared and introduced measures for the *Apella,* or assembly of citizens, and it could block any measure passed by the assembly. The *Apella,* comprising all citizens over thirty years of age, elected the magistrates and the members of the *Gerousia.*

In foreign policy, it was no longer feasible to conquer new areas and enslave their populations. As a result, the Spartans formed (by 505 B.C.), the Peloponnesian League, a system of alliances with local governments favorable to Sparta, Every state in the Peloponnesus except Argos and the Achaean *poleis* was a member.

SPARTAN SOCIAL LIFE

From birth, the life of a Spartan was circumscribed by the state. The newborn infant was inspected, and if it did not appear strong or perfectly formed, it was exposed to the elements on a mountaintop. At the age of seven, a boy entered a troop and learned a rigorous discipline. His clothing and food were minimal even in the winter, and he was thus forced to depend on furtive theft (detection brought disgrace). He was taught to look with downcast eyes, lest external stimuli force him to think and break his discipline. When he reached the age of twenty, he was enrolled in the army and in a *syssition*, or common eating group, and had no family life. It was only at the age of thirty that he received voting rights. He spent a large part of his life in military exercises until the age of sixty, when he was at last freed from military obligations. Spartan women kept in excellent physical shape, in order to bear healthy, bellicose offspring. They had more freedom, especially in property rights, than women in most parts of Greece. Commerce and industry were left to the *perioikoi,* for Spartans could not be spared from military duties.

The *helots* appear to have had a serflike status, and they were owned by the state. They were placed on Spartan farms, but they could keep some of the produce for themselves. They were perpetually terrorized by the *krypteia* (secret police), consisting of disguised Spartan youths who could murder any restive serf.

Some later Greeks, including the historian Xenophon, who were tired of the excesses of democracy, idealized the Spartan way of life. But it was a system that stifled all creative and intellectual endeavor. In the fifth and fourth centuries B.C., although Athenian life had enormous flaws, it shone in brilliance contrasted with Sparta.

THE DEVELOPMENT OF HELLENIC CULTURE

The Archaic period (ca. 750–500 B.C.) witnessed the first flowering of Greek culture. In every field of endeavor, Hellenic creativity reached new heights. The wide range of literature included the works of Hesiod, lyric poetry, and historical and geographical writings. The ancient world saw the birth of philosophy, which helped men attain a better understanding of the universe. Official religion was rationalized, and the visual arts that were created for its glorification, as well as secular art, reached new levels of refinement.

Literature

The Greeks were essentially of one linguistic group divided into several dialects. Attic-Ionian, Doric, Aeolian, and Arcado-Cypriote were employed for literary purposes. During the Middle Age, when isolated strongholds and heroic deeds in war were the norm, the oral epic tradition was the primary literary form. Cycles of legends going back to the Mycenaean period were related about the famous Greek royal houses. If a bard was skillful, he would interweave myths, legends, and the deeds of his patron. With the adaptation of the alphabet from the Phoenicians, oral tradition became literature, although the works of Homer display much of their spoken or chanted origin. As in other cultures, the religious-mythical basis of literature was expressed first in poetry. Artistic prose developed only at a later period.

HESIOD

More than any book in modern European tradition save perhaps the Bible, the works of Homer formed the basis of a nation's education. The *Iliad* and *Odyssey* were memorized, quoted, and credited with possessing a panacea of wisdom. Not far behind in the estimation of future generations were the poetic works of Hesiod.

Hesiod was born in Boeotia during the eighth century B.C., a period when population was increasing faster than the land could support it. His father left his estate to his two sons, but Hesiod's brother, Perses, was avid to obtain Hesiod's share. Hesiod's *Works and Days,* written as an admonition to Perses, contains a veritable treasure house of farming and calendar lore. It also includes a section on the "Five Ages of Man," which exemplifies the pessimistic past-oriented attitude of these times, declaring that from a race of gold, mankind had degenerated to one of iron.

Hesiod's *Theogony* ("Birth of the Gods") is an attempt to rationalize the variety of prevalent myths into one system. In a sense, for the prephilosophical world, this was the explanation of the creation of the universe. Subsequent Greek attempts at synthesis were to be in terms of natural philosophy.

THE LYRIC POETS

The singing of verse accompanied by a musical instrument was a very old form of Greek literature. With the expansion of culture on the Ionian coast and islands during the seventh and sixth centuries B.C., a new form, personal lyric poetry, was born. Many of these lyrics survive only in fragments.

Archilochus, born on the island of Paros around 700 B.C., wrote verses in a great variety of meters. In his poems, a new attitude toward life becomes evident. In the works of Homer, at least in the *Iliad,* the greatest virtue was the heroic ideal, *arete,* or excellence in warfare. The highest achievement for an individual was glory. In the *Works and Days* of Hesiod, the advisable way of life was that of a parsimonious farmer who was thankful for a good year but was basically pessimistic. Archilochus rejected these attitudes and related with abandon how he threw away his shield and fled during battle.

Alcaeus (ca. 620 B.C.), a native of Mytilene on the island of Lesbos, spent much of his life fighting political opponents, including the tyrant Pittacus. His verses, written in several meters, concern politics, wine, and love. Sappho, a contemporary of Alcaeus, was also a native of Lesbos. She was the mistress of a finishing school for girls, and her love poems reflect the bond between teacher and pupils.

Other lyric poets were Alcman, who wrote choral odes, and the martial Trytaeus, who composed in Sparta during the seventh century B.C., before that state made literature superfluous. Anacreon of Teos (ca. 570 B.C.) wrote at the court of the tyrant Polycrates of Samos. Anacreon's poems cover a variety of subjects, and his drinking songs are excellent.

The art of lyric poetry spread to other parts of Greece, as can be seen from the works of Theognis of Megara, in the second half of the sixth century B.C. Lyric verse continued into the fifth century, but most of its creative effort was absorbed by drama.

THE BIRTH OF DRAMA

The first drama appears to have grown out of the dithyramb, a lyric ode sung to the god Dionysus by a chorus. Thespis, director of the chorus for a Dionysiac Festival during the administration of Peisistratus (ca. 530 B.C.), is said to have appeared as a character apart from the chorus. He recited a prologue and changed masks to represent a variety of characters. While Thespis was out of sight, the chorus related the action.

History and Geography

With the advent of the *polis* form of government, records of the various administrations of magistrates began to be kept. In many cases, the list of archons of a city served as a calendar. However, there was no true sense of chronology, for the past was invariably considered in a mythological framework. In the sixth century B.C., when a critical concept of the universe was evolved by the natural philosophers, the writing of history began. Hecataeus of Miletus (ca. 500 B.C.) wrote *Genealogies,* tracing important family lines of his city. This was a critical work that attempted to discredit irrational myths.

Hecataeus also wrote a geography, *Description of the Earth.* The conception of the world at this time had not changed much from that of Homer's *Odyssey.* Faraway places were regarded as the lairs of magical figures, and the circle of earth was thought to be surrounded by the Stream of Ocean. Against those views, the Pythagoreans proposed a spherical earth, and Hecataeus wrote a rational description of it.

Philosophy

The Ionian islands and coast were in constant touch with the older civilizations of Asia; as a result, a more open intellectual attitude developed there than in Greece proper. It has also been suggested that, when the Ionians migrated from mainland Greece, they left behind many of their religious biases, which had been tied to the soil. By the seventh century B.C. a new school of thought, which attempted to find a rational rather than mythical explanation of the universe, had matured at Miletus.

Thales (ca. 626 B.C.) was extremely interested in celestial phenomena and mathematics. From his investigations, he concluded that everything on earth has water as its primary substance. Thales taught his students that the gods were not responsible for such natural phenomena as earthquakes and thunder. To understand why such things occurred, a person had to study nature itself.

Anaximander (ca. 610–545 B.C.), author of the first extant Greek literary prose, was a student of Thales. He thought that all things had separated from a boundless substance and that the earth was cylindrical.

Anaximenes (ca. 585–525 B.C.) stated that the primary substance was air, from which fire and water arose and on which the earth was suspended.

The Persian conquest of the Ionian cities sent many intellectuals as refugees to Magna Graecia (southern Italy and Sicily). Xenophanes of Colophon (fl. ca. 540 B.C.) dismissed religious myths and substituted the idea of a world created by one deity. He made fun of the anthropomorphic gods by saying that if oxen had artistic abilities, they would represent their gods as oxen. Pythagoras (d. ca. 496 B.C.) left his native island of Samos because of the tyranny of Polycrates and emigrated to Croton in southern Italy, where he founded an important school of philosophy. His followers, the Pythagoreans, were a semimystical order who believed in successive rein-carnations of the soul and observed strict dietary and other regulations in order to purify their lives. In studying the structure and harmony of the universe, they considered numbers the underlying reality.

Heracleitus of Ephesus (fl. ca. 500 B.C.) added introspection to the study of philosophy, for he held that the ruling force of the universe was divine flame (called *Logos,* or the Word), which also guided the soul. Thus, the basic reality was in becoming rather than being and all things were in ceaseless flux.

Religion

The Greeks were never so dominated by religious fatalism as were the Mesopotamians. In the works of Homer, the gods were controlled by Fate *(Moira),* as were mortals, but the hopelessness present in other regions was lacking. The gods themselves were delightfully amoral in the *Iliad* and the *Odyssey,* but if a mortal exceeded himself in arrogance *(hubris),* he invited divine retribution *(nemesis).* This concept carried over to later centuries. Afterlife was a shadowy affair, providing little hope for immortality. In addition to worship of Zeus, Hera, Apollo, and Aphrodite (and the rest of the Twelve Olympians), there appears to have been a belief in daemons that entered the body and induced madness. (Some scholars, including Bruno Snell, believe that decisions of Homeric heroes were arrived at not by cogitation but by divine agency.)

With the systematization of religion, similar gods of various cities were identified with each other. For example, Zeus had attributed to him all kinds of erotic adventures in many city-states, which thereby claimed connection with his divinity. Every *polis* had heroes (such as Erechtheus in Athens) who were worshiped as demi-gods. Every tribe, clan, and *phratry* also had its semidivine founder.

Fear of religious pollution and the resulting *nemesis* was extremely great, for it was contagious like a plague and was visited upon subsequent generations. It did not matter whether or not the original offense was committed intentionally. Ritual purification was essential in order to guard against it.

The coming of philosophy challenged the supremacy of religion at the same time that the traditional cults had themselves become too official and public to help those in need of comfort. Certain mysteries, such as those at Eleusis, offered a fuller spiritual life to the initiate by rites celebrating rebirth and immortality. Throughout this and subsequent periods, oracles—voices of the gods passed on to mankind—were vital to decision making in the Greek *poleis.* The oracle of Apollo at Delphi was the most prestigious.

Religion also played a role in bringing Greeks closer together. Religious leagues, or *amphictyonies,* centering on such shrines as those of Apollo at Delphi and Delos, provided a common ground for many *poleis.* If the property of the god was infringed upon or his temple desecrated, a sacred war was declared by members of the *amphictyony* against the offending state.

Another international Greek institution was also based on religion: the Olympic games. Founded in 776 B.C. and held every four years, these games were part of the worship of Zeus at Olympia. During these festivities, no wars were fought. Similar games were held at Delphi (the Pythian games) and at Isthmia.

Pottery

By the sixth century B.C., a truly native Archaic style, attempting to achieve naturalism, had emerged. Because the *symposium* (drinking party) held such an important place in the intellectual development of Greece, the vessels used in what often became a literary bout were of the highest artistic caliber. Most Greek painting on large surface areas has been lost, but pottery offers some means of understanding it.

During the Greek Middle Age, there developed a very sophisticated form of art, which has been called *Geometric* because of its severe stylization. The earliest vases of the Geometric period were decorated in a severe rectilinear manner. Later, when human and animal figures appeared, they were silhouettes composed of triangles with few curved lines.

The Geometric manner lasted until about 750 B.C., when Greek art became influenced by art objects imported from the Near East that had rounder and more exotic motifs. Griffins, goats, lions, and floral motifs entered the repertory of Greek decoration, in a style now called *Orientalizing*. The figures were often black, or sometimes they were drawn in outline on the natural color of the baked clay or an added clay slip that served as a background. Internal details were drawn or incised, and sections were sometimes overlaid with various colors of paint. This variety of styles reached a high point during the seventh century B.C. when the proto-Corinthian (ca. 650 B.C.) and the ripe Corinthian (625–580 B.C.) vases were made. Characteristic of the earlier phases of this style was the preponderance of rosettes used as a fill for the background.

The Attic styles developed in a similar manner to those of Corinth. During the sixth century B.C., Attic vases were more prized than their Corinthian counterparts because of the higher quality of clay from which they were made. In addition, Corinthian draftsmanship had deteriorated, while that of Athens had improved, as at the same time Athenian commerce grew to surpass that of Corinth. In the sixth century B.C., Attic vases were made with parallel bands having black figures on clay background in the style known as *Archaic*. In a more naturalistic mode than that of the decorative figures of the previous century, they depicted myths and other events. By the last third of the sixth century B.C. Attic black figure vases were of such high quality that many were signed. One of the finest potters and painters of this period was Exekias. By the end of the century, a new style had developed: red-figure decoration. Instead of having black figures on the orange background of the clay, the vase was painted black, and space for figures was left on the buffed clay surface. Thus, details could be drawn freely without incision.

Sculpture

Little sculpture remains from the Geometric period except for several small bronzes and terra-cottas. The earliest extant reliefs and statues, often of a votive nature, representing youths *(kouroi)* and maidens *(korai)*, are in the Orientalizing style. The free standing figures are rigid in the Egyptian style, with one leg forward and with hands clenched. Some of the hairdresses of early female sculptures also betray Eastern influence. Nonetheless, from the earliest Greek sculptures, there were attempts to achieve greater naturalism. The first device used to represent a relaxed face has been called the Archaic smile, which appears today as a grimace. In the sixth century

B.C., greater relaxation and naturalism of body were represented, although the Archaic smile and stylized hair continued throughout the century. Examples of the height of Archaic art are the famous *Calf-bearer* and reliefs from the Siphnian treasury at Delphi.

Architecture

The most characteristic of early Greek buildings was the temple. From an early date, it took on the rectangular plan of a *cella,* or inner room, surrounded by columns supporting a pitched roof. The first temples were made of wood and mud brick. Their exposed beams and open areas were covered with terra-cotta reliefs. In the sixth century B.C., limestone replaced wood and terra-cotta in construction, but much of the new stone structure still represented crossbeams (in coffered ceilings) and other details of carpentry.

Two main orders of architecture arose, the *Doric* and the *Ionic*. The Doric order revealed a closer affinity to the original wooden structure, with a simple column and rounded capital. The original ends of the beams were represented by projecting tablets known as *triglyphs;* the spaces between them in which reliefs were sculpted were known as *metopes*. The pediment or *tympanum* (the triangle formed by the pitch of the roof) was also filled with sculpture. The most renowned standing Archaic temples are found at Paestum (Poseidonia) in southern Italy. One such structure is the Temple of Hera, which was constructed in the Doric order. The Ionic order, which originated in Asia Minor, was more ornate. The column had a base and its capital included two large volutes (spiral-shaped forms). The entablature was dominated by a running frieze. The most renowned Ionic temple of the Archaic period is that of Artemis at Ephesus.

In the fifth century B.C., the Greek culture would advance further, while the Greeks would check Persian advances into the Hellenic world. But instead of continuing their cultural development in peace, the various Greek states would fall to fighting among themselves. The result would be weakened Greek city-states that would not be able to stand up to a new outside threat.

Selected Readings

Andrewes, A. *The Greek Tyrants* (1963)

Bowra, C. M. *Greek Lyric Poetry from Alcman to Simonides* (1961)

Burn, A. R. *The World of Hesiod* (1962)

_____. *The Lyric Age of Greece* (1961)

Burnet, J. *Early Greek Philosophy* (1962)

Desborough, V. R. d'A. *The Greek Dark Ages* (1972)

Fontenrose, J. *Python: A Study of Delphic Myth and Its Origins* (1959)

Forrest, W. G. *A History of Sparta, 950–192 B.C.* (1962)

Freeman, K. *The Life and Work of Solon* (1926)

Greenhalgh, F. A. L. *Early Greek Warfare* (1971)

Hignett, C. *History of the Athenian Constitution to the End of the Fifth Century B.C.* (1956)

Huxley, G. L. *Early Sparta* (1962)

Lorimer, H. L. *Homer and the Monuments* (1950)

Nilsson, M. P. *Homer and Mycenae* (1950)

Richter, G. M. A. *Archaic Greek Art* (1949)

Snodgrass, A. M. *The Dark Age of Greece* (1971)

Starr, C. G. *Origins of Greek Civilization* (1961)

Woodhead, A. G. *Greeks in the West* (1962)

7

Greece in the Fifth Century B.C.

499–428 B.C.	Persian Wars
499	Ionian revolt against Persian rule
496–406	Sophocles—writer of tragedies
495–430	Empedocles—natural philosopher
494	Miletus destroyed; Ionian revolt crushed
493–492	Themistocles archon
490	Athenians defeat Persians at Marathon
487	Archons selected by lot at Athens
485–410	Protagoras—Sophist
484–425	Herodotus—historian of *Persian Wars*
480	Battles of Thermopylae, Artemisium, and Salamis
480	Syracuse defeats Carthage at Himera
480–406	Euripides—writer of tragedies
479	Battles of Plataea and Mycale
478–477	Creation of the Delian League
470	Themistocles ostracized
469–399	Socrates—philosopher
464	Third Messenian War; Cimon expelled by Spartans
461	Cimon ostracized
461–431	Administration of Pericles
460–406	Thucydides—historian of the Peloponnesian War
460–377	Hippocrates—physician
460–370	Democritus—atomist

459–380 Lysias—orator

454 Treasury of the Delian League transferred to Athens

451 Five Years' Peace between Athens and Sparta

450–380 Aristophanes—writer of Old Comedy

445 Thirty Years' Peace between Athens and Sparta

433 Athens intervenes with Corcyra against Corinth

431–404 Peloponnesian War

431–421 Archidamian phase of war

430–429 Plague at Athens

429 Pericles dies and is succeeded by Cleon

422 Cleon and Spartan general Brasidas killed at Amphipolis

421 Peace of Nicias between Athens and Sparta

420–347 Plato—philosopher

415–413 Syracuse expedition

411 Oligarchy of Four Hundred at Athens

410 Alcibiades defeats Spartans off Cyzicus

410 Democracy restored in Athens

404 Athens falls to Spartans

The fifth century B.C. has been considered by many to represent the high point of Greek culture, for during this time all of the potential inherent in the polis reached fruition. War and imperialism dominated politics throughout the century. After the Persian threat subsided, the unity of spirit brought on by fighting a common enemy disappeared, and in its place stood the excesses of the Athenian imperial adventure. Athens and Sparta were now face-to-face as archrivals for the dominance of Greece. The result was the disastrous Peloponnesian War.

THE IONIAN REVOLT

Cyrus of Persia had conquered the lands of the Near East with relative ease. His imperialist accomplishment by 540 B.C. included Persian dominance of the Hellenized Asia Minor coastline. As in other areas, the

Persians did not subjugate the newly conquered Greeks, but they did see to it that friendly governments were established in the Ionian *poleis*. The strategy of replacing budding democracies with pro-Persian tyrants ran contrary to current Greek political tendencies. It is not surprising that the Greeks sought to rebel with greater intensity and frequency than did other Persian subjects, for due to their fierce spirit of independence they could hardly join with one another for their own common good, much less bear control by a foreign power.

In Miletus, first Histiaeus and then his son-in-law, Aristagoras, were appointed tyrants; both were adventurers. In 499 B.C. the Ionian cities revolted from Persian rule. They were led by Aristagoras, now in the bad graces of the emperor. After initial success and modest aid from Athens and Eretria (twenty and five ships respectively), the Ionians burnt the Lydian capital, Sardis. The Persians could endure the situation no longer, and by 494 B.C. they had destroyed Miletus and crushed the revolt. Those Miletans who did not die in the fighting were sold as slaves in other parts of the Persian Empire. Darius, who was now ruler of the Persian Empire, treated the Greeks leniently and allowed them more local autonomy than they had previously possessed.

THE PERSIAN WARS

The Persians desired as a buffer zone the silver- and gold-rich land of Thrace, in addition to other lands stretching to the Danube River. In 513 B.C., Darius had crossed the Hellespont and succeeded in conquering Thrace. However, the land of the Scythians to the north proved impossible to take, as the natives fled the Persians, scorching the earth behind them. The Ionian revolt temporarily stopped Persian ambitions in Europe, but in 492 B.C. Darius was ready to cross the Hellespont once more, apparently in order to seek revenge on Athens and Eretria because of their part in the Ionian revolt. An army under Darius' son-in-law, Mardonius, crossed into Thrace but was defeated, and the Persians' accompanying fleet was destroyed in a storm.

The Preliminaries to War

By the time of Themistocles' archonship (493–492 B.C.), the Athenians were ready for war with Persia. Themistocles had the port of Peiraeus fortified, but it was another ten years before the Athenian fleet was appreciably increased. In the meantime, Hippias, who had fled to Persia, advised Darius on the best strategy for securing a toehold on the Greek mainland. Instead of repeating the strategic errors of Mardonius, the new invasion was planned to cross the Aegean and land in Attica. In 491 B.C., Darius sent envoys to the Hellenic cities to demand earth and water (symbols of surrender), but Athens and Sparta not only refused to comply, but they mistreated the envoys. The story was told by Herodotus that the Athenians threw their envoy into a pit and the Spartans threw theirs into a well—one for the earth and one for the water. However, many other Greek cities, as well as the strategic island of Aegina, bent to the Persian will. This turn of events united the Athenians, as never before, against the Persian host.

The Battle of Marathon

In 490 B.C., a Persian fleet headed by Darius and Artaphernes set sail across the Aegean, conquering Delos among other islands. When the Persians landed on Euboea, they destroyed the city of Eretria, killing its men and selling its women and children into slavery. (The punishment far exceeded the Eretrian crime of having sent five ships to aid the Ionian revolt.) The Athenians, in panic, sent envoys to Plataea in Boeotia, Sparta, and other cities for assistance. The Plataeans complied, but the Spartans, despite the unprecedented two-day run of the Athenian messenger Pheidippides, would not make the inauspicious move of leaving the city in the middle of a religious ceremony.

Presumably guided by the advice of Hippias (who had accompanied the Persian generals), the armies of Datis and Artaphernes landed at the plain of Marathon, where they could use their cavalry to greatest advantage. Ten thousand Athenian troops, aided by one thousand Plataeans under the able command of Miltiades, prepared for battle. The Athenian strategy was to form a relatively weak center and very strong wings, so that the Persian cavalry would be crushed before it was prepared. The plan worked admirably, and after suffering many losses, the Persians retreated. Nonetheless, they still hoped to gain a toehold in Attica by a surprise landing at the undefended port town of Phalerum. Anticipating this attempt, the Athenians rushed to Phalerum in time to repel it. The second effort of Darius to land in Greece had failed, and his armies retreated. The prestige of Athens was at an all-time high, as was the feeling of patriotism within the city. When the Spartans finally arrived after the battle was over, their feeling of disappointment was overcome by their admiration of the Athenians.

Athens Between Invasions

Of the heroes active during the first episode of the Persian Wars, Miltiades fared badly, but his rival Thermistocles did well. Miltiades' unsuccessful attempt to avenge Athens on those islands that had gone over to the Persian side was most disagreeable to the Athenian people. Miltiades was prosecuted for the fiasco at Paros, which he besieged for a month without effect, but he died at his trial from a wound incurred in that campaign. Since his archonship, Themistocles had seen clearly that if Athens were to defend itself against Persia, defeating its Hellenic enemies in the process, it must build up its naval power. Money was lacking to complete the job in 493–492 B.C., but ten years later a new vein of silver was found in the mines at Laurium. Aristides, who headed the conservative noble faction, wanted to divide the new wealth among the citizens in the traditional manner, but Themistocles carried the day. He used the silver to build a fleet of about two hundred ships, as well as port facilities for the fleet. Themistocles, conservative rival, Aristides, was exiled by ostracism.

The Athenian constitutional base for power now became greater, as after 487 B.C. the archonships were selected by lot, and the office was thereby weakened. Replacing the *polemarch* as commander-in-chief of the armed forces was the *strategos* (general), one of a board of ten now elected from the citizen body rather than one from each of the ten tribes as before. The great advantage of this magistracy, created at the end of the sixth century B.C., was that those who held it could succeed themselves in office indefinitely. In 480 B.C., Themistocles held the extraordinary post of sole general.

Xerxes' Invasion

For several years after his accession to the throne, Xerxes, son of Darius, plotted his strategy for an invasion of Greece. His forces included a vast army, which has been estimated by scholars and contemporaries as containing anywhere from 100,000 to 500,000 men. This army crossed the Hellespont on pontoon bridges and a fleet sailing parallel to it (481 B.C.). In order to avoid the storms and consequent wrecks that had befallen Mardonius ten years before, the Persians performed the unusual engineering feat of cutting a canal across the Athos peninsula. Representatives of the Greek states met at Corinth to work out a common policy of defense, which gave Sparta the leadership of the allied armies and navies. Athens, however, was able to carry out its policy of defending the areas to the north of the Peloponnesus. The Spartan policy to take a stand at a wall across the Isthmus of Corinth would have been the height of folly, for the Persian fleet could easily have landed somewhere on the extensive Peloponnesian coastline.

THERMOPYLAE–ARTEMISIUM

The Persian advance was rapid, and it became obvious that the states of northern and central Greece were not going to fight against the enemy. Even the Delphic oracle, apparently fearing for its own safety, offered small encouragement to the allied forces. The narrow pass at Thermopylae was of crucial importance, because through it passed the only road south to Boeotia and Attica. King Leonidas of Sparta led the defense of the pass (480 B.C.). At the same time, the combined Greek fleet under the Spartan Eurybiades defended Cape Artemisium, the northern tip of the island of Euboea. The Persian navy fared badly because many of its ships were destroyed by storms. On land, the forces of Leonidas bravely defended Thermopylae, destroying many Persian troops, but after a local traitor showed the Persians a path

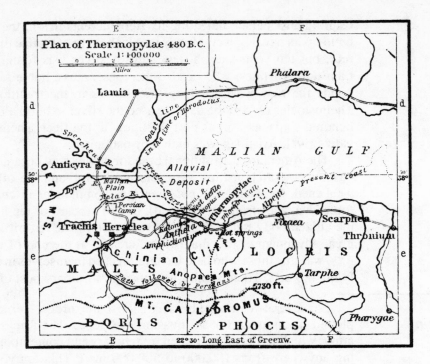

Plan of Thermopylae 480 B.C.
Scale 1:100000

behind the pass, the allies were trapped. All escaped but Leonidas and his three hundred Spartan Equals, who died martyrs' deaths.

SALAMIS

The Persian advance continued southward and Athens lay open to attack. The population fled for safety to Salamis and Troezen, while the Persians ravaged the city, burning the Acropolis. Themistocles planned a strategy of luring the Persian fleet into the narrow waters between Salamis and Attica, where the ships would not be able to maneuver. The Spartans in the meantime had built a wall across the Isthmus of Corinth and retreated. Themistocles sent a false report to Xerxes that the Athenians were thoroughly demoralized and that a quick attack would break them. The ruse was successful, and the subsequent sea battle in the Strait of Salamis (480 B.C.) resulted in a crushing defeat for the Persians.

PLATAEA–MYCALE

Xerxes retreated northward, leaving Mardonius in command of the Persian armies in Greece. Meanwhile, the Spartans were coaxed and threatened into reentering the fray. The next year (479 B.C.), the Spartan general Pausanias, commanding an allied army of about 100,000 men, fought the Persian host near Plataea in Boeotia. The Persians were thoroughly routed, and Mardonius was killed. In the same year, the Greeks destroyed the Persian navy, which had landed at Mycale in Ionia. It now remained for the allies to establish safeguards to contain Persia.

THE DEFEAT OF CARTHAGE

Much has been made of the similarity between the Greek defeats of the Persians in the east and that of the Phoenicians (Carthaginians) in the west. Perhaps there was a connection, but it must be remembered that major western Greek *poleis* and Carthage had always been antagonists. In 480 B.C., Syracuse under the tyrant Gelon was the most powerful Hellenic city in Sicily, controlling much of the eastern portion of the island. The Carthaginians ruled western Sicily. After a variety of Greek and non-Greek states appealed to Carthage for aid against Syracuse, a battle ensued at Himera (480 B.C.). The Syracusans were victorious, and the Greeks were freed from foreign domination in the western Mediterranean.

THE RISE OF ATHENIAN IMPERIALISM

When Sparta withdrew to the Peloponnesus after the Persian defeats, Athens remained the sole protector of Greece. However, in a short period of time it appeared that Athens, not Persia, was the major threat to the smaller Aegean powers.

The Fall of Pausanias and of Themistocles

The last and most unsuccessful example of Spartan leadership in Greece during this period was Pausanias, who had commanded the victorious armies at Plataea. Herodotus attributed the beginning of the general's corruption to his astounded Spartan reaction at Mardonius' plush campaign tent. At Byzantium, which Pausanias took in 478 B.C., his lust for power alarmed both Spartans and Athenians. In addition, there were reports that he was intriguing with the Persians. Pausanias was tried several times, but each time was acquitted. Finally, when he was to be tried again (470 B.C.), he fled to a temple for asylum, but was starved to death there.

Themistocles fared no better at the hands of his countrymen. His bold conservative rival, Aristides, had been recalled in 480 B.C., and the aristocratic faction was further strengthened by Cimon, son of Miltiades. In 478 B.C., Themistocles had been the hero of the day when he ordered the fortifications of Athens rebuilt. But after he was implicated in a plot linking him with Pausanias and thus with Xerxes, Athens turned against him and ostracized him (470 B.C.). The former hero of the Persian Wars was subsequently forced to flee to the Persian Empire, where he became a governor of several Asia Minor cities. He died in 462 B.C.

The Delian League

In 478–477 B.C., the Delian League, or Confederacy, was organized by Athens as a defense against future Persian imperialism. Its members were Aegean coast and island cities, and its seat was on the island of Delos, where worship of Apollo had centered for many centuries. Each of the member states had a vote in the league assembly, but since Athens was the leader *(hegemon)* of the confederation, its power far exceeded that of the smaller states. Each state was assessed a certain amount of money for maritime defense, and treasurers at Delos saw to its expenditure. Members of the league swore that they would remain within its confines until iron rose to the surface of the sea, little realizing that within several years they would be chafing to break away. Some islands, including Scyros, were forced into the confederation. The first state to try to achieve independence was Naxos in 468 B.C. Although the Persian menace had receded beyond the horizon, Athenian military tactics compelled the rebellious island not only to reenter the alliance but to become a direct vassal of Athens.

SIMON

Athens' imperialistic policies were engineered by Cimon, the aristocratic successor to Themistocles. Cimon held the office of *strategos* for a few years and was instrumental in several victories against the Persians and also against straying members of the Delian League. However, his star waned when, in 464 B.C., he led an expedition to help Sparta suppress a revolt of Messenian *helots* (Third Messenian War). The former allies did not get on together, and the Spartans dismissed the Athenians. Cimon was blamed for this great loss of face, and in 461 B.C. he was ostracized.

THE ATHENIAN EMPIRE UNDER PERICLES

The Athenian democratic rivals of Cimon were Ephialtes and Pericles, who had succeeded in stripping the Council of the Areopagus of its last vestiges of power. After Ephialtes was assassinated (461 B.C.), Pericles, grandnephew of Cleisthenes, became leader of the democratic party. The pendulum had swung to the side of the democrats, and Pericles was ruler of Athens' Golden Age for the next thirty years (461–431 B.C.).

Athens' Expansion in Greece

Athens now had territorial ambitions on land as well as at sea. Pericles began the expansionist venture by building an extensive series of fortifications around Athens and its port, Peiraeus. He connected the two cities with a series of "Long Walls" so that Athens could withstand a long siege without losing its imported grain supply.

Following the Third Messenian War, Athens was able to populate the port of Naupactus, on the west coast, with refugee *helots*. Athens was now in conflict with Sparta and Thebes, as well as with Corinth, whose zone of influence had included Naupactus. The enemies of Athens won a battle at Tanagra in Boeotia (457 B.C.), but soon afterward Pericles succeeded in seizing Aegina and forcing it into the Delian League. The next year Cimon returned from exile, and in 451 B.C. he signed a truce of five years with Sparta. Pericles made peace with Persia in 448 B.C., after defeating her forces off Cyprus. This so-called Peace of Callias is thought by some scholars to have been spurious and by others to have been an oral agreement that recognized the spheres of influence of the two states, with Athens controlling the coast of Asia Minor.

Although the Athenian navy was peerless, the land force was overextended. In 447 B.C., the Thebans won a battle at Coronea in Boeotia, which resulted in Athens' loss of its vassal states in central Greece. In 445 B.C., a Thirty Years' Peace was established that recognized Spartan hegemony on land and Athenian maritime dominance.

The Extension of the Empire

In 454 B.C., the treasury of the Delian League was transferred from Delos to Athens, ostensibly as protection against the Persians. The expenditures for the league were now decided by the Athenian assembly and the assessments were established by the *Boule*. Athena had replaced Apollo as the patron deity of the league. Why, the Athenians asked, should not the tribute be spent to glorify her hill, the Acropolis, which had been destroyed during Xerxes' invasion? By 440 B.C., only the islands of Chios and Lesbos remained autonomous states within the Delian League. The Athenian Empire was now ripe for expansion.

CLERUCHIES

Athens was three centuries late in the colonization movement, and its colonies *(cleruchies)* took on a different form from those of other Greek states. In cities that Athens wished to punish or to keep under control, groups of Athenian citizens were allotted pieces of land *(cleroi)* and hence were known as *cleruchs*. In contrast to older forms of Greek colonization, which provided for local citizenship and autonomy from the mother city, *cleruchies* were extensions of Attica abroad, and each *cleruch* was just as much an Athenian citizen as a man living in the shadow of the Acropolis.

Although Athenian attempts to make inroads against Persia in Egypt ended in failure (453 B.C.), the forces of Pericles were able to found settlements in Thrace, including Amphipolis (437 B.C.), which controlled the Black Sea trade. The colonization (443 B.C.) of Thurii in southern Italy as a potential competitor of Syracuse was not successful, because its citizens later broke with Athens.

REORGANIZATION OF THE EMPIRE

In order to facilitate collection of tribute, the empire was divided (442 B.C.) into five districts: the Aegean Islands, Thrace, the Hellespont region, Ionia, and Caria (the last two were combined after 438 B.C.). Athenian-style democracies were imposed in the three hundred odd city-states, resulting in a considerable decrease in local autonomy. Eventually these states, under pressure, took over Athenian coinage, which proved a boon to Aegean commerce. Now that the Persians had been eliminated, the empire became a prosperous economic unit free from external interference.

PERICLEAN DEMOCRACY

Full democracy was not established in Athens until after 450 B.C., when state pay for officials was introduced by Pericles. An unfortunate aspect of this extension of rights to all classes was the limitation of citizenship to a smaller number of Athenians (451 B.C.). Another gross defect of the democracy that became very evident after the death of Pericles was that, not only did it not respect minority opinion, but it censured it severely.

The People of Attica

The population of Attica varied in occupation as well as in class. The number of Athenian citizens during the time of Pericles is estimated by many scholars to have been around 172,000 and the total number of resident aliens, about 28,000. The slave population is said to have been around 115,000. All citizens, whether rural or urban, were enrolled in *demes,* the same political and religious units organized by Cleisthenes. An Athenian once registered in a *deme* remained in it even if he moved to a cleruchy in the islands.

THE RURAL POPULATION

The noble families continued to own large tracts of land, but since the time of Peisistratus the number of free small-scale farmers had been steadily increasing. Methods of agriculture were far from advanced, and olives and oil were the chief crops. About a quarter of the grain consumed in Athens was grown in Attica, and the rest was imported.

THE URBAN POPULATION

The increase in trade and prosperity was accompanied by growth in the urban middle classes, whose livelihood was gained in commerce or in the owning of workshops. Equal to them in all respects under the Periclean regime were the artisans and laborers. *Metics* (resident aliens) were protected under the law, and their loyalty to the government matched that of the citizens. Their activities were largely connected with trade and finance, and they lived in the cities of Athens and Peiraeus. Pericles relegated offspring of marriages between Athenian men and foreign-born women to *metic* status; formerly, they had been entitled to citizenship.

State slaves were engaged in public works, and some (the Scythian archers) even served as a kind of police force. The treatment of those unfortunates who worked the mines was lamentable, for they were considered objects to be used and discarded. However, slaves fared quite well in private industry, where they formed part of the unskilled labor class. In the home they were often treated as members of the family, and sometimes served as teachers.

The Government

One of the final steps toward democracy undertaken by Pericles was the transfer of the supervision of magistrates from the Council of the Areopagus to the Council of the Five Hundred *(Boule)*. The other was state payment to officials. It was now possible for anyone, regardless of class or wealth, to hold office; potential graft was also obviated. The rich were charged with liturgies, or taxes on their fortunes, which, among other public benefits, paid for the production of plays.

THE ASSEMBLIES

The *Ecclesia* (assembly) continued to include all citizens with a working quorum of six thousand, and from it juries were selected each year by lot. These formed the *Heliaea,* or law courts. Once a year, a measure was set before the assembly concerning individuals considered dangerous to the state. Balloting was on bits of pottery *(ostraka),* and the person with the most votes was ostracized (sent into exile for ten years). The institution, although credited to Cleisthenes, appears not to have been used before 487 B.C.

The *Boule,* comparatively unchanged since the reforms of Cleisthenes, was still divided into ten rotating *prytanies* during a calendar year. Its functions now included supervision of magistrates and preparation of the agenda for the *Ecclesia.*

THE STATE EXECUTIVES

The law providing for the selection of archons by lot meant that their function as chief executives of the state was eclipsed. Instead, the offices tended to acquire a judicial or religious cast. The *archon eponymous* continued to name the year and was in charge of domestic cases, while the *archon basileus* had jurisdiction over religious affairs. The real rulers of the state, the Board of Ten Generals *(strategoi),* were elected annually and could repeat their tenure in office. They were in charge of the armed forces as well as serving as chief executives of state. The official position of Pericles was that of *strategos,* who because of critical external circumstances was made general-in-chief. All officials were watched with hawk eyes by the people and could be ostracized if they failed to satisfy the public.

THE PELOPONNESIAN WAR

The disaster impending due to the excesses of Athenian foreign policy was not long in coming. By 431 B.C., the enemies of Athens were galvanized into action. By the time of the death of Pericles (429 B.C.), the Athenian leadership had lost all sense of proportion. Now a series of demagogues, interested only in self-aggrandizement, played upon the emotions of the people and involved them in a reckless war with Sparta that nearly resulted in the destruction of Athens.

The First Causes of the War

The Thirty Years' Peace had proved a sham, and most of the mainland cities, alienated by Athens' land-grabbing activities, looked to Sparta for leadership. Among them was Corinth. It will be recalled that Athens became deeply involved in the politics of the western regions of Greece because of its seizure of Naupactus at the mouth of the Gulf of Corinth. An opportunity to expand in this area occurred in 433 B.C. The island state of Corcyra had been founded by Corinth and, together with its mother city, had established a series of colonies along the west coast of Greece and Epirus, among which was Epidamnus. This city had found itself in a state of civil war, with both

Corinth and Corcyra involved on opposite sides. Corcyra, refusing to be stifled by its mother city, offered its support (including a very large fleet) to Athens if it intervened. The offer was gladly accepted. Corinth considered this alliance not only a breach of ethics but also an alarming threat to its westward trade, and began inciting Sparta, head of the Peloponnesian League, to take action.

Potidaea, Megara, and Plataea

The next offense against Corinth took place in 432 B.C. In the seventh century B.C., Corinth had founded several colonies along the coast of the Chalcidice (in Thrace), among which was Potidaea. Since this colony was situated along the Athenian route to the grain areas of the Black Sea, it was incorporated into the Delian League, but the chief city magistrate was sent each year from Corinth. Now, as Potidaea was about to revolt after being assessed an increase in tribute, Athens demanded that the city exclude its Corinthian magistrate and tear down its fortifications. Corinth and Sparta agreed to invade Attica if Athens attacked.

Megara had always been a sore spot to Athens, because it occupied the area directly to the west of Attica and provided a link between the Isthmus of Corinth and Boeotia. So long as Megara was under the control of the Peloponnesian League, the enemies of Athens were joined by land. Now Athens passed measures intended to keep Megarian commerce out of the

Aegean Sea, thus wrecking it financially. The Megarians thereupon appealed to King Archidamus of Sparta for help.

The final violation of the Thirty Years' Peace took place when Thebes tried to seize Plataea, which although located in Boeotia was a traditional ally of Athens.

The Archidamian War

The war began in 431 B.C. with raids by Athens in the Peloponnesus and the devastation of Attica by Sparta under King Archidamus. From the outset, it was evident that neither Athens nor Sparta could win. Athens had control of the seas, but commanded few mainland areas outside Attica. If Attica were invaded, its citizens could retreat within the walls of the city, while food imported by sea could be sent from Peiraeus to Athens between the "Long Walls." Sparta was leader of the Peloponnesian League, but had no navy. However, it could obtain grain from its allies, and the ravages of Athenian sea raids bothered it little. Apparently the strategy of Pericles was to fight a war of attrition during which the Peloponnesian League would fall apart.

THE PLAGUE

In 430–429 B.C., a terrifying plague from the East struck Athens. Because of overcrowding in the city, its spread could not be arrested, and people died in the streets with no one to take care of them. Fully a third of the population perished, and many others were crippled. Due to the universal horror of the disease, traditional Athenian religion and social behavior proved ineffective. The nadir was reached when Pericles himself, after having been removed from office and then reelected, died of plague (429 B.C.). Whatever logic and moderation there had been in Athenian policy died with him. His successor was the rash demagogue Cleon, whose rhetoric raised the Athenian masses to the highest hopes of destroying Sparta; nothing short of that would do.

CLEON

The emotionalism of Cleon was matched by that of the Athenian assembly, whose temper was very short and whose moods changed rapidly. Mytilene on the island of Lesbos, although relatively independent, had been chafing under Athenian hegemony and was planning to revolt (428 B.C.). When Cleon got wind of this situation, he whipped the Athenians into such a frenzy that they decided to kill all of the men on the island and sell the women and children into slavery. A boat was sent off to execute that order, but the next day more rational opinion prevailed and the orders were countermanded. Nevertheless, Mytilene suffered the loss of its freedom with the imposition of higher tribute and Athenian *cleruchies*.

The theory behind Cleon's actions was that Athens could win the war and must do everything possible to ensure a rapid victory. The theater of war now shifted westward, and an able general, Demosthenes, was placed in command. After defeats in Aetolia, the Athenian forces began to win and, thus encouraged, landed at the back door of Sparta, the narrow hilly peninsula of Pylos off the west coast of Messenia. In a totally unexpected move, the Spartans blockaded on the island of Sphacteria, adjacent to Pylos, asked for a truce (425 B.C.). The Athenians refused, and Cleon himself arrived and took command. By luck, the Spartans were defeated, and Cleon returned to Athens in triumph.

BRASIDAS

The euphoria of Cleon and the Athenians did not last long, for Brasidas was now (424 B.C.) in command of the Spartan forces, and his skill matched Cleon's rashness. Athenian attacks on Megara and Boeotia ended in failure. The new strategy of the Spartans was to cut the Athenian lifeline to the Black Sea grain supply by offering to liberate the Thracian coastal cities and by intriguing with the Macedonian king.

The balance now shifted in favor of the Peloponnesians, and Athens was ready for peace. But war began again and Cleon rushed to the important city of Amphipolis, which had revolted (422 B.C.). There his forces were defeated by the Spartans, but in the fray of battle both Brasidas and Cleon were killed. The Athenian people, tired of the continual ups and downs of the war years, elected as general the leader of the aristocratic peace party, Nicias (421 B.C.).

The Peace of Nicias

The resources of both Sparta and Athens had been depleted in the war, and neither side had won any advantage. As a result, in 421 B.C. a peace treaty was negotiated that recognized the status quo, with Athens in control of Pylos and the Thracian cities independent. The peace was to last for fifty years.

THE DISAFFECTION OF SPARTA'S ALLIES

Megara, Corinth, and Thebes had nothing to gain from peace; but with the defeat of Athens, they would become major powers. As a result, they broke away from the Spartan alliance; and Sparta temporarily joined with Athens for protection. Further trouble for Sparta occurred in 421 B.C., when a Thirty Years' Truce with Argos expired. Argos, never a friend of the Spartans, made moves to combine against them with the former members of the Peloponnesian League.

THE RISE OF ALCIBIADES

The situation played into the hands of Alcibiades, a young disciple of Socrates from the prestigious Alcmaeonidae clan. Alcibiades wanted the democratic leadership, and he clamored for an alliance with Argos against Sparta (420 B.C.). A treaty was approved, but in 418 B.C. the Spartans defeated their former allies at Mandnea and restored the Peloponnesian League.

With peace and prosperity, the Athenians again acquired expansionist ambitions. The leadership of Nicias seemed unexciting and stodgy in comparison with the charismatic personality of Alcibiades, who incited them to reckless adventures.

The Melian affair lacked even the pretense of legality present in earlier Athenian transgressions. In 425 B.C., the Dorian island of Melos, never a member of the Delian League, was assessed tribute by Athens, which it rightly refused to pay. In 416 B.C., Athens tried to pressure the island into her empire; when it refused, its men of military age were slaughtered and the women and children were sold into slavery. Athenian *cleruchs* replaced the population. Punishment which had been wisely rejected twelve years before in the case of a disaffected ally, Mytilene, was now executed on a neutral. Athens was well on the way to self-destruction.

The Syracuse Expedition

By 415 B.C., Alcibiades had conceived of a grand design to spread Athenian power to the lands of Magna Graecia at the expense of Syracuse, then the most powerful city in the western Greek world. The immediate chance for intervention occurred when Segesta in Sicily asked for Athenian aid in its military problems.

THE DEFECTION OF ALCIBIADES

It was decided (415 B.C.) that a fleet should be sent to Sicily under the command of Nicias (who opposed the expedition), Alcibiades (who favored a coalition with the enemies of Syracuse), and Lamachus (who wanted an immediate attack on Syracuse, then relatively unprepared). However, the night before the expedition set sail, the Athenian *herms* (pillars surmounted by busts of the god Hermes, which were thought to protect the buildings they fronted) were mutilated. Since Alcibiades had a reputation for nocturnal carousing, his aristocratic enemies accused him of the desecration. The expedition left, but Alcibiades was recalled to face trial on charges of impiety. He fled to Sparta, where he divulged the Athenians' designs. The loss of the prime mover and planner of the Syracuse venture did not augur well for its success.

THE SIEGE OF SYRACUSE

The siege of Syracuse did not take place until 414 B.C. By that time, the Syracusans were ready, and the Spartans had sent a contingent under Gylippus to aid them. Despite reinforcements from Athens headed by the war hero Demosthenes, the Athenians were defeated (413 B.C.). The escape of the fleet was still possible; but Nicias, a conservative by nature, feared the portent of a lunar eclipse and did not permit withdrawal for twenty-seven days. In the meantime, the Syracusans had blocked all exits from the harbor, and two-thirds of the Athenian fleet was destroyed. Survivors managed to land, but their attempted retreat was stopped. The Athenian leaders were executed, and the remnants of the troops were sold to work in stone quarries as disposable slaves.

The Last Stages of the War

On the urging of Alcibiades, the Spartans had fortified Decelea in Attica so that they could ravage enemy fields in a more systematic way (413 B.C.). The empire started to disintegrate, and internal strife began in Athens. In 411 B.C., an oligarchic group of four hundred seized power and attempted to limit citizenship to a chosen few. Their allies, the moderates led by Theramenes, wanted a broader citizen body based on those who could afford to be *hoplites* (five thousand in number). Alcibiades, who had left Sparta for Persia, was now recalled and became chief of the Athenian fleet at Samos, which had remained loyal to the democratic cause. The "Four Hundred"— who had alienated their moderate allies—now fell from power and were replaced by the "Five Thousand."

RESTORATION OF THE DEMOCRACY

The Spartans were dismayed at this turn of events, which culminated in their naval defeat off Cyzicus by the forces of Alcibiades (410 B.C.). Now that the oligarchy which it had favored was gone, and after the Athenians rejected a peace offer, Spartan policy required that Athens be humbled militarily. The only way to do this was by sea, with the cutting of the Athenian grain route from the Hellespont in the process. The Persians, ever eager to recover the Ionian cities from Athens, began supplying Sparta with the necessary funds to build a navy.

In 410 B.C., the democracy was restored in Athens. There ensued a bloody massacre of the four hundred oligarchs; and in 407 B.C., upon his return to Athens, Alcibiades was once more made *strategos*. The fortunes of both Alcibiades and Athens were running out, however, for the new Spartan navy had a most able commander, Lysander. After the Athenians lost the Battle of Nofium (407 B.C.) and many ships were destroyed, Alcibiades once more left Athens. The final victory of the Athenians in the war was a desperate one. At the Arginusae Islands, an Athenian fleet consisting of virtually anything that could float, manned by all kinds of Athenians, defeated the Spartans (406 B.C.). Because of storms, however, many Athenian ships were destroyed, and their commanding generals were rashly condemned to death for failing to rescue the crews.

THE DEFEAT OF ATHENS

The end came at Aegospotami (405 B.C.) in the Hellespont region, where Lysander surprised the Athenian fleet despite the alertness of the *strategos,* Conon (who managed to escape with several ships to Cyprus). The Athenian grain supply was now cut, and it remained for the Spartans to take Athens. A state of siege lasted until 404 B.C., when the city fell. The Long Walls were ordered destroyed, but Athens itself was spared; the Spartans were sentimental about the "School of Hellas." Under the guidance of Sparta, an extreme oligarchy ("the Thirty") led by Critias (like Alcibiades, a pupil of Socrates) was established in Athens. It began the slaughter of its enemies, matched in deadliness only by the plague of 430–429 B.C. In 402 B.C., there was a democratic reaction under Thrasybulus, but Athens, depleted in resources and without control of a tributary empire, was no longer the same city. Sparta, too, was far from strong, for the war had eroded its powers.

INTELLECTUAL AND CULTURAL DEVELOPMENT AT ATHENS

The fifth century B.C. is considered one of the periods of highest cultural development in the history of Western man. Drama absorbed lyric poetry and created a form of literature unique in the ancient world. Historical writing flourished, and philosophy revolutionized thought processes. Sculpture and architecture were so highly refined that they became the classical standards for future generations.

The Sophistic Revolution

Greek literature of the fifth century B.C. can be divided into two categories: that before the Sophists and that after. The influence of these men cannot be underestimated. In the first half of the century, Athenian thought was still rooted in the aristocratic ideals of the past. Traditional virtues embedded in the state, gods, and family, rather than in the individual, were the norm, and as a result the orientation was toward the past. With the coming of full democracy under Pericles, new needs were felt by citizens who had never before participated in government, and traditional education was found wanting. In addition, the plague and other disasters of the Peloponnesian War destroyed faith in the traditional values of religion.

The field was open for the Sophists, who traveled from place to place receiving pay for their lectures, a most daring innovation. They taught practical subjects such as elocution, and their new concept of the individual can be summarized by the saying of Protagoras of Abdera (ca. 485–410 B.C.): "Man is the measure of all things." Henceforth, individuals would look within themselves, rather than speculate about the universe as had the natural philosophers. The teachings of the Sophists tended to be hypercritical of the traditions of state and religion and thus brought them into disrepute with the older generation.

Lyric Poetry and Drama

After Pindar (ca. 518–438 B.C.), who wrote his odes for athletes in the old aristocratic tradition, and the *Bacchylides* (fl. ca. 450 B.C.), the greatest creativity in lyric poetry was represented by Attic drama. Since these plays were attended by the whole population of Athens, they reflected contemporary thought. Aeschylus was rooted in the traditions of the past, while Sophocles put more characterization, albeit idealized, into his plays. Euripides was influenced by the Sophists, and his characters are more like everyday individuals. The comedies of Aristophanes, at least in their political viewpoint, reflected the older aristocratic traditions.

TRAGEDY

All Athenian tragedies had approximately the same form, since they were part of the Dionysiac Festival. On each morning of the festival, a playwright entered three tragedies and a light satyr play in the competition for a prize. A rich citizen *(choregus)* produced the plays, using his own funds. The dramas took place on the slopes of the Acropolis in the Theater of Dionysus, which had wooden seats surrounding a circular flat area for the chorus *(orchestra),* with an altar to the god. A wooden building *(skene)* served as a backdrop for the orchestra and a place from which the actors emerged.

The chorus, which moved in dancelike motions, was a most important component in the actions of a play. It sang choral odes and continued the action when the actors were offstage. It also gave the background of events preceding the action of the tragedy. Aeschylus introduced a second, and Sophocles a third, actor who could change masks in the skene and thus represent several characters. The performers also wore padded robes and thick-soled boots *(kothoriwi).* Since music played such an important role in ancient drama, its loss leaves a somewhat austere air to the surviving texts.

Aeschylus. Among the plays of Aeschylus (525–456 B.C.), the best-known are those of the *Oresteia* trilogy. In the *Agamemnon,* the hero of the Trojan War returns home, but is killed by his wife Clytemnestra and her lover, Aegisthus, the ostensible reason being that he had sacrificed his daughter Iphigenia in order to obtain favorable winds for the Greek fleet. In the *Choephoroi* ("Libation Bearers"), Agamemnon's son Orestes avenges his father's death, but since the murderess is his mother, in killing her he commits an enormous pollution. In the *Eumenides,* Orestes is pursued by the Furies (goddesses of vengeance), but after much suffering is pardoned. It should be noted that it is not feelings of guilt, but the mythologized Furies that plague Orestes. He is finally saved through the compassion of Zeus.

Sophocles. Sophocles (496–406 B.C.) belonged to a later time and a different world than Aeschylus. The tragedy of *Oedipus the King* illustrates this best. Before the beginning of the tragedy, Laius, king of Thebes, had been told by the Delphic Oracle that his newly born son was destined to kill his father and marry his mother. He therefore exposed the young child, who was however saved by a servant and raised by the King of Corinth. The child (Oedipus) grew up and heard the oracle's predictions. Thinking that Corinth was his native city, he left it forever. On the road to Thebes, he killed an old man (Laius) who blocked his way. Subsequently, he guessed the riddle of the monster Sphinx, who was then plaguing the city. The monster killed herself and Oedipus became king, marrying Laius' widow Jocasta (his mother). In the play, upon Oedipus' probing, all is revealed to him, and Jocasta hangs herself. Oedipus blinds himself out of guilt, and then goes into exile. In *Oedipus at Colonus,* Oedipus goes through a metaphysical change after his suffering and cleansing, and becomes a demigod.

Although there appears to be a fatalistic framework to the play, the characterization of Oedipus is of paramount importance. His rashness causes the death of Laius, and his impatience leads to the disclosure of his identity. Finally, in his guilt and pollution, he himself—not an external deity—puts out his eyes, and he voluntarily goes into exile. His final deification is, however, more in the traditional vein.

Euripides. In future generations the most popular of the great fifth-century B.C. tragedians was Euripides (ca. 480–406 B.C.). His plays deal even less with the divine element than do those of Sophocles. Indeed, the *Medea* concerns the emotions of an abandoned passionate woman from a half-barbaric country. Jason had taken Medea, a Colchian princess, back with him to Corinth after she helped him obtain the Golden Fleece. She was passionately in love with him, and they had two sons. But Jason was extremely opportunistic; and, as the play opens, he has decided to abandon Medea for the daughter of Creon, king of Corinth. Medea's passion causes her to become deranged, and she kills the princess as well as her own two children. Oracles and prophecies play no part in this drama; only the jagged emotions of a woman predominate. The same individualization and realism in characterization can be found in the other plays of Euripides, including *Trojan Women* and *Bacchae.*

COMEDY: ARISTOPHANES

Comedies entered the competition of the Dionysiac Festival in the afternoon. The genre appears to have originated early in the fifth century B.C. from slapstick and erotic fertility skits. By the end of the century, such writers as Aristophanes wrote masterpieces combining astringent satire with uproarious fantasy along a minimal story line. Since comedy was part of a religious festival and appears to have acted as a safety valve for the community, much could be ridiculed in such a play which would not be permitted in the Assembly or the Agora (marketplace).

The outlook of Aristophanes (ca. 450–380 B.C.) was conservative. He had no use for the extreme democracy of the period, nor could he abide Euripides and the Sophists. In his plays, no one was spared: Cleon was devastated in *The Acharnians;* Euripides in *The Frogs;* Socrates in *The Clouds;* and the Peloponnesian War in *Lysistrata,* which depicts the Athenian women rejecting their men until they stop fighting.

History

With the fusion, in the writings of Herodotus, of the annalistic-genealogical tradition and geographic description, an integrated form of history was created. The new emphasis on individuals brought motivation and acute characterization into the *History* of Thucydides. The two epic events of the century, the Persian and Peloponnesian Wars, are both described in the new genre.

HERODOTUS

Herodotus (ca. 484–425 B.C.), who was born in Asia Minor, traveled all over the ancient world and eventually joined an expedition of Athenians to found Thurii in southern Italy. He wrote in the Ionic dialect and continued the analytic thought of that area. In the *History* of the Persian Wars, Herodotus made an attempt to write a universal history by delving into the past and giving the background for the events that he described. He liked nothing better than a good story (at times at the expense of the truth), and his respect for gods of other peoples as well as of the Greeks was great. Indeed, in his writings divine forces punish those who exceed the bounds of propriety.

THUCYDIDES

Thucydides (ca. 460–406 B.C.) had been an unsuccessful general of Athens at Amphipolis in 424 B.C. (after his recovery from the plague a few years earlier). Following his ostracism for this defeat, he turned to historiography. The *History of the Peloponnesian War* is not complete, for it does not go past the events of the year 411 B.C., but it is a landmark in objective writing. The revolution in thought that occurred in the latter part of the fifth century B.C. dictated the form of the *History;* the events of paramount importance are shaped by men rather than gods. Thucydides analyzed the causes of the war in terms of the reality of the times. The speeches put in the mouths of the characters were not aimed at verbatim journalistic rendering, but were written to give a clearer insight into the psychological make-up of individuals.

Philosophical and Scientific Thought

During the first part of the fifth century B.C., natural philosophy and science were intertwined in speculative thought, but in the latter part of the century, philosophy began to deal more and more with ethics and with man as an individual. Science, although only in its embryonic state, was now separated from natural philosophy. The ideas of Socrates brought about the transformation of philosophy, and Hippocrates inaugurated scientific studies.

NATURAL PHILOSOPHERS AND A PHYSICIAN

It will be recalled that in his search for the truth, Heracleitus of Ephesus (fl. ca. 500 B.C.) had speculated that the universe consisted of opposites constantly battling. Opposed to this view was the Eleatic school of southern Italy, which believed in the nondestructibility and nonmotion of matter. Empedocles of Acragas (ca. 495–430 B.C.) combined these points of view and said that the universe consisted of four elements: earth, air, fire, and water, sometimes in motion and sometimes at rest. Anaxagoras of Clazomenae (ca. 500–428 B.C.) believed in a divine force or intelligence *(Nous)* that directed a universe consisting of seeds, conceived in a materialistic, nonmythological way. The theory closest to modern science was that of Leucippus of Miletus (fl. ca. 440 B.C.) and his pupil Democritus (ca. 460–370 B.C.), who believed that the universe consisted of indestructible, indivisible particles called atoms.

Hippocrates of Cos (ca. 460–377 B.C.) achieved a large measure of scientific medical knowledge, with which he treated patients. Magic and miracles had no place in his system. Instead, he believed that if people followed a healthy diet and paid attention to their personal hygiene, they would remain healthy. Hippocrates' "oath" is still used by medical graduates as a pledge of ethics.

SOCRATES

Socrates (469–399 B.C.) is considered one of the most important thinkers of Hellenic culture. Little is known about his actual ideas, because he never committed them to writing, but much of the philosophy of his pupil Plato seems to have been Socratic in origin. Socrates was primarily a teacher who devoted his life to achieving a critical, logical, probing attitude on the part of his pupils. He did this by his famous method of cross-examination that resulted in the deflation of foolish and prejudicial ideas. Yet in the strictest sense of the word, Socrates was no Sophist, for although he urged his students to be critical of all things, he was devoted to the state. In addition, his private religion of a god *(daimon)* who guided him was not incompatible with traditional cults. Perhaps the most important difference between Socrates and the Sophists was that he taught out of dedication and they for money. The execution of Socrates in 399 B.C. was due to the fact that the newly reestablished democracy needed a scapegoat: who could be a better one than Socrates, whose disciples had included Alcibiades and Critias?

Art

Throughout subsequent periods of the ancient world, the fifth century B.C. was known as the classical age when all of the canons of style and dimensions were established. The last frontier to realism had been surmounted, and new techniques made possible the representation of anything. Artists, however, did not choose literal realism but an idealized form that typified mankind.

PAINTING

Vase paintings and descriptions by later writers are the only evidence for painting in the fifth century B.C. Red figure was now the predominating form of pottery design (although white background was also present), and such advances as foreshortening and full-face appearances of figures were achieved. Also, in profile views of a face, the eye was now represented laterally rather than frontally. According to tradition, Polygnotus of Thasos (fl. ca. 475–447 B.C.) was the greatest painter of the period. Apparently the most ambitious artists did large murals of epic cycles, and one of the masterpieces of Polygnotus was *The Destruction of Troy (Iliupersis).*

SCULPTURE

The Archaic smile and rigidity in sculpture disappeared in the fifth century B.C. During the first decades of the century, the "Severe Style," best exemplified by sculptures from the Temple of Aphaia on Aegina and the Temple of Zeus at Olympia, still revealed some stylization, but faces were now completely relaxed. The intent of all sculptural representation of man and the gods was similar to that of Sophocles in the delineation of his tragic characters: the depictions were to be universal, bigger than life, and idealized versions of man.

Myron's (fl. ca. 480–445 B.C.) sculpture of the *Discus Thrower (Discobolus)* shows the new freedom of representation, although the statue is seen to best advantage only from the front. Polycleitus (fl. ca. 450–405 B.C.) created what in future generations was known as the canon, or system of ideal proportions of parts of the body. In his statues of athletes such as the *Spear Carrier (Doryphorus),* the weight of the body rests on one foot, giving the figure a slight twist. Pheidias (ca. 490–415 B.C.) worked on the sculptures for the Parthenon, one of which was the gigantic cult statue of Athena Parthenos, made of gold and ivory (chryselephantine). Because of Pheidias' influence, drapery was sculpted realistically with lush folds.

Original bronze statues of the fifth century B.C. are rare, but many marble copies from later periods survive, so that a good idea can be achieved about the appearance of the originals. Except for architectural decorations and complements, most freestanding masterpieces of this period were of bronze.

ARCHITECTURE

The destruction of the Acropolis during the Persian Wars supplied the need, and the treasury of the Delian League the means, of achieving the most remarkable architecture of Hellenic culture. The original Parthenon, destroyed during the Persian Wars, had been the shrine of Athena; therefore Pericles gave priority to its new construction. The result of the work of the architects Callicrates and Ictinus is a masterpiece of the Doric order. The subtleties of adjustments to avoid visual distortion were never equaled in the Greek world. The Erechtheum (completed in 407 B.C.,), a temple built on the site of the ancient Achaean palace, was hardly less hallowed. Because it was constructed on sloping ground, the flexible Ionic order was employed. Its Porch of the Maidens was a daring departure for Athens insofar as it was supported by statues instead of columns. By the last quarter of the century, other structures completed the architectural ensemble on the Acropolis. The Temple of Athena Nike is a small gem of Ionic construction. The monumental Acropolis entrance for the Sacred Way of the Panathenaic processions, the Propylaea (designed by the architect Mnesicles), is a masterpiece of Doric architecture.

The Acropolis was not the only part of Athens affected by the Periclean building program. Other temples, as well as theaters, courts, and marketplaces, were constructed throughout the city. This construction activity provided not only architects, stonemasons, and sculptors with employment, but the urban poor as well.

In the next century, several city-states besides Athens and Sparta would achieve dominance, but it was a century marred by conflict. At the end of the century, another outside power would threaten the Greek states and this time subjugate them.

Selected Readings

Ashmole, B. *Architect and Sculptor in Classical Greece* (1972)
Bolkenstein, H. *Economic Life of Greece's Golden Age* (1958)
Bowra, C. M. *Periclean Athens* (1962)
Burn, A. R. *Persia and the Greeks* (1962)
Calhoun, G. M. *Business Life of Ancient Athens* (1926)
Conner, W. R. *The New Politicians of Fourth Century Athens* (1971)
Corbett, P. E. *The Sculpture of the Parthenon* (1959)
De Ste. Croix, G. E. M. *The Origins of the Peloponnesian War* (1972)
Dover, K. J. *Aristophanic Comedy* (1968)

Gomme, A. W. *Commentary on Thucydides*. 3 vols. (1945–56)

————. *The Population of Athens in the Fifth and Fourth Centuries B.C.* (1933)

Henderson, B. W. *The Great War Between Athens and Sparta* (1927)

Hammond, N. G. L. *The Classical Age of Greece* (1975)

Jones, A. H. M. *Athenian Democracy* (1957)

Meiggs, R. *The Athenian Empire* (1972)

Murray, G. *Aeschylus, The Creator of Tragedy* (1940)

Pickard-Cambridge, A. W. *The Theatre of Dionysus in Athens* (1957)

Pollitt, J. J. *Art and Experience in Classical Greece* (1972)

Webster, T. B. L. *Greek Theater Production* (1956)

8

The Greek World in the Fourth Century B.C.

395–387 B.C.	Corinthian War
387	King's Peace
384–322	Demosthenes—orator
384–322	Aristotle—philosopher
382	Sparta occupies Thebes
378	Epaminondas and Pelopidas free Thebes from Sparta
371	Thebans defeat Spartans decisively at Leuctra
367–344	Dionysius II and Dion rule Syracuse
362	Thebans win Battle of Mantinea, but Epaminondas is killed
359	Philip gains throne of Macedonia
356	Second Athenian Confederacy breaks away
356	Alexander born to Philip and Olympias of Macedon
351–340	*Philippics*—Desmosthenes' invectives against Philip
348	Chalcidian League falls to Philip
346	Peace of Philocrates between Macedonia and Athens
341–290	Menander—writer of New Comedy
341–270	Epicurus—founder of Epicureanism
338	Philip defeats Athens and other Greek states at Chaeronea
338	League of Corinth formed

*F*ollowing the defeat of Athens in the Peloponnesian War, Sparta, with no real rival left, became the tyrannical ruler of much of Greece. Persia, who controlled the balance of power, then began to support Thebes and Athens against the Spartans, and Athens reestablished a defensive confederation. Thebes subsequently defeated Sparta and constructed a large empire in Greece, but it was short-lived. After the states in Greece had sufficiently worn themselves out with war, Macedonia under Philip was able to conquer the peninsula, thus ending seven hundred years of Greek independence.

SPARTAN HEGEMONY

After the Peloponnesian War, much of Greece was in a difficult economic situation, for there was little unruined land to absorb excess population. In victorious Sparta, on the other hand, the number of Equals able to serve in the army had dwindled. *Perioikoi* and even *helots* were used by the military, but if Sparta were to follow the plan of its leader, Lysander, even more soldiers would be necessary. The expedient of hiring unemployed Greeks and veterans of the Peloponnesian War was now used, and within fifty years mercenary troops were displacing citizen armies in the Greek world. The rationale was simple: a leader, if supported by sufficient funds, could have unquestionable loyalty from paid troops, instead of the uncertainties of a citizen army.

Spartan Tyranny

The Spartan promise to liberate Greece from tyranny was to prove false. In addition to imposing oligarchies favorable to its policies, Sparta stationed garrisons and military governors in many places. Corinth and Thebes, who had rejoined the Peloponnesian League only after their defeat by the Spartans (418 B.C.), were extremely dissatisfied with the new defenders of Greece. The Spartan mentality now revealed itself singularly unfit to rule; it could not cope with world problems beyond a Peloponnesian scope, and events were shortly to demonstrate that members of the Spartan Empire did not like being treated like *helots*.

The Expedition of the Ten Thousand

For the Persians, Greece had become a source of excellent mercenary troops. The king of Persia, with his great wealth, had been able to offer subsidies that had built a navy and won the Peloponnesian War for Sparta. In consequence, Persia hoped to have a permanent hand in Hellenic affairs and to also retain the Ionian cities. The Spartans felt that they would have to turn against the Persians in order to keep their image as liberators.

After the death of Darius II in 405 B.C., his two sons, Artaxerxes II and Cyrus, engaged in combat as Cyrus claimed the throne from his elder brother. The pretender, who was in control of Asia Minor, hired a large army of mercenaries, including thirteen thousand Greeks (the "Ten Thousand"), and obtained aid from the Spartans. The forces of the two brothers met at Cunaxa in Mesopotamia. To the total surprise of all concerned, the Greeks won a smashing victory, but Cyrus was killed, and the Ten Thousand found themselves in the middle of a vast land area far from the sea (always a traumatic experience for Greeks). They organized under the leadership of the Athenian Xenophon (who wrote about the march in the *Anabasis*), and finally made it to the port of Trapezus, shouting with joy as they sighted the Black Sea.

Spartan Involvement in Asia Minor

The Spartans chafed at the loss of Cyrus, but one fact remained: a small group of Greeks had been able to defeat the army of the "King of Kings" on its own territory. Under King Agesilaus of Sparta, many of the Ten Thousand were reemployed in an invasion of Asia Minor (396 B.C.). Although it first appeared that Sparta would soon be in control of the Ionian cities, things did not go well and the expedition was unsuccessful. In 402–401 B.C., democracy had been restored in Athens, contrary to Spartan policies. In 395 B.C., Thebes and Corinth joined with Argos (which had always hated the Spartans) to form a coalition against the new tyranny—and Athens also joined.

The Corinthian War

The Spartans and the new alliance clashed in the Corinthian War (395–387 B.C.). Persia, now an enemy of Sparta, sent a fleet under the Athenian Conon to Cnidus, where the Spartan navy was crushed (394 B.C.). Artaxerxes, preferring to see Greek states balancing each other in strength, sent money to Athens to rebuild the Long Walls destroyed by Sparta in 404 B.C. Athens was once more on the way to becoming a major power, but only on a relative basis, for all of Greece was being rapidly depleted. Athens recovered certain islands, including Scyros and Lemnos, and an Athenian army under Iphicrates badly defeated the Spartans on land. Sparta sent to the Persian king for terms to end the war, and in 387 B.C. Artaxerxes imposed the terms in the "King's Peace": the Ionian cities of Asia Minor would now belong to Persia and all power blocs in Greece, including the Boeotian League, were to be broken up. Sparta was to be Persia's agent in supervising the peace terms. This provision was a great mistake, for the Spartans were only waiting for a chance to regain their lost power and now they began to oppress all of Greece. After forcing the inhabitants of Manfinea to destroy their city (384 B.C.), they occupied Thebes (382 B.C.).

The Second Athenian Confederacy

In the meantime, Athens was reestablishing an overseas confederation. The Second Athenian Confederacy was created, with checks to avoid another Athenian Empire. The league congress met in Athens and was completely separate from the city. Its aggregate power on the workings of the confederacy was equal to that of Athens, but safeguards such as the prohibition of tribute were imposed. Although Athens had been at war with Sparta since the inception of the Second Confederacy, the aggressive designs of Thebes against Phocis had pushed her toward the Lacedaemonians.

THEBAN HEGEMONY

Under the able leadership of Pelopidas and Epaminondas, Thebes was freed from Spartan control (378 B.C.), and began to reorganize the Boetian League (374 B.C.). The new fighting force of the league, the "Sacred Band," and new military tactics made Thebes into a formidable power.

In 371 B.C., a peace conference was held in Sparta, and was attended by representatives from most Greek states. The aim of Athens and Sparta was to restore the *status quo* on the mainland according to the King's Peace, which meant the dismemberment of the Boeotian League. This did not augur well for peace, and when all of the powers signed a pacification treaty, the Theban delegate Epaminondas inscribed the words "Boeotian League," which he claimed to represent. The Spartans did not recognize this organization of states and therefore deleted the signature. The Thebans left, and that same year the Spartans sent an army under King Cleombrotus to Boeotia, but it was crushed at Leuctra (371 B.C.) . The Spartans never recovered, and within a few years all of the Peloponnesian states had become independent.

Reorganization of the Peloponnesus

The defeat at Leuctra was not only a military catastrophe but also resulted in a tremendous loss of prestige for the Spartans. Member states of the Peloponnesian League one-by-one declared their independence and began to form into leagues of their own; although in a very imperfect form, federalism seemed to be in the air. The newly rebuilt Mantinea joined with neighboring states in the Arcadian League, which Thebes defended. A capital for the league, Megalopolis, was constructed under the military protection of the Boeotians. Only Sparta itself, secure in its primordial frontiers, remained untouched. The Messenian *helots,* on being liberated by Thebes, built a new city, Messene, thereby depriving Sparta of manpower and much fertile land.

The Height of Theban Influence

Thessaly, chafing under the tyrant Alexander, asked Thebes for help, and by 370 B.C., the area was liberated, but the Theban general Pelopidas was killed during the campaign. Thessaly, too important strategically to be left free, was forced into alliance with Thebes, as were other cities. The Thebans' destruction of Orchomenus for planning a revolt put Thebes into that condition of unpopularity hitherto incurred only by Athens and Sparta. The next challenge for Epaminondas was Athens, and he set about building a navy to defeat her (363 B.C.). During these years, several peace conferences had been held, but to no avail.

THE DECLINE OF GREECE

In 363 B.C., Athens and Sparta, together with Mantinea and other Peloponnesian states, joined in an alliance to liberate Greece. The resulting battle at Mantinea (362 B.C.) pitted the Thebans against the new coalition. The Thebans won, but their great leader Epaminondas was killed, and Thebes like the rest of Greece trod the road of decline.

The client states of Thebes broke away, and by 357 B.C. the Second Athenian Confederacy was on the brink of revolt. The Persians aided the rebels, and in 356 B.C. Athens lost its Second Confederacy. The Greek states never recovered military and political vitality, and their unification was to be achieved only with the loss of independence to Macedonia.

EVENTS IN THE WEST

Syracuse, which since its defeat of the Carthaginians at Himera (480 B.C.), had been considered the liberator and defender of Sicily, still faced the Carthaginian challenge. Carthage, located on the strategic peninsula jutting out from Africa toward Sicily, was the most powerful commercial state in the western Mediterranean. It controlled the north African and the Spanish coasts, as well as the western part of Sicily.

Dionysius I

Dionysius I, who in 405 B.C. had supplanted Syracusan democracy with his own dictatorial rule (although keeping democratic forms), became the new liberator of the island from Carthaginian incursions. His success in Sicily was at first moderate, but his real intent was to build an empire, making himself master of Magna Graecia, then perhaps of Greece.

Using newly invented military techniques for besieging cities, Dionysius I met with outstanding success in his expansionist drive. In the process, he enslaved entire cities, and when he died in 367 B.C., the western Greek cities were in a state of chaos similar to that of their mainland mothers.

Dionysius II and Timoleon

Dionysius II, the son of Dionysius I, was too affable and ineffectual to hold his father's conquests. The situation was not helped by his uncle Dion, who became a rival for power. In a brief attempt to bring enlightenment into government, Dion's friend, Plato, was sent for in 366 B.C. to convert Dionysius into the Philosopher King, but he failed dismally. By 344 B.C., the Syracusans had had enough, and they sent to their mother city, Corinth, for help. Timoleon, a most able Corinthian statesman and general, succeeded in freeing Sicily from tyranny, while coming to favorable terms with the Carthaginians. In 317 B.C., however, Syracuse once more fell to a tyrant.

THE RISE OF MACEDONIA

If to the early Greeks, Thessaly was half-barbarous, then Macedonia—to the north of it and west of Thrace—was beyond the pale. Nonetheless, the Macedonians were Greeks and spoke a dialect remotely connected with those in use in Greece. The regions developed separately and, perhaps because of the greater geographic unity of Macedonia, the *polis* form of government did not arise there. Instead, a series of local chieftains ruled until the country was partially united in the middle of the seventh century B.C. by King Perdiccas I. By 450 B.C., under the rule of Alexander I, a veneer of Hellenic civilization appeared on the ruling class of Macedonians, and cities had begun to develop.

The Plans of Philip II

Of the three sons who succeeded King Amyntas II (reigned ca. 390–369 B.C., the unifier of the disparate parts of Macedonia), Philip II (382–336 B.C.) ruled for the longest period. His training for the throne had been excellent; as a youth he had been held hostage in Thebes, and he there learned from Epaminondas the most advanced military techniques. On gaining the throne in 359 B.C., Philip set about to modernize the Macedonian army. His primary military objective was the Chalcidice, for with it Macedonia would gain a much-needed Aegean coastline. For the past century, Athens had been closely tied to the area, which secured the grain route from the Black Sea. A clash between the two powers thus loomed on the horizon.

The whole Macedonian nation was welded into an excellent military machine, and Philip developed to perfection the Theban phalanx. The cavalry was made up of nobles, the "King's Companions."

Philip's Early Conquests

Philip's true character is hard to evaluate, for in history he is seen only through the eyes of two opposing Greek factions. Those such as Isocrates, who favored his policies, believed that he was the savior of the Hellenic world and would at last unite a prostrate Greece. The anti-Philip faction, under the leadership of Demosthenes, was convinced, or wanted the Greeks to think, that Philip was an arch-villain who desired to enslave Greece for his self-aggrandizement. Many modern historians have followed Demosthenes, perhaps because of his superb Attic prose, perhaps because he represented the ideal *polis* of the fifth century B.C.

It does seem clear that, whenever possible, Philip bribed and cajoled to get what he wanted, for he had informants everywhere. Only as a last resort did he use military force, and if that failed he tried again. In order to facilitate his diplomatic and military efforts, Philip took over the gold-producing section of Mount Pangaeus in Thrace (358–357 B.C.), and he was soon embarked on conquering the coastline and Thessaly. Athens was so alarmed that she declared war in 357 B.C., but her involvement in the revolt of the Second Confederacy prevented effective action. By 348 B.C., Philip had conquered the major cities of the Chalcidian League, of which many, including Olynthus, were destroyed. Athens was in no position to pursue a policy of war with Philip, and in 346 B.C. the Peace of Philocrates was signed.

The Sacred War (356–346 B.C.)

The Delphic Amphictyony had long been an important Panhellenic body, for it took charge of the Oracle of Apollo and the Pythian games. In the fourth century B.C., Thebes had gained control of Delphi, thereby incurring friction with Phocis and the consequent declaration of a sacred war (355 B.C.). Phocis in turn committed sacrilege by taking over the Delphic treasury to hire mercenary troops. The Phocians advanced rapidly, and finally (356 B.C.) Thebes sent to Macedonia for aid.

Phocis was forced out of Thessaly, but it was not until the Peace of 346 B.C. with Athens that Philip felt free to destroy the state. The Macedonians then took over the Phocian votes on the Delphic Amphictyony and at last felt themselves to be true Hellenes.

The Defeat of Athens and Thebes

Philip had a great respect for Athens, as was shown by his later behavior. The peace party, led by Aeschines, not wanting to risk a retrogression into chaos, therefore tried to abide by the treaty of 346 B.C. However, Demosthenes did not permit matters to rest and his will finally prevailed; Athens decided on war against the Macedonians.

Since Athens was now the great obstacle for a Macedonian takeover of Greece, Philip decided to attack the city in its most vulnerable spot: the grain route from the Black Sea area. Accordingly, he besieged the cities of Perinthus and Byzandum, but without success. Athens in the meantime had constructed a formidable alliance that included much of central Greece and the Peloponnesus. Philip used a sacred war against the city of Amphissa as an excuse for entering central Greece. Athens was in a state of panic, for its only real chance against Philip was an alliance with Thebes. Finally, after making exorbitant demands, Thebes joined forces with Athens. In 338 B.C., the Macedonians completely defeated the coalition at Chaeronea in Boeotia. Their strong left cavalry wing headed by Philip's son, Alexander, made the decisive attack.

The League of Corinth

Philip, now in physical control of all Greece except Sparta, set about to organize a system of alliances in order to avoid further dissipation of the Hellenic *poleis*. He made separate treaties with the various Greek cities. Athens, despite its defeat, was spared. Thebes fared badly, for it was no longer head of Boeotia and it suffered the indignity of having a Macedonian garrison in its citadel.

In 338 B.C., a conference was held at Corinth to form a league of Greek cities (excluding Sparta). In order to achieve stability, all member states were forbidden to change their forms of government or to engage in acts of violence. All members of the league were required to help one another militarily under the leadership of Philip of Macedon and his successors.

Plans were now afoot for an invasion of Persia by the combined forces of Macedonia and Greece. The Greeks were extremely anxious to colonize Asia Minor, and the defeat of Artaxerxes by the Ten Thousand had struck the Hellenic imagination. The expedition had to wait, however, for Philip was assassinated in 336 B.C. and was succeeded by his son, Alexander.

The long history of *polis* government had now come to an end. To be sure, Athens and other Greek cities retained their institutions into the Roman period, but the predominating forces in the world would be those of kingdoms and empires.

CULTURE

To many who consider the fifth century B.C. the Golden Age of Greek culture, subsequent endeavors are regarded as a decline. The fourth century B.C., however, was as great as the previous age in many respects, and in the fields of philosophy and rhetoric surpassed it. The tendency in all of the arts was toward greater individualization and deeper psychological insight. In the visual arts, emotions began to appear on the faces of more freely represented figures.

Rhetoric

The Sophists were the first true teachers of rhetoric, and the fourth century B.C. was their heir. The art of human expression reached its height with Isocrates and Demosthenes, although the works of Lysias had their own importance. In seeking human motivations and psychological insights, rhetoric became one of the bases of education.

Lysias

In the restored Athenian democracy, there was much opportunity for litigation, but not everyone could write suitable speeches for it. As a result, a group of orators, among whom was Lysias (ca. 459–380 B.C.), were paid to write for clients. Lysias' speeches were direct, reflecting the class of his patrons.

Isocrates

Isocrates (436–338 B.C.) was a remarkable man. Because his voice was inadequate for the rigors of public speaking, he devoted much of his efforts to education. His school at Athens became world famous, and his methods of teaching aimed at a psychological understanding of the human being. In addition, Isocrates wrote political works, for he was a confirmed Panhellenist and the washing away of Hellenic energy pained him. Style was so important to Isocrates that he is said to have worked ten years on his *Panegyricus*, in which he beseeched the Greeks to unite. Finally, in his *Philippus*, he exhorted Philip of Macedon to unite Greece. Besides bringing oratorical prose to a high point of aesthetic development, Isocrates wrote what appears to have been the first true biography, the *Evagoras*, a eulogy for the dead king of Cyprus.

Demosthenes

Demosthenes (384–322 B.C.) was well versed in the art of rhetoric; his teacher was the famous orator Isaeus. In order to excel, Demosthenes trained himself to strengthen his voice. He studied prose writing of past and present and learned much from the logical, direct style of Thucydides. Many scholars view Demosthenes as the last potential savior of Greek independence, but others consider him to have been insensitive to the political realities of his day. His speeches were instrumental in Athens' abrogation of the Peace of

346 B.C. and in its final clash with Macedonia in 388 B.C. The *Philippics* (351–340 B.C.) and the *Olynthiacs* (344 B.C.) are masterpieces of rhetorical invective.

History

The fourth century B.C. produced no giants of historiography like Herodotus and Thucydides. Nonetheless, the historical works of the period have their importance. Xenophon (ca. 434–354 B.C.), a disciple of Socrates and a leader of the Ten Thousand, wrote works about both of these aspects of his life. His *Memorabilia* presents a view complementary to that of Plato's concerning the Socratic school. The *Anabasis* gives an account of the adventures of the Persian expedition against Artaxerxes and the retreat to the Black Sea, while the *Hellenica* continues history from where Thucydides left off to the Battle of Mantinea. Although Xenophon has been condemned for his journalistic style, he has also been praised for his delineation of character.

Surviving only in fragmentary form are rhetorical universal histories called *Atthides*, composed by a number of writers, which became an important genre around 350 B.C.

Philosophy

In the fourth century B.C., the development of philosophy reached its height with the works of Plato and Aristotle. Not only were their writings immediately important, but they became keystones in the structure of Western thought. Other schools of philosophy, including the hypercritical Cynics, founded by Diogenes (ca. 400–325 B.C.), and the overindulgent, sensationalist Cyrenaics, founded by Aristippus of Cyrene, also made their appearance at this time.

PLATO

Of all the disciples of Socrates, only Plato (ca. 420–347 B.C.) appears to have ingested his master's most profound thoughts, and his *Dialogues* reflect them. After the execution of his teacher, Plato became embittered with democracy and began to evolve his own plan for an ideal state. He has been criticized by some for being inconsistent, because he changed his opinions later in life, but it must be remembered that wisdom comes with learning and perfection is long in arriving, if it arrives at all.

Theory of Ideas. Like Socrates, Plato wanted his pupils to achieve a knowledge of truth. His success can be seen by the fact that his school, the Academy, outlasted the ancient world. Not only is the dialogue form didactically sound, but, as written by Plato, the genre became a small drama, filled with humor and pathos. In his dialogues, the true world is not that collection of imperfect things that one perceives with the senses, but it exists in the realm of abstract ideas, to be grasped only by philosophical application and training. Thus, a chair that one sees on earth is only an imperfect reflection of the ideal form of chair existing beyond the material world. The same relation might apply to political institutions and to such qualities as beauty and goodness (see Plato's *Phaedo*).

Political Theories. In his *Republic*, Plato delineated the ideal form of state. Tired of the excesses of democracy, he looked approvingly to certain aspects of the Spartan constitution. To Plato, an ideal *polis* should have about five thousand inhabitants and consist of three classes: the workers, the soldiers, and the rulers. The first would remain in ignorance and take care of the mechanical workings of society, while the two upper classes would receive an intensive education from the earliest age. Poets (including Homer) were to be omitted from the curriculum because they talk of the irrational and the superstitious. Both the upper classes were to have military training, so that when they reached the age of twenty it could be seen who would be a soldier and who a ruler. By the age of thirty-four, after intensive intellectual training, most rulers would become members of the administration. Those who truly excelled, after five additional years of probing for the truth, were to become the overlords (guardians). There was to be no private property, nor were private families to be permitted.

Plato himself realized the impracticability of such a state, and later, in the *Laws*, he revised his concepts. The new *polis* conceived in this work was closer to Greek realities, for it contained a *boule* and an assembly. But all aspects of life were to be supervised by examiners who would write and revise laws governing the most minute activities of men.

Conception of Immortality. To the Greeks, traditional religion provided little hope for the afterlife beyond a shadowy existence in Hades. Earlier philosophers, including Pythagoras, had adopted a theory of metempsychosis, or transmigration of souls on their way to purification. Plato elaborated this doctrine and combined it with his ideas of truth and beauty. In his view, the body imprisons the soul, which is created by the Divine Being but sullied by a sinful corporeal life. If a person leads a good life in accordance with the highest principles of philosophy, his soul enters the dwelling place of the gods. If life is spent in vice, the soul has to go through a series of cleansings in order to return to its pure state.

ARISTOTLE

Aristotle (384–322 B.C.), a native of Stagira in the Chalcidice, went to Athens in 362 B.C. to become a student of Plato. In 343 B.C., he was asked by Philip of Macedon to become the tutor for his son, Alexander. This instruction was a success, an exceptional achievement, for in similar attempts neither did Plato succeed with Dionysius II, nor was Seneca to accomplish anything with Nero. In 335 B.C., under the protection of Alexander, Aristotle opened the Lyceum or Peripatetic ("Walk Around") School in Athens. Aristotle's dialogues have been lost; only his lecture notes remain.

Divisions of Knowledge. Aristotle believed in Platonic ideas, but held that they were inseparable from the material world. His main interest was in objects, beings, and institutions as they actually existed. His great strength was logic and the resulting classification of things. Aristotle experimented, but not in a strictly scientific way. He divided knowledge into categories, among which were ethics, or the principles of social life; natural history, or scientific exploration into everything on earth; and metaphysics, or the study of the primary laws of the universe.

Political Theories. Like Plato, Aristotle disliked extreme democracy. After an exhaustive study of the various constitutions of the Greek city-states, he developed a theory of government cycles from monarchy to democracy. In his *Politics*, he categorized three main types of government—the monarchy, the aristocracy, and the republic—and their respective corrupt forms: tyranny, oligarchy, and democracy (the last of which he thought easily degenerates into ochlocracy, or mob rule). In government, as in all other aspects of life, Aristotle advocated a balance, the "golden mean." He thought that the ideal state was a small *polis* with a mixed constitution and a powerful middle class to prevent extremes.

Other Contributions. Aristotle had a truly encyclopedic mind. He began the classification of plants and animals, in addition to analyzing the arts, including drama. His celestial theories, based on the concept of an earth-centered universe, remained in force until the Renaissance.

Drama

Poetry all but disappeared as a vital art form during the fourth century B.C., and no first-rate tragedies were written. Middle Comedy can be seen in the *Plutus* ("Wealth"), among the last plays of Aristophanes. This new type of play was a comedy of manners with more character delineation and fewer laughs than Old Comedy.

Art

Painting, sculpture, and architecture broke away from the conventions of the fifth century B.C. Greater emphasis was put on specifics such as shadowing, facial expressions, and architectural decoration.

PAINTING

The art of vase painting declined considerably. Surfaces were now covered with a plethora of figures; too much was attempted for one vessel. Large-scale painting, all examples of which have been lost, achieved greater realism than before. Not only were foreshortening and perspective more clearly understood, but a great innovation was made in shadowing and subtle blending of textures to achieve a three-dimensional effect. According to ancient sources, Zeuxis, in the early part of the century, put emotion as well as realism into his work. His contemporary, Parrhasius, was noted for his elegance and subtlety of execution; and Apelles, who worked later in the century, was famous for his portraits.

SCULPTURE

Actual knowledge of fourth-century B.C. sculpture is more accurate than that of painting, for some originals and a great many later copies are extant. Like painting and literature, sculpture was marked by increasing characterization and realism. Statues from this period display emotion, pensiveness, and a variety of poses not present before. Although the art of portraiture has been said to begin in this century, there was still a large measure of idealization compared with the individuality of the Hellenistic period and the brutal realism of the Roman Republic.

The great masters of fourth-century B.C. sculpture were Praxiteles, Scopas, and Lysippus. Praxiteles, during the first half of the century, represented figures in a new half-turned position so that they could be appreciated from several angles. The faces of the statues display a pensive, dreamy expression, and this softness is enhanced by the translucent quality of the sculpted marble surface. *Hermes Holding the Infant Dionysus* is considered by many an original work of Praxiteles, although its authenticity has been doubted by some authorities. Scopas, a contemporary of Praxiteles, specialized in representing strong emotions, above all expressions of deep pathos. (These qualities also characterize certain aspects of Hellenistic art.) Lysippus, who lived later in the century, created an entirely new set of bodily proportions. Heads of figures were now smaller, and bodies were slimmer, twisting around so as to represent action momentarily frozen. One famous statue by Lysippus is the *Apoxyomenos* ("the Scraper"), which exists only in later copies.

ARCHITECTURE

In keeping with the spirit of the period, architecture broke from the canons of the fifth century B.C. On the Greek mainland, temples were not so common as before, but they appeared in Asia Minor on a colossal scale (for example, the Ionic Temple of Apollo at Didyma). Detail was richer than in previous periods. The Corinthian order, a development of Ionic with acanthus leaf capitals, was popular, especially on small monumental buildings such as the circular monument to Lysicrates in Athens. The greatest monumental structure of this period was the mausoleum at Halicarnassus in the Ionic order, one of the Seven Wonders of the Ancient World. Magnificent theaters were now built of stone; an outstanding example is the one at Epidaurus. It is ironic that they were constructed after the art of drama had begun to decline.

In the next century, the dominant political entities in the Greek world would be kingdoms, not the city-states. Artists and intellectuals would continue to flourish, but would inhabit a different world from that of their ancestors.

Selected Readings

Cawkwell, G. L. *Philip of Macedon* (1978)
Ellis, J. *Philip II and Macedonian Imperialism* (1976)
Jaeger, Werner. *Desmothenes* (1938)
———. *Aristotle* (1948)
Johnson, F. P. *Lysippos* (1927)
Jebb, R. C. *The Attic Orators from Antiphon to Isaeos.* 2 vols. (1962)
Parke, H. W. *Greek Mercenary Soldiers* (1933)
Webster, T. B. L. *Art and Literature in Fourth Century Athens* (1956)

9

The Conquests of Alexander and the Hellenistic Period

336 B.C.	Philip assassinated
336–150	Hellenistic Period
336	Alexander becomes king of Macedonia
336	Darius becomes king of Persia
335–263	Zeno—founder of Stoicism
334	Alexander lands at Troy
333	Alexander defeats Darius at Issus
332–331	Alexander in Egypt; Alexandria founded
331	Alexander enters Babylon
330	Darius III killed
327	Alexander crosses Khyber Pass into India
327	Alexander defeats King Porus
324	Alexander returns to Babylon and is deified
323	Alexander dies
315	Cassander in control of Macedonia
312	Seleucus controls the East
306	Alexander's other generals declare themselves kings
287–212	Archimedes of Syracuse—mathematician and inventor
275–195	Eratosthenes—geographer
242	Aegis III rules Sparta
223–187	Reign of Antiochus III (the Great) of Seleucids

221–179 Reign of Philip V of Macedonia

215–205 First Macedonian War with Rome

200–120 Polybius—historian

200–197 Second Macedonian War

197 Romans win Battle of Cynoscephale

171–168 Third Macedonian War

168 Battle of Pynda

146 Macedonia becomes first Roman province in the East

63 Last portion of Seleucid Empire becomes Roman province of Syria

30 Egypt becomes a Roman province

In the fourth century B.C., the personality and achievements of Alexander the Great brought the dawn of a new age. The extent of the Hellenistic period has been variously reckoned, for some scholars deem it to have begun with Alexander's reign and some date it after his conquests. Agreement on the end of the age is also far from unanimous. To some, it ends with Rome's conquest of Macedonia and Greece in the middle of the second century B.C.; to others, it ends with the death of Cleopatra in 30 B.C. Still others extend the Hellenistic Age to cover the revival of Greek letters during the Antonine period, while a stalwart few continue it through the Byzantine period. For all practical considerations, however, Hellenistic civilization can be said to begin with Alexander and continue to about 150 B.C., at which time the Greek and Roman cultures coalesce.

ALEXANDER'S EARLY REIGN

At the death of Philip II of Macedonia in 336 B.C., his son Alexander was only twenty years of age, and the young king had to prove his fitness to rule. Barbarians threatened the north as they had done during his father's reign. In 335 B.C., Alexander, who had been well trained in Philip's army, decisively defeated the Triballi and the Getae. In the meantime, the Greek city-states, feeling constrained within the League of Corinth, sought an excuse to break away. When a rumor spread that Alexander had been killed in the north, Athens and Thebes led a revolt. The king of Macedonia appeared, and to make an example for the rest of Greece, he completely destroyed Thebes, although leaving the house of the poet Pindar intact. This brutal move has been said to have alienated Greek opinion, but the *poleis* had always been against anyone who infringed upon their autonomy. Greece was to prove a problem to Alexander and his successors. Alexander's general, Antipater, was left there when the young king set off to conquer Asia.

Reasons for Alexander's Conquests

The character of Alexander had been molded from many sources, but basic to his political theories was the thought of Aristotle. Unlike Philip, Alexander was a practical romantic, and the glories of Greece's past were ever-present before him. He revered Homer and slept on the *Iliad*. His curiosity about the world—geography, society, and history—went far beyond the narrow horizons of the *polis*. Indeed, an attitude that continued to develop and grow in Alexander was that of the brotherhood of man; he rejected the Greek division of the world into Hellene and barbarian.

Besides his worldwide vision, some very practical considerations motivated Alexander's conquest of the Persian Empire. Greece was overcrowded, and new lands in Asia Minor would relieve this pressure. In addition, the Persian royal treasure would not only refill empty Macedonian coffers, but, as coins, would raise economic levels of the Hellenic world. Last but not least was the appeal of Panhellenism; now a Greek (the distinction between Greek and Macedonian was becoming blurred) would avenge himself on the Persians for their invasions of Greece and their destruction of the Acropolis. Besides, since the march of the Ten Thousand, the Hellenic imagination had been captivated with the idea of defeating in their own territory the "invincible" Persians.

The Conquest of Asia Minor and Egypt

In very romantic fashion, Alexander crossed the Hellespont and landed in Ilium (334 B.C.), visiting the famous sites of the Trojan War. The same year, he met the Persian forces at the Granicus River and won his first encounter with the Oriental host. The Greek cities of Asia Minor were at last liberated, but the native inland areas were taken over as *satrapies* ruled by Alexander's appointees. There was a legend that the man who could untie the complicated knot at Gordium would be master of Asia; when Alexander arrived, he cut it with his sword.

THE BATTLE OF ISSUS

A real threat to the Macedonian expedition was the Persian navy commanded by the Rhodian, Memnon. In order to avoid losing newly conquered areas, it was essential for Alexander to seize potential naval bases. At Issus in the southeast corner of Asia Minor, he defeated the forces of Darius III (333 B.C.). (Darius had become king the same year as Alexander, and much was made of this coincidence by the ancients.) The victory over the Persians, the subsequent capture of the royal family, and the flight of Darius made

Alexander successor to the Persian kings. Alexander treated the mother, wife, and daughters of the king very well, for it was his wish that East and West unite under peaceful conditions.

ALEXANDER AS PHARAOH

Everywhere Alexander was hailed as a liberator, and he had little trouble with the Phoenician cities. The notable exception was Tyre, which held out for seven months, but finally fell (333 B.C.). When he arrived in Egypt (332–331 B.C.), Alexander was greeted as the new pharaoh, a god incarnate. He set about founding a city, the most successful of the Alexandrias, which was to become the capital of the western regions of his empire. Alexander even visited the oracle of Zeus-Ammon, at the Oasis of Siwa, who ascertained his divine origins.

The Conquest of Central Asia

The forces of Alexander once more took up their eastward march. In 331 B.C., they won a smashing victory against the Persian forces on a plain near Arbela in Mesopotamia, but Darius again was able to flee. Alexander then entered Babylon, where he was made representative on earth of the god Marduk, thus following in the footsteps of such a renowned king as Hammurabi. The same year, the palace complex of Persepolis was burned to the ground as revenge for the Persians' destruction of the Acropolis, and the royal treasure fell into Macedonian hands. In 330 B.C. at Hecatompylos, the Macedonians found the body of Darius; he had been killed by his own *satrap*, Bessus, who wanted the throne for himself. (Bessus was eventually caught and executed.) Alexander was now truly king of the Persian Empire, and he generously buried his predecessor with royal honors. Alexander's sense of mission pushed him ever eastward, although many of his men were becoming tired. On his way, cities were founded and princes pacified. In 327 B.C., Alexander set an example of the union of East and West by marrying Roxane, the daughter of a Bactrian prince living on the eastern borders of the Persian Empire. He urged his men likewise to marry Asians and also to adopt Persian clothing; this seemed a bit too radical for the Hellenic mind.

Penetration to India

Alexander now wanted to conquer the world, for he believed that he was nearing the Stream of Ocean, thought to surround the continents. In 327 B.C., he crossed the Khyber Pass into India, where he allied himself with King Taxiles and defeated the forces of King Porus and his elephants. By this time, however, mutiny was in the air, as the Macedonian troops refused to advance any farther. Consequently, Alexander turned back and followed the course of the Indus River southward into the Persian Gulf. From there, he led part of the army on a course parallel to the gulf (325 B.C.). The rest were transported by a fleet constructed for the purpose under the admiralship of Nearchus. The voyage back to Mesopotamia was disastrous, for many soldiers died en route. In 324 B.C., upon his return to Babylon, Alexander

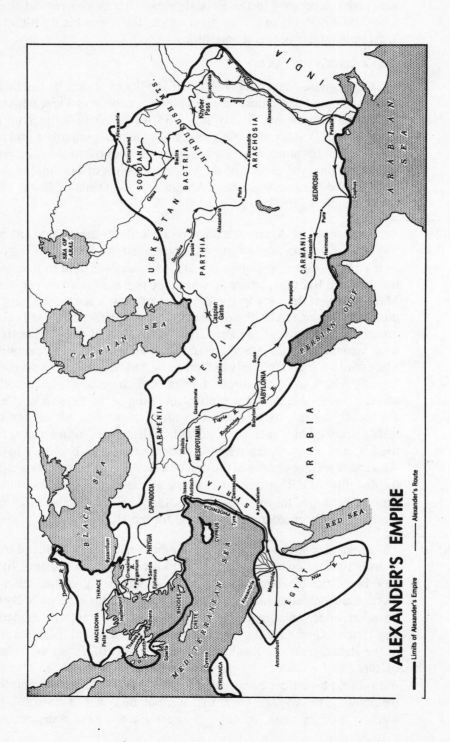

ALEXANDER'S EMPIRE

Limits of Alexander's Empire

Alexander's Route

was officially deified by the League of Corinth. Since Alexander's feats had truly been extraordinary and his personality charismatic, the members of the league could not but approve. Besides, there were precedents for this in the giving of divine honors to founders of tribes and *poleis*. In 323 B.C., Alexander died of a fever.

The Results of Alexander's Conquests

Because of Alexander's conquests, the Greek world became part of a vast empire including the ancient lands of the Near East. The East now entered the Greek economic system. The excess population of the *poleis* colonized the new cities, but Hellenic cultural penetration to the hinterland was very limited in most cases. The administrative apparatus of the Persian Empire was taken over, with Greeks as well as Orientals employed in it.

The loss of Alexander's great magnetism spelled the demise of his empire after his death, for there was no one to replace him. The only heirs were his demented half-brother Philip III Arrhidaeus and his posthumous son, whom his mother, Roxane, called Alexander IV.

ALEXANDER'S SUCCESSORS AND THE BIRTH OF THE HELLENISTIC KINGDOMS

The individual greed of Alexander's generals did not allow the empire to remain undivided. After spheres of influence had been established, a gradual formation of separate kingdoms under three generals took place. The descendants of Ptolemy ruled in Egypt; those of Antigonus in Macedonia; and those of Seleucus in the Asiatic portion of the empire.

The Successors (Diadochi)

At first, the Macedonian generals who had been in charge of certain areas remained there and recognized the regency of Perdiccas for Alexander's infant son. Antipater was in command of Macedonia and Greece; Lysimachus of the Hellespont region; Antigonus of Asia Minor; Perdiccas himself of the rest of Asia; and Ptolemy of Egypt. In 323 B.C., the Lamian War involving a revolt of Greece was suppressed by Antipater. In 322 B.C., Perdiccas was killed by his own troops while trying to eliminate Ptolemy. Antipater then was made regent, and Seleucus became *satrap* of Babylon. When Antipater died in 319 B.C., a vacuum was left. His son, Cassander, thereupon seized parts of Greece and by 315 B.C. was in control of Macedonia. Philip Arrhidaeus, Alexander's mother Olympias, and eventually Alexander IV and Roxane were killed by Cassander's forces. Demetrius of Phaleron was made master of Athens by Cassander. Meanwhile, Antigonus challenged Cassander, and in 314 B.C. he temporarily liberated Greece. By 312 B.C., Seleucus had control of the East, but he lost the Indian provinces about 304 B.C.

Demetrius Pohorcetes ("Sacker of Cities"), son of Antigonus, took Athens in 307 B.C., and both father and son became kings. In 306 B.C., the other generals followed suit, thus ending once and for all the fiction of a united empire. Although Antigonus still tried to rule over all of Alexander's domains, the other generals turned against him and in 301 B.C., in the Battle of Ipsus, he was killed. By 294 B.C., Demetrius had become king of Macedonia, but eleven years later he died a prisoner. Lysimachus then gained ascendancy in Greece and Macedonia, but he was killed in battle in 281 B.C.

The New Generation (Epigoni)

In 279 B.C., Celtic (Gallic) invasions of Macedonia shattered all balance of power and led to a treaty between Antigonus II Gonatas (son of Demetrius Poliorcetes) and Antiochus I (son of Seleucus), delineating spheres of influence. By 277 B.C., Antigonus II had become king of Macedonia; Antiochus I, king of the East; and Ptolemy II, pharaoh of Egypt. In addition, there developed a series of smaller kingdoms, such as Pergamum, and powerful commercial states, such as Rhodes. Greece was divided among the Aetolian League, the Achaean League, and the independent states of Athens and Sparta.

THE PTOLEMAIC KINGDOM

The Nile Valley, flanked by desert and delta, was always a rich prize in conquest, for its supply of wheat was enormous. In general, the civilization of Egypt continued the traditions begun in the Old Kingdom, and each new conqueror was proclaimed a god incarnate. Under the Ptolemies, a veneer of Hellenistic civilization was added; but in time the dominant Egyptian culture won out in the countryside, even while the capital, Alexandria, remained a cosmopolis.

Expansion of the Ptolemies

In the traditional chronology of Egypt, Ptolemy I Soter (367–282 B.C.) founded the Thirty-first Dynasty. Ptolemy had a great psychological advantage over the other Hellenistic rulers, for he had managed to obtain Alexander's body, which he placed in a sumptuous tomb in the heart of Alexandria. The kingdom expanded into the west with the conquest of Cyrene and into the east with seizure of the Phoenician coast and parts of the

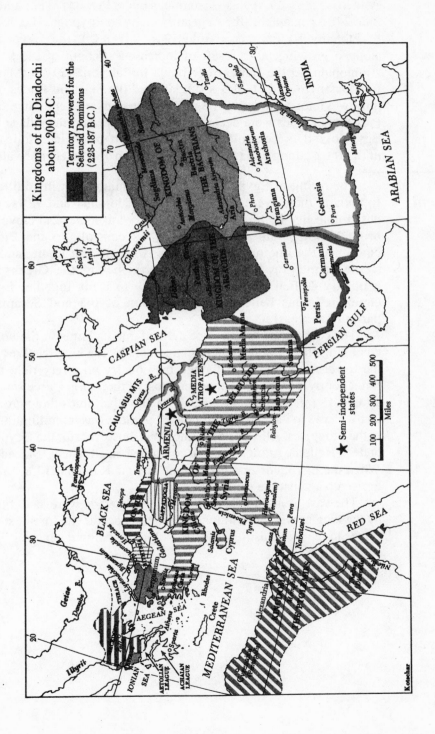

Kingdoms of the Diadochi about 200 B.C.

Territory recovered for the Seleucid Dominions (223-187 B.C.)

Semi-independent states

Miles
0   100   200   300   400   500

INDIA

ARABIAN SEA

KINGDOM OF THE BACTRIANS

Sogdiana
Bactria
Antiochia Margiana

Oxus
Choresmia

Sea of Aral

CASPIAN SEA

Gedrosia
Pura

Arachosia
Alexandria Arachotorum

Drangiana
Phra

KINGDOM OF THE ARSACIDS

Carmania

Persis
Persepolis

PERSIAN GULF

CAUCASUS MTS.

Cyrus R.
Araxes R.

ARMENIA

MEDIA ATROPATENE

Ecbatana
Media Magna

SELEUCID

Susiana
Susa

ARMENIA

CAPPADOCIA

KINGDOM OF THE

Tigris R.
Babylon
Babylonia
Seleucia

Euphrates R.

MESOPOTAMIA

Antioch
Seleucia
Syria
Damascus

Hierosolyma (Jerusalem)

Phoenicia
Tyre
Petra
Nabataei

Gaza

BLACK SEA

Sinope
Trapezus

Paphlagonia

THRACE

Geitae
Danube

Illyria

IONIAN SEA

AETOLIAN LEAGUE
ACHAIAN LEAGUE

Sparta

AEGEAN SEA
Athens

Crete

Pergamum
Rhodes
Salamis
Cyprus

MEDITERRANEAN SEA

Alexandria

KINGDOM OF THE PTOLEMIES

RED SEA

Kotschar

Asia Minor coast. Expansion continued under Ptolemy II Philadelphus (ruled 282–246 B.C.), making the Aegean virtually an Egyptian lake. After the reign of Ptolemy III Euergetes (ruled 246–221 B.C.), the Egyptian kingdom stopped growing, as a result of increased strength of the Seleucids and Antigonids. At the Battle of Raphida in Palestine (217 B.C.), Ptolemy IV Philopater (ruled 221–205 B.C.) defeated the Seleucid forces, but it was a hollow victory, one resulting in dissension at home. In 200 B.C., the Ptolemaic armies were decisively defeated by the Seleucids at Panion, and Egypt lost all its acquisitions. Still, it managed to hold its Nilotic region intact until 30 B.C., long outlasting its Macedonian and Seleucid rivals.

Ptolemaic Government

The ruling of Egypt was not an easy matter, for in addition to native Egyptians there were Greeks and Macedonians and Jews, each group desiring to live by its own laws. Ptolemy I used several clever devices to bring his disparate subjects under his control. To the Egyptians, he continued the line of pharaohs, was Amon-Re incarnate, and owned the whole country as his private property; but to the Greeks he was an officially deified monarch. An attempt to bring together Egyptian and Greek religious beliefs by the creation of the god Serapis was only partially successful.

The country continued to be divided into its immemorial *nomes,* but the chief magistrates were Hellenes appointed by the king. Natives perpetuated the lower bureaucracy. Although the country was very rich, the peasants fared poorly, for the king obtained most of their crops. Free small farms run by Greeks *(cleruchs)* also existed. Each of the three ethnic groups lived by its own laws in its own communities, but there was intermingling, especially in the provinces. All was not harmonious, however, for the Egyptians chafed under a Hellenic ruling class that controlled an all–Greek-Macedonian army. When the Egyptians finally obtained arms at Raphia (217 B.C.), they began to rise up against the Hellenes.

The vast wealth of Egypt and its luxury trade were as tightly regulated by the king as was agriculture. Alexandria became the foremost commercial center in the Hellenistic world, as well as its cultural center.

THE SELEUCID KINGDOM

The descendants of Seleucus inherited a less cohesive empire than did the Ptolemies; it included the ancient lands of the Fertile Crescent as well as Persia and lands east. It is not surprising that this empire lost its eastern territories at an early date, and had to struggle to hold other lands.

Seleucid Government

The king of the realm succeeded the local monarchs or rulers. Hence, he was at once an official god to the Greeks, the representative on earth of the god Marduk to the Babylonians, and the King of Kings to the Persians. Two main capital cities were built: Antioch, on the Orontes River in Syria, and Seleucia, on the Tigris River near Babylon. The Persian system of *satrapies* was retained, with governors appointed by the king. In order to unify the realm further, a systematic program of urbanization was established, since, unlike Egypt, the Seleucid Empire had a tendency toward fragmentation. Some cities were directly controlled by the king, while others were essentially self-governing *poleis*. As a result, the Near East acquired a facade of Hellenism. The Greek language was used throughout the area, especially in commerce, although it did not supplant Aramaic. Meanwhile, the peasant of Mesopotamia continued his serflike existence without the benefits of Greek culture.

The Height and Decline of the Seleucid Empire

The greatest extent of the Asiatic empire was reached during the reign of Seleucus I (358–280 B.C.). In about 304 B.C., Seleucus lost the Indian provinces to the Indian emperor, Chandragupta. However, this loss was more than compensated for by the defeat of Lysimachus at Corupedium in 281 B.C., resulting in Seleucid hegemony over Asia Minor. Under Antiochus I (ruled 280–261 B.C.), an agreement was reached with Macedonia (279 B.C.), but the northern tier of Asia Minor *satrapies* broke away. In addition, Egypt obtained large sections of the Asia Minor coast. The eastern provinces were lost under Seleucus II (ruled 247–226 B.C.), with the establishment of the Parthian Empire in Persia (247 B.C.). A revival under Antiochus III, the Great (ruled 223–187 B.C.), who made a treaty with Philip V of Macedonia, brought the empire into conflict with Rome. Within decades, the Seleucid Empire began to disintegrate as a result of Parthian incursions from the east and Roman conquests from the west. In 83 B.C., the truncated Seleucid kingdom of Syria was taken over by Armenia, and in 63 B.C. it became a Roman province.

THE ANTIGONID KINGDOM

Antigonus II Gonatas (320–239 B.C.) won control of Macedonia (277 B.C.), by his defeat of the invading Gauls. Thereafter, the dynasty ruled a kingdom more homogeneous than that of the Ptolemies or the Seleucids. It was, after all, the Macedonian homeland and thus a continuation of the monarchies of Philip II and Alexander the Great. The Macedonians failed to hold Greece for any extended period of time, but they stood poised over it.

Under Antigonus III Doson (ruled 229–221 B.C.), Macedonia gained control of much of Greece, organizing the Hellenic League in 224 B.C. Under his successor, Philip V (ruled 221–179 B.C.), Antigonid influence became very widespread. Indeed, the expansionist aims of Philip and his ally, Antiochus III were so great that Rome entered the Greek world, eventually making Macedonia a province (146 B.C.).

GREECE

Most of the Greek *poleis* were too weak to defend themselves against the Hellenistic monarchies and, as a result, banded together into two leagues, the Aetolian and the Achaean. Athens felt strong enough not to join; and Sparta, which had despised all such unions, remained aloof. Unfortunately, parts of Greece were often treated as pawns in the power politics of Macedonia and Egypt.

The league concept was not new to Greece. Besides the defunct Boeotian and Peloponnesian Leagues, several such organizations had been formed in the fourth century B.C. In addition, the Delphic Amphictyony served as an important Panhellenic body.

The Aetolian League

The Aetolian was the more powerful of the third-century B.C. leagues, since it included north-central and western Greece, controlling Delphi and the Amphictyony. Indeed, its great self-confidence made it a bulwark against Macedonian, as well as Gallic, inroads into the Greek peninsula, although it was not loath to join the Antigonids to undo its archrival, the Achaean League.

A *strategos* (general) was president of the league, and its legislative body, the *Synedrion*, was elected with representatives proportionate to the population of member states. Full citizenship was limited to Aetolians.

Natives of other member states were granted *isopoliteia*, or full league citizenship, when they took up residence in Aetolia.

The Achaean League

It was not until after 251 B.C., when Aratus of Sicyon entered its generalship, that the Achaean League became a force with which to be reckoned. Its early stance against Macedonia changed after a war with Sparta, and it was assimilated into the Hellenic League in 224 B.C.

The main organs of the Achaean League were similar to those of the Aetolian except that, as each member state entered, it received full federal citizenship while retaining a local citizenship.

Athens

Athens could not consider itself a minor state, and its foreign policy during the Hellenistic period reflects this attitude. An early revolt against Macedonia (the Lamian War, 323–322 B.C.) was frustrated. Under Chremonides, Athens joined with the Ptolemies and Peloponnesians against Macedonia and was once more defeated (266–262 B.C.). When the Romans entered the Greek world, Athens chose well in allying itself with the Colossus of the West. In 167 B.C., Rome made Delos a free port as an Athenian *cleruchy*, and it supplanted Rhodes as the major Aegean transit port. Unfortunately, Athens allied itself with Mithridates, and Athens' prosperity was ended when it was sacked by Sulla in 87–86 B.C.

Sparta

An attempted revival of Sparta under Aegis III (242 B.C.), who enfranchised the *perioikoi*, ended with his death. His successor, Cleomenes III, succeeded in extending the right of Spartan citizenship, but his ventures in trying to restore the Peloponnesian League ended in his defeat by the combined forces of the Achaean League and Macedonia (221 B.C.). The last revival of Sparta under Nabis ended with Roman conquest in 195 B.C. After this, the future of Sparta lay with the other Peloponnesian cities as states within the Roman Empire.

PERGAMUM AND RHODES

Essential in maintaining the balance of power between gigantic empires were the kingdoms of Pergamum and the island state of Rhodes. Both enjoyed great prosperity, and they were responsible for Rome's eventual entry into Greek Asia.

Pergamum

Pergamum, near the coast of Asia Minor, was given to Philataerus (ca. 343–263 B.C.) after he deserted Lysimachus for Seleucus. His successor Eumenes I (d. 241 B.C.), gained independence from the Seleucids by allying himself with the Ptolemies (262 B.C.). Under Attalus I (ruled 241–197 B.C.), Pergamum reached its high-point, and its prosperity matched that of the great monarchies. Indeed, the city of Pergamum was a rival to Alexandria in the splendor of its wealth and culture. When the last Attalid died in 133 B.C., his kingdom was willed to Rome.

Rhodes

The strategic location of Rhodes off the coast of Asia Minor made it a major commercial power. The process was speeded around 400 B.C., when the three parts of the island joined to form the city of Rhodes. Rhodes was successful in holding off Demetrius I, the "Sacker of Cities," in 305–304 B.C., and in ridding the seas of pirates who had ravaged the Aegean after the demise of Athenian power. The city increased its wealth by charging a two percent transit tax to passing ships. However, this prosperity disappeared when, after Rhodes had alienated Rome, Delos was made a free port.

HELLENISTIC CULTURE

The radical change in the world after the conquests of Alexander cannot be underestimated. The great new cities, such as Alexandria, Antioch, and Pergamum, were not just Greek cities but cosmopolitan centers. As a result, the narrow if profound ideas of the *polis* broadened to a worldwide scope. The patronage of kings such as the Attalids and the Ptolemies created unsurpassed cultural institutions, including the library at Pergamum and the museum complex at Alexandria, which comprised teaching facilities presided over by the eminent scholars of the day, scientific collections, and the greatest library the Greek world had yet seen. Urban life created a culture that led to a new awareness of man and of the universe.

Literature

The Greek *koine*, based on the Attic dialect, became the standard language of the Hellenistic world. Such was the interest in language, growing out of rhetoric, that a new discipline, *philology*, was created. In a sense, the Greeks of the Hellenistic Age considered themselves heirs to all previous epochs. As a result, they collected and cherished past literature. This eclecticism gave Hellenistic literature its broad scope, for all fields of letters were eagerly attempted, with lyric poetry making a remarkable recovery. Nonetheless, dry pedanticism, fostered in the great institutions such as the

Alexandria Museum, predominated; and perfect rhetorical form of prose and exquisite handling of meters and sounds in verse were considered more important than spirit and content.

Philology

Of all books, the works of Homer continued to be the most important to the Greeks. Aristarchus of Samothrace (215–145 B.C.) divided the *Odyssey* and the *Iliad* into twenty-four books each, ending the traditional practice of reading them together as one continuous scroll. Some scholars, such as Apollodorus of Athens (fl. 150–130 B.C.), wrote the first grammars of the Greek language. Others wrote analyses and commentaries on Homeric and other works.

History

The Greek traditions of history writing continued into the Hellenistic period, and exited great interest in the world at large. Fragments still exist of Hieronymus of Cardia's work, *On the Successors*, which inspired part of the late Hellenistic *Universal History* of Diodorus Siculus (fl. 60–20 B.C.). The greatest historian of the period, however, was Polybius of Megalopolis (ca. 200–120 B.C.), who was held hostage by the Romans after their war with Macedonia. His *Universal History* deals chiefly with the expansion of Rome. Although dry in style, Polybius had a profound understanding of historical processes, and has been ranked with Thucydides.

Poetry

The revival of verse during the Hellenistic era gave rise to exotic meters and poems. Some took on an epic cast, some a scientific aspect. Pastoral poetry, a new genre reflecting yearnings of the urban middle classes, evoked escape to a simple life among shepherds.

The *Argonautica* of Apollonius of Rhodes (b. 295 B.C.) is a Hellenistic epic relating the deeds of Jason in his pursuit of the Golden Fleece. Apollonius' rival at the Museum of Alexandria, Callimachus of Cyrene (ca. 305–240 B.C.), in addition to cataloguing works of the Alexandrian library, wrote the *Aetia* ("Causes"), a combination of myth and quasi-science. Perhaps the greatest of all Hellenistic poets was Theocritus of Syracuse (fl. ca. 275 B.C.), whose *Idylls* describe with longing a simple country life. Theocritus was to have a great influence on future poets.

Drama

The new middle classes wanted to be entertained and, in addition to the repertory works of the fifth-century B.C. greats (especially Euripides), and mime, New Comedy redefined their needs. All unevenness of Middle Comedy disappeared, and extremely polished comedies were written. Menander of Athens (341–290 B.C.) was the greatest writer in this genre. One complete play of his, the *Dyscolos* ("The Curmudgeon"), survives, as well as fragments of other works. They typically portray slices of everyday life with complications of plot, such as mistaken identity. The characters tend to be reduced to types, such as the grumpy father, the prodigal son, and the courtesan with a heart of gold.

Science

Science in the Greek world, especially during the Hellenistic period, was a paradox. Fertile minds probed into the workings of the universe and discovered hitherto unknown facts and principles. Indeed, some went so far as to apply these newly discovered laws to working models. Yet, by and large science was not utilized to better the lot of man, and as a result there was not even a hint of an industrial revolution. After all, the scientists were men of leisure—philosophers—who considered practical matters demeaning. Besides, the menial work was done by the lower orders and slaves, and none of these men had any desire to cause a social upheaval by tampering with this arrangement.

BOTANY AND MEDICINE

Following the tradition of Aristotle in zoology, Theophrastus (ca. 370–285 B.C.) established botany as an independent science in such works as *On the Origins of Plants*. The science of medicine continued to be improved upon, especially by Herophilus of Chalcedon (fl. 300–250 B.C.), who worked in Alexandria and performed dissections of the human body. Besides accurately describing the nervous system, he discovered the function of the arteries.

GEOGRAPHY AND ASTRONOMY

Geography was one of the more popular sciences during the Hellenistic period. The greatest achievements in this field were those of Eratosthenes of Cyrene (ca. 275–195 B.C.). In a most ingenious way, Eratosthenes was able to compute the circumference of the earth within an accuracy of a few hundred miles. His map of the world was remarkably accurate for his time. As a result of his studies of tides, he could suggest that by sailing westward, one would eventually reach India.

In many cases, Hellenistic thought achieved a profound understanding of science; yet practical application was not forthcoming. Indeed, some theories appeared too radical for the Greek mind. This was so with the ideas of Aristarchus of Samos (ca. 310–230 B.C.), who discovered that the sun is many times larger than the earth and concluded that it was the center of the universe. It was most difficult for the Hellenistic mind to believe that the earth, the habitat of man—the measure of all things—was but an insignificant cosmic particle. Hence, the geocentric theories of Hipparchus of Nicaea (b. ca. 190 B.C.) were readily accepted. Besides, these concepts more easily explained celestial phenomena than did the circular orbits postulated by Aristarchus. Hipparchus also discovered the precession of the equinoxes and made an accurate estimate of the length of the year. (His theories were based on the assumption that all celestial bodies revolve in cycles around the earth as well as in their own cycles.)

MATHEMATICS AND PHYSICS

None of the Hellenistic advances in geography and astronomy would have been possible without development of mathematics. Euclid of Alexandria (fl. ca. 300 B.C.), in his *Elements,* established plane geometry. Archimedes of Syracuse (ca. 287–212 B.C.) went much further. In addition to discovering approximately the value of *pi,* he worked in the realm of higher mathematics. However, since the Greeks had not discovered the concept of zero, there was a limit to their mathematical capabilities. The Hellenic number system, although not so awkward as Roman numerals, did not lend itself to mathematical complexities. Archimedes' inventions, such as the water screw, the compound pulley, and war engines, received some application, but his discovery of specific gravity did not lead to a revolution in science.

Philosophy and Religion

As the world became increasingly Roman, larger and more complex, the traditional gods of the small community had become outdated. The intellectually oriented turned more and more to the comforts and delights of philosophy. The masses were attracted to the mysterious side of traditional Greek religion, Oriental cults, or astrology. Of the various schools of philosophy current during this period, Epicureanism, Stoicism, and Skepticism, in addition to the earlier Cynicism, were the most important.

EPICUREANISM

Epicurus of Athens (341–270 B.C.) founded one of the major schools of philosophy in the ancient world. Epicureanism was created to cope with the problems and perplexities of mankind. It held that the greatest pollution in life is an irrational fear of death. If man understands that the universe, even including the gods, consists of atoms and that death only dissolves the human being into his component parts, there is no need to fear dying. Life itself is fraught with tensions, and in order to live it to its utmost fulfillment, man must withdraw from the turmoils of the world and devote himself to pleasure. This does not mean total sensual indulgence, as the Cyrenaics believed, but a limited amount of enjoyment, preferably intellectual. The result will be *ataraxia*, or release from the negative aspects of life.

STOICISM

Stoicism was to prove most congenial to later generations of the ancient world, and as a result it grew and developed with the passage of time. Zeno of Citium (335–263 B.C.) founded the Stoic school in Athens, stating that the divine force of the universe is Reason (*Logos*). The wise man should be able to partake of cosmic virtue and be oblivious to everything else, including changes in everyday life. Periodically, there are universal conflagrations, but afterward everything, having returned to Reason, begins again. Under Panaetius of Rhodes (185–109 B.C.), these doctrines were modified, resulting in the ideal of the wise man aiding his unfortunate brethren, since every man partakes of the divine spark. Still, in order not to be caught in snares, the Stoic must refrain from getting unnecessarily involved. He thus maintains a sense of numbness *(apatheia)* for the good as well as the bad, so that life will not be an unending cycle of ups and downs.

SKEPTICISM

An outgrowth of the Platonic Academy, Skepticism was essentially a negative school of thought. One of its great proponents, Carneades of Cyrene (214–129 B.C.), challenged dogmatic aspects of existing philosophies and severely criticized superstition. Skepticism was important as a gadfly, and led its adherents to a critical understanding of life and a selective choosing of beliefs.

DEVELOPMENTS IN RELIGION

The traditional form of Olympic religion, with the accretion of emperor-worship, continued unabated, although much of the populace only half-believed, if that. The gods and king stood for the state, and their worship formed an integral part of citizenship. More immediate for the masses desiring solace and salvation were mysteries based on such agricultural deities as Dionysus, Demeter, and Persephone. Ptolemy's creation of the Greco-Egyptian god Serapis opened the mysterious cycles of Nilotic cults to the West. In addition, traditional Mesopotamian star-gazing was corrupted into astrology by self-styled seers who claimed that they could foretell the future. The goddess Tyche (Fortune) was worshiped in hope of avoiding the vagaries of life. Finally, magic was increasingly employed in an attempt to bend the forces of nature to human will. When Rome conquered the Hellenistic world, it fell heir to this legacy.

Art

As did most other aspects of culture, the visual arts expanded during the Hellenistic period. Painting developed in scope, and sculpture became so diversified, reflecting the eclectic tastes of the new age, that one cannot refer to a single Hellenistic style. This range is reflected by the various schools of sculpture, such as those of Rhodes and Pergamum. Architecture also developed new forms, resulting in a new type of urban environment.

Painting

Hellenistic painting was often done on a grand scale, as can be seen from mosaic copies of it from the Roman period. The famous Alexander mosaic from Pompeii, a copy of an original by Philoxenus of Eretria, represents the Battle of Issus. It reveals mastery of shadowing, foreshortening, and depiction of intense emotion. Small-scale paintings, also extant only in mosaic copies, were popular. Panels attributed to Dioscurides of Samos represent theatrical scenes while others show still life. The older idealization was absent from historical and everyday scenes, but apparently continued in divine and mythological subjects. This can be seen from later Pompeiian painting, sections of which are copies of Greek masterpieces. Landscape elements began to appear in painting; but in contrast to Roman landscapes, man—and not the forces of nature—dominates the scene.

SCULPTURE

In many respects, Hellenistic sculpture continued trends established during the fourth century B.C.. Complete fluidity in posture was achieved, and an element of turbulence entered statues and reliefs. Many cult statues retained their immemorial calm, although mythological subjects were often represented in a most agitated fashion. Thus, the Aphrodite of Melos, although presented in a twisted posture, is the very model of Olympian tranquillity. On the other hand, the Pergamene school, in representing the battle of the gods and the Titans on the Great Altar of Zeus, shows extreme emotion, agitation, vigorous movement, and huge musculature. In the same spirit are the pictures of Laocoon and his sons being killed by snakes and the Rhodian *Farnese Bull*, a baroquelike pastiche.

After the Gallic invasions, barbarian warriors provided material for sculptors, and the style representation was very emotional, as in the *Dying Gaul*. Followers of Praxiteles developed sculpture with such translucent surfaces that the results often resembled soap statues. Especially popular during the period, presumably holding most appeal for the urban middle classes, was genre sculpture. Subjects that the fifth and fourth centuries B.C. would have considered alien to the realm of art were now represented, including strikingly realistic fishermen, farm people, drunks, and broken-nosed pugilists. However, portraits of the famous still tended toward idealization, and the Hellenistic kings were represented in divine guise.

ARCHITECTURE

Because of the great number of cities founded during this period, urban planning became a science. The gridiron plan of Hippodamus first used in the fifth century B.C. was now applied to such cities as Alexandria, Antioch, and Seleucia. Public buildings were disposed in an orderly and rational way. The focal point of most of these cities was the *agora*, or central marketplace and forum. Facing this square were *stoas*, public centers with an alignment of shops and offices fronted by a colonnade. Building was on a more colossal scale than ever, and temples, palaces, and gymnasia were richly decorated with a predilection for the Corinthian order. One of the wonders of ancient architecture was the Pharos (Lighthouse) at Alexandria.

Selected Readings

Baily, C. *Epicurus* (1926)

Bell, H. I. *Egypt from Alexander the Great to the Arab Conquest* (1948)

Bieber, M. *Alexander the Great in Greek and Roman Art* (1964)

Cary, Max. *A History of the Greek World, 323–146 B.C.* (1951)

DeWitt, N. W. *Epicurus and His Philosophy* (1954)

Dudley, D. R. *A History of Cynicism* (1937)

Ehrenberg, Victor. *Alexander and the Greeks* (1938)

Elgood, P. G. *The Ptolemies of Egypt* (1938)

Fox, J. R. *Alexander the Great* (1973)

Fyfe, D. T. *Hellenistic Architecture* (1936)

Griffith, G. T. *The Mercenaries of the Hellenistic World* (1935)

Hadas, Moses. *Hellenistic Culture* (1959)

Hansen, E. V. *The Attalids of Pergamon* (1947)

Hicks, R. D. *Stoic and Epicurean* (1962)

Jones, A. H. M. *The Greek City from Alexander to Justinian* (1940)

Lawrence, A. W. *Later Greek Sculpture* (1927)

Macurdy, G. H. *Hellenistic Queens* (1932)

Robinson, C. A. *Alexander the Great* (1963)

Rostovtzeff, M. I. *The Social and Economic History of the Hellenistic World*. 3 vols. (1941)

Tarn, W. W. *Greeks in Bactria and India* (1951)

———. *Hellenistic Military and Naval Developments* (1930)

10

The Emergence and Expansion of the Roman Republic

3000–2000 B.C.	Neolithic Period in Italy
2000	Small communities on stilts in Lake District
1600	Bronze Age begins—Terramarans
1200	Arrival of Indo-Europeans
1000–800	Iron Age begins
850–800	Arrival of Etruscans
753	Traditional date for foundation of Rome
750	Cumae in southern Italy founded by Greeks
524	Etruscan expansion ended by Greeks at Cumae
509	Traditional date for expulsion of Tarquin kings
509–264	Early Roman Republic
493	Battle of Lake Regillus
450	The Twelve Tables
445	Canuleian Law permits intermarriage between orders
396	Destruction of Veii by Romans
390	Gallic invasion and sack of Rome
367	Licinian-Sextian Laws
338	Defeat of Latin allies—dissolution of Latin League
338	Roman domains extended into Campania
326–290	Samnite Wars
321	Samnites defeat Romans at Caudine Forks

312   Via Appia connects Rome with Capua
295   Romans defeat Etruscans, Sabines, and Samnites at Sentinum
287   Hortensian Law
284–204   Livius Andronicus—translator of *Odyssey* into Latin
280–275   Rome at war with King Pyrrhus of Epirus
270–201   Naevius—author of first Roman epic, *De Bello Punico*
264–134   Middle Roman Republic
264–241   First Punic War
259–184   Plautus—writer of comedies
239–169   Ennius—author of *Annals,* first Roman dactyls
234–149   Cato—archconservative senator, author of *On Agriculture*
227   Organization of first provinces: Sicily, Sardinia, and Corsica
225–222   First Illyrian War
220–219   Second Illyrian War
218–201   Second Punic War
216   Romans defeated at Battle of Cannae
215–206   First Macedonian War
206   The younger Scipio expels Carthaginians from Spain
202   Romans victorious at Battle of Zama
200–197   Second Macedonian War
197   Rome defeats forces of Philip V of Macedon at Cynoscephale
195   Aetolian League and Sparta join in alliance with Antiochus III
195–159   Terence—writer of Roman New Comedy
189   Romans defeat forces of Antiochus III at Magnesia
185–109   Panaetius—bringer of Stoicism to Rome
171–168   Third Macedonian War
149–148   Fourth Macedonian War
149–146   Third Punic War
148   Macedonia becomes first Roman province in the East

*I*n the eighth and seventh centuries B.C., the relationship of Greece to Italy
was somewhat like that of Europe to the Americas in the sixteenth and
seventeenth centuries. When it was conquered and colonized, Italy was a vast
land full of open spaces, whose inhabitants were below the Greek level of
civilization. The Hellenic city-states in the south eventually grew into some of

the most important areas in the ancient world. The northern and central regions were occupied by other peoples, foremost of whom were the Etruscans. Much Etruscan culture was borrowed from the Greeks in the south, but in Etruria it took on a special tone that was eventually transmitted to the Romans. The unique circumstances of early Rome, its strategic location, and its people gave it predominance in Italy. After the Romans conquered the Etruscans and the cities of Magna Graecia, the Carthaginian world and the Hellenic homeland fell to their might, also.

THE GEOGRAPHY OF ITALY

The lag in cultural developments in Italy during the prehistoric period was part of that process of cultural diffusion whereby the elements of civilization traveled from the Near East in a westerly, then northwesterly, direction. When the advances of the Neolithic period arrived in the Italian peninsula, its cultural aspects were tempered by the geographic conformation of the land.

Unlike the fertile Nile and Tigris-Euphrates river valleys and Greece, whose small fertile areas are cut up by an indented coast and ever-present mountains, Italy has few large rivers and but a single spine of mountains running the length of the peninsula. To the north and west are the Alps, which form a natural land barrier. South of this are the Lake District and the Po Valley. The distinctive natural features of the area now known as Tuscany are foothills of the Apennines, which were easily fortified. Running through central Italy in roughly a north-south course is the Tiber River, which could serve as a waterway for the area known in ancient times as Umbria and Latium. To the south is Campania with its extremely rich volcanic soil and indented coastline, ideal for ports. The toe of the Italian boot was known as Bruttium and the heel as Apulia. The nearby large islands of Sicily, Sardinia, and Corsica were closely related to Italian cultural developments. The climate of Italy is typically Mediterranean, with warm summers and fairly mild winters. Rainfall is more abundant than in Greece and the soil, especially in the volcanic areas of Campania, is more fertile.

PREHISTORY

The latter phase of the Neolithic period (ca. 3000–2000 B.C.) brought agriculture to Italy. By the year 2000 B.C., small communities on stilts, an ingenious adaptation of the Neolithic hut to marshy areas, were established in the Lake District. As in all regions of the ancient world, there were continual migrations. At this time, they were mostly from Central Europe; among the invaders (ca. 1600 B.C.) were the Terramarans, a bronze-working people. By 1200 B.C., large numbers of Indo-Europeans had begun to settle in the peninsula. Between 1000 and 800 B.C., the Iron Age spread throughout Italy. This period, beginning in Greece with the Dorian invasions, saw the extensive use of iron. The chief culture was that of the Villanovans, who clustered in the area of modern Bologna. By the end of the ninth century B.C., new bands of settlers—the Phoenicians and the Etruscans—had come to the peninsula in ships. The Phoenician influence was minimal except in Sicily. The Etruscans, however, were instrumental in the development of Italy.

THE ETRUSCANS

The best philological and archaeological evidence indicates that the Etruscans came from the East, although some scholars still believe that they were indigenous or came from Central Europe. They settled into the foothills of north-central Italy and founded a series of fortified cities that were independent of one another, but nonetheless formed a league. The area of Etruscan domination spread southward until it was stopped at Cumae in 524 B.C. by the Greeks. Among other occupied cities was one smallish Latin settlement known as Rome.

Etruscan Towns and Houses

The cities of the Etruscans, perched on the tops of hills for easy defense, were the direct ancestors of the medieval hill towns that later arose on the same spots for similar reasons. On each site, there was a walled city and a *necropolis*. Modern Italian practice still follows this custom; each hill town in Umbria and Tuscany has its own burial ground.

The major public buildings of Etruria seem to have been temples. Their architectonic elements were taken over from primitive Greek techniques, but the form and orientation were indigenous. The temple usually faced south and was built on a high podium with a flight of steep stairs in the front. It will be recalled that, by the sixth century B.C., stone had replaced wood in the construction of Greek temples. But the Etruscans' basic conservatism (shared with their neighbors, the Romans) retained the wood and terra-cotta of an earlier period. Decoration, however, kept pace with the Hellenic world, for there was close contact between the two peoples.

It is not clear what the private houses were like, but if, as most scholars believe, tombs and cinerary urns represented homes after death, then *necropoleis* such as the one at Caere (Cervetri) give a rough idea of such structures. The earliest houses were doubtless huts, either circular or rectilinear in form. Tombs at Caere indicate that the *liwan*, or tripartite house of Near Eastern origin, was also found in Etruria. This appears to have been combined with a primitive *atrium*, or small entrance courtyard.

Etruscan Tombs and Their Contents

Tombs contain a wealth of information about the Etruscans. The vessels they used were either imported from the Greek world or imitations, and not always very good ones. The native form of pottery, the shiny black *bucchero*, had its origin in metalworking. The stone couches on the sides of the burial chambers seem to have been intended for reclining at a perpetual feast. Both sarcophagi for inhumation and urns for incineration were used, indicating the diverse burial customs of the Etruscans and the people whom they had conquered. Depending on the area, stone or terra-cotta was used for the burial vessel. At times, the tombs were painted. As in the case of terra-cotta styles, the varieties of painting range from Archaic in the sixth century B.C. to Hellenistic in the third and second. The earlier representations show banquets, while later works, created during the decline of Etruria, indicate a morbid preoccupation with punishments of the otherworld.

Etruscan Writing and Religion

The Etruscan alphabet, taken from the Greeks, was used in a language that, in part because of the scarcity of documents, is only now beginning to be understood. It is interesting to note the purposes to which writing was put in primitive ancient societies. The relatively secular society of the Mycenaeans seems to have used its syllabary for uninspiring inventories. The religious nature of extant Etruscan texts denotes an intense preoccupation with gods and ritual. Two specialties of Etruria were *augury* (watching the flights of birds in relation to quadrants in the sky) and *haruspices* (observing sections of animal livers). By these techniques, it was thought that the attitude of the gods could be divined and future events foretold.

The major Etruscan god was Tinia, a sky god roughly equivalent to Zeus (Jupiter). With him, Uni (Hera-Juno) and Menerva (Athena-Minerva) formed a triad, to be inherited by the Romans. Other gods were taken over from Greek mythology and re-formed for Etruscan purposes. One of these was Charun (Charon), who instead of being the deathly ferryman transporting souls to Hades, became the devilish punisher of the deceased. Vanth, the benign winged spirit who carried the dead, was a native Etruscan goddess.

The Importance of the Etruscans

The Etruscans had control of much of north and central Italy, including Rome, and they passed on the benefits of civilization to their subject Italic peoples. In this way, writing and other elements of Hellenic civilization, which had been absorbed, assimilated, and changed by the Etruscans, were diffused. Many religious practices of the Romans and other peoples came from Etruria. The Etruscans were superior engineers, as indicated by the astounding water storage units at Veii; this skill, also, was bequeathed to the Romans. Thus, the basis of civilization for the future conqueror of the Mediterranean was Etruscan. This influence endured even after the decline of Etruria and its absorption by Rome.

THE EARLY ROMANS

The Latins were one among many groups of Indo-Europeans in the Italian peninsula. Unlike the various Greek dialects, the languages of Italy were not mutually comprehensible. For example, Oscan and Umbrian, which are considered linguistically close to Latin, would not have been understood by a Roman. The Latins, like other groups, settled in strategic and easily defensible sites, especially the hill towns. One branch chose one of the most vital spots: the Tiber near its island.

The Settlement of Rome

About fifteen miles from its mouth, the Tiber encircles an island. On the left (eastern) bank is a series of easily defensible hills. In the ninth and eighth centuries B.C., much of the land between these heights was swampy, and they were thus isolated from one another. The major hills are the central Palatine, in the earliest period actually four separate outcroppings; to the west the Capitoline with its double elevation; to the north the Quirinal and Viminal; to the east the Esquiline and Caelian; and to the south the Aventine. Whoever controlled the hills also controlled the island in the Tiber and its ford, thus acquiring a stranglehold on the river-borne trade of central Italy.

According to Roman tradition, Romulus founded the city on the Palatine Hill in the eighth century B.C. (The dates vary in the writings of the ancients; 753 B.C. was used by the first-century-B.C. historian Livy.) Romulus was its first king, and he was succeeded by a line of monarchs until the last, an Etruscan tyrant, was overthrown in 509 B.C. A republic was then established. There appear to be some elements of truth in these legends. On the base rock of the Palatine, holes for the supports of a village of round huts have been found, apparently dating from the ninth or eighth century B.C. In addition, the then swampy area to the north of the Palatine, which later became part of the Roman Forum, has revealed an early Iron Age settlement and cemetery of the ninth to sixth centuries B.C.. There were early settlements on other hills, including the Esquiline and the Quirinal; the latter, according to legend, was inhabited by the Sabines, who eventually joined with the Romans, although probably not in the melodramatic way depicted in the legend of the Rape of the Sabine Women.

The Kingdom

The kingdom of Rome is not well understood by modern scholars; knowledge about it is based mostly on legends, and there are few extant inscriptions from the period. However, since the Romans were very conservative when it came to religion and the outward form of political traditions, it is possible to trace later institutions back to the era of kings.

SOCIAL LIFE

The population of Rome comprised three tribes which were divided into clans (*gentes*, related to the Greek *gene*). Each clan *(gens)* was composed of groups of families. Modern scholars have a multitude of theories to explain the presence of *patricians* (cf. Greek *eupatrids*) and *plebeians* in Roman society. Some say that the patricians, or nobles, were the original Romans and that the plebeians were of a racially diverse group (like the *perioikoi* in Sparta). Others deny the presence of plebeians during the early kingdom. It appears clear, however, that there were a noble and a common class at a very early period. The patricians, so called because they formed the group of *patres* (fathers), or senators (elders), have counterparts in most ancient Indo-European societies from the Hittites, Persians, and Mycenaeans to the Spartans and early Athenians. They were the privileged element of the community who had political rights. They also acted as a council of advisers to the king.

Because the government had little mechanism for the protection of its citizens, this task fell to the individual families. The father of the family *(paterfamilias)* had the power of life and death over individuals in his household. He was also the priest of the domestic religious cult. In addition, he was a patron to *clients*, who were commoners. In return for services to the patrician family, such as appearing as its retainers and coming to its aid in public, the clients received political and judicial protection. Thus, the family unit in early Rome consisted of its members; free clients; and, once wars of expansion began, slaves—all ruled by the *paterfamilias*.

POLITICAL LIFE

In a sense, the entire community was a super-family and the king *(rex)* was its father. The fact that he was the head of religion as well lent a divine air to his being. He was advised and, to some extent, limited by his council of elders, or senate. His supreme power, or *imperium*, made him undisputed master of the community in judicial affairs as well as in time of war. It seems that the kings were elected, and not hereditary rulers.

The Assembly of the People at this time was called the *Comitia Curiata*. It consisted of thirty *curiae* (wards), ten to each tribe, each with its own cult. In later times, when other assemblies represented the people, the *Comitia Curiata* still continued to meet. It is unclear how the citizen army was organized, for the military reforms traditionally attributed to King Servius Tullius appear to be of a much later date.

RELIGIOUS LIFE

The early Italic gods were unlike the anthropomorphic Greek gods. They derived more from the animistic beliefs of primitive man, which held that every rock, tree, and flower was inhabited by a spirit. As time went on, the Romans absorbed elements of Etruscan and Greek religion, and by the end of the Regal period, the sky god, Jupiter, was personified. His accompanying deities in the Capitoline triad were Juno and Minerva. As father of the state, the king was chief priest, and he resided near the hearth of the city, the temple of Vesta. Haruspices and augury were most likely taken over during the Etruscan occupation, as was the form of the temple itself: a sanctuary built on a high podium with a flight of steep stairs leading to the entrance, which was often part of an area set apart for religious purposes.

The domestic religion of the early Romans was highly developed. As the king was the chief priest of the state religion, so the *paterfamilias* presided over the household cult. The protecting gods of the household were known as *lares* and *penates*. In addition, ancestors were worshiped and their death masks were kept in a chapel of the house.

ESTABLISHMENT OF THE REPUBLIC

History and legend present a curious admixture when it comes to studying the kings of ancient Rome. Tradition states that the Etruscan dynasty was begun by Tarquinius Priscus, who was followed by Servius Tullius. Etruscan domination of Rome probably began in the sixth century B.C. The last king of Rome was Tarquinius Superbus, who was overthrown about 509 B.C. because of his tyrannical practices. The reasons for the end of the kingdom have been much discussed. There are probably three distinct ones: the tyranny of the last Tarquin; the desire of the Romans to be rid of the Etruscans; and a political evolution parallel to that of the Greek city-states, whereby the noble classes chafed under the restraining influence of the monarch and overthrew him, establishing an aristocratic form of government in the process.

THE BEGINNING OF ROMAN CONQUEST

The early Republic witnessed a period of turmoil and change. Not only did the Romans lack external security, but there was an internal struggle taking place between the two social classes, the patricians and the plebeians. Expansion to protect their own territories drew the Romans into ever-increasing involvement with the surrounding peoples, which in turn led to new territorial acquisitions and further involvement.

The Latin League

From a very early period, the Romans were joined to their fellow Latins by religious and military bonds. The shrine of Jupiter Latiaris on the Alban Mount was a focal point of unity where once a year all Latins came to worship. The military alliance, at least during the time of the early Republic, was known as the Latin League.

During the monarchy, Rome had been a dependent state of the Etruscans. When it abolished the Tarquin dynasty, it found itself free, republican, and weak. Tradition describes rivalry between Rome and an alliance of other Latin states which came to a head at the Battle of Lake Regillus in about 493 B.C. The peace treaty put Rome in the position of leadership of the Latin League, although the Etruscans were by no means crushed, and such peoples as the Hernici and the Volsci and Aequi from the hills posed a perpetual threat. This was alleviated by an alliance with the Hernici, but it appears that by the middle of the fifth century B.C. the hill people were getting the upper hand. However, within a few decades the balance of power had shifted in favor of the Latins, and Rome geared itself for a new threat: the south Etruscan metropolis of Veii.

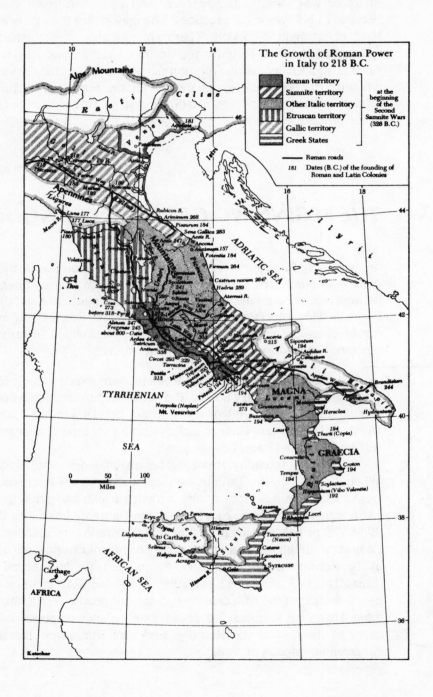

The Growth of Roman Power
in Italy to 218 B.C.

	Roman territory	
	Samnite territory	
	Other Italic territory	at the beginning of the Second Samnite Wars (326 B.C.)
	Etruscan territory	
	Gallic territory	
	Greek States	

——— Roman roads

181 Dates (B.C.) of the founding of Roman and Latin Colonies

THE DESTRUCTION OF VEII AND THE GALLIC INVASION

Veii seems to have been a rival of Rome in the commercial as well as the military sphere, and, insofar as it was less than fifteen miles away, it presented a definite threat. After a lengthy siege by the Romans, Veii was captured and destroyed (ca. 396 B.C.). Its land was taken over by the Romans, expanding their then very limited horizon. As the Veientine land was being distributed among the plebeians, a horde of Gauls was making its way down the Italian peninsula. They were part of an extensive Celtic migration, which followed the pattern of earlier Indo-European wanderings. Despite legends about the heroic behavior of the Romans when the Gauls attacked and sacked the city in about 390 B.C., the result was nothing less than a catastrophe. Upon the departure of the Gauls, Rome was rebuilt and adequate fortifications, hitherto lacking except for the high point of the Capitoline Hill, were built. Rome was never sacked again until A.D. 410, although the wall around the city, wrongly attributed to Servius Tullius, was in ruins by the late Republic.

Dissolution of the Latin League

The enemies and some of the former allies of Rome decided to strike while the city was still in a convalescent state. To their regret, the Aequi, the Hernici, and finally the Volsci found the Romans far from prostrate, and they were severely beaten while the Etruscans were pushed back. By the last third of the fourth century B.C., Roman territory had expanded manyfold and was secured by colonies of Roman citizens.

During this time of strife, the Latin allies, long chafing at Roman leadership, as they would have at any hegemony, broke away from the Latin League. After a treaty in 358 B.C. that reestablished the league in a form not unlike that of the Second Athenian Confederation, Rome was its undisputed leader. However, citizens of each member city had the legal rights of commercial transaction *(ius commercium)* and marriage *(ius connubium)* with the citizen's of any other league city. Still, the Latins resented the Romans, and they abrogated any allegiance to Rome until after their revolt and subsequent defeat in 338 B.C., when they became part of the Roman system of government. At that times, some cities received the rights of full Roman citizenship, while others received only partial enfranchisement that became full for individuals from those cities when they moved to Rome. Less favored cities became only allies of Rome. The least favored lost all the local rights that in other communities were corollaries of Roman citizenship or alliance, and such areas were absorbed by the young colossus.

The Samnite Wars

Alliances had brought the Romans as far south as Capua and, after the readjustment of 338 B.C., a goodly chunk of Campania was absorbed into the Roman political system. This expansion brought Rome face-to-face with the dominant people in the area, the Samnites.

The Samnites were hill people who felt it was their right to control Campania. When Neapolis (Naples) became associated with Rome and it was threatened by the hill people, conflict between Romans and Samnites was inevitable. The war can be divided into three sections, the first of which reached a climax in 321 B.C., when the Romans suffered a disastrous defeat at the Caudine Forks. In 316 B.C. the struggle began again, and Rome gradually tipped the balance of power in her favor. One of the reasons was the construction (312 B.C.) of the *Via Appia* (Appian Way) from Rome to Capua; on it, troops could easily be rushed to Campania. The Samnites allied themselves with malcontent peoples around Rome, including the Etruscans, Sabines, and even Gauls, all of whom were finally defeated by a massive Roman military effort at Sentinum in 295 B.C. As a result of these wars, Rome obtained a wide belt of land across Italy from the Tyrrhenian Sea to the Adriatic and from southern Etruria to the Bay of Naples. The assimilation of these new lands took place by the establishment of colonies of Roman citizens within their confines, while, following the now-established principle of Roman policy, the other conquered areas were affiliated with Rome, with varying degrees of autonomy.

CONQUEST OF THE GREEK SOUTH

The Greek city-states of southern Italy and Sicily offered an impressive cultural legacy. Although there had been major powers among them, such as Syracuse and then Tarentum, there was little unity. Indeed, rivalry was the common condition. As a result, when the Roman sphere of influence began to spread southward, not a few Hellenic cities allied themselves with the new master of central Italy. This brought Rome into conflict within the Greek world and led to Roman absorption of its Italian portion.

As central Italy had never been assimilated by the Etruscans, so the southern part of the peninsula had never been fully Hellenized. Many peoples lived beyond the limited boundaries of the Greek city-states and often proved dangerous to them. Tarentum, however, had the ambition if not the power to be the leading city in the area, and it considered all of southern Italy within its sphere of influence.

The Lucanians were becoming quite aggressive and threatened several of the cities in the south, including Thurii. The self-proclaimed leadership of the Tarentines proved ineffectual, and the Thuriians turned to Rome for protection, much to the resentment of the Tarentines. The Romans placed a garrison in Thurii and sent ships to the area, which were duly attacked by the Tarentines, some being sunk in the process. Rome demanded reparations; Tarentum refused to even make apologies. War resulted, and the Tarentines appealed to King Pyrrhus of Epirus for aid.

Pyrrhus not only had territorial ambitions in the Balkans, but once he was given the opportunity for involvement in Italy, his dreams of empire began to encompass the West. He landed with a large army (twenty-five thousand men) and those animal war tanks, elephants (hitherto unseen in Italy), which terrified the Italians. Pyrrhus won victories at Heraclea in 280 B.C. and at Asculum in 279 B.C., but they were hollow, for he lost many troops and much strength (hence the expression, "Pyrrhic victory"). Rome and Carthage then made an alliance for mutual protection.

In the meantime, the Greeks of Sicily felt themselves threatened by Carthage and called Pyrrhus to help them. Pyrrhus' dream of empire became more focused, and he saw himself not as the savior of Hellenic Sicily but as its king. However, after expelling the Carthaginians from most of the island, Pyrrhus alienated the Sicilians by his high-handed attitude and, as a result, had to withdraw to Italy. There he returned to hostilities with the Romans. But after suffering severe losses at the Battle of Beneventum (275 B.C.), he left for his homeland, where he died shortly thereafter. Rome now found itself in command of the southern Italian peninsula, which it assimilated as it had the north and central sections.

POLITICAL LIFE IN THE EARLY REPUBLIC

As the military ventures of Rome took a downward turn in the fifth century B.C., so did the political rights of the plebeians. The king had been a father figure to the state and had guaranteed certain rights for the whole population. With the coming of the Republic and aristocratic government, many rights were taken away from the lower order. But through violence and stubbornness, the plebeians were able to regain their lost rights and add to them. The resulting changes in the Roman constitution included the creation of an inviolable plebeian magistrate known as the *tribune*.

The Government

The magistracies and assemblies were quite different from those of the monarchy. During an early phase of the Republic a new assembly, the *centuriate*, was created. This, because it was based on wealth rather than birth, diluted the power of the patricians. In addition, the even newer tribal assembly aided in breaking the patrician stranglehold.

CONSULS

When the monarchy was abolished, the executive power was vested in two consuls. In the manner of the archons of Athens, new consuls were elected annually and gave a name to each year. It appears that the term *consul* came into use toward the middle of the fourth century B.C. and that in the earlier period no distinction was made between consuls and praetors. This highest of public offices inherited from the monarchy the *imperium* (supreme power) and its symbolic accompaniment, the *fasces* (bundles of rods enclosing an ax that at public events were carried by officials known as *lictors*). Each consul could veto any move made by the other, and each could convoke the assemblies. If through misfortune both consuls died, the senate selected one of its own number, known as the *interrex*, who took over supreme power until elections could be held. If an emergency arose requiring supreme power to be vested in the hands of one person, a *dictator* was chosen.

PRAETORS, QUAESTORS, AEDILES, AND CENSORS

In the fourth century B.C. the praetorship became an office distinct from the consulship. The *praetor* assumed judicial functions while retaining the *imperium* and military attributes. In the early Republic, there were only two *praetors*, but during the third century B.C., with the expansion of Rome overseas, the number increased. The office of *quaestor* went back to the beginning of the Republic. This official was originally the assistant of the consuls in judicial matters, but, within a short time, his primary function was financial supervision. The *aedile* was a magistrate ranking between the *quaestor* and *praetor*. The office was originally held by two plebeians, but in the fourth century B.C. two patrician *aediles (curules)* were added to the magistracy. The *aediles'* concerns were the maintenance and construction of public buildings, care of the grain supply, and the unenviable task of supplying entertainment for public festivities. Another office was that of the two *censors*, who every four years made lists of citizens and their property qualifications. In time, the *censors* became so powerful that they would revise the rolls of members of the senate, deleting the names of individuals whose attitude or behavior they considered objectionable.

THE SENATE

In the early Republic, the senate symbolized the aristocracy. To be sure, by the fourth century B.C., there were plebeian senators, but they were in the minority and were not given the same respect as the patricians. The number of senators was three hundred, based on the original three tribes. The power of the senate was enormous, for the tenure of its members was for life, while that of most elected officials was for only one year. In addition, since the senate was the repository for former consuls, there was a very close tie between the senators and the highest magistrates. Besides, the senate selected the candidates for public office who were elected by the centuriate.

THE CENTURIATE ASSEMBLY *(COMITIA CENTURIATA)*

As Rome increased in size and in commitments abroad, a new military organization was essential to replace the tribal *curiae*. About the middle of the fifth century B.C., the so-called Servian reforms (many good things were attributed to the benign king Servius Tullius) reestablished the military in accordance with wealth. The citizen body was divided into two parts: those who could afford to buy their own military gear and those who could not. The former were divided into two groups, both of which were able to support a horse: the cavalry and the first class. The cavalry, also known as *equestrians* or *equites*, was the basic kernel for the later growth of upper-middle-class merchants who formed a buffer between the senatorial and lower classes in the second century B.C. The first class was composed of the senatorial order. The following five classes, categorized by diminishing riches, were all lumped together in a single have-not group. The citizen body, thus arranged, met in an assembly, the *comitia centuriata*, so called because each category consisted of groups called centuries, which varied in size according to rank. The greatest number of centuries was in the first class. Voting began with the cavalry and then continued by class, but it usually did not get beyond the first or second class. If the cavalry and first class voted as a bloc, a not-infrequent occurrence, a majority was reached. Thus, the largest part of the citizen body had the fewest votes, and wealthy landowners, both patricians and plebeians, dominated the proceedings. The centuriate assembly elected major magistrates, but obviously in a very undemocratic fashion. Still, it was an improvement over the curiate assembly, which was retained as that type of vestigial ceremonious body so dear to the Romans.

THE TRIBAL ASSEMBLIES

As a result of the Servian reforms, the number of tribes was increased and the plebeians were enrolled in four new urban units. They met in a council *(concilium plebis tributum)*, which acted as a pressure group on the patricians. As time went on, it seems that this council became an assembly with the right to vote on legislation. By the fourth century B.C., the assembly *(comitia tributa)* included all of the Roman citizens voting by tribe. Since each tribe voted as a unit, the seemingly democratic aspect of this assembly was minimal, for the rich applied great pressure to their clients to vote their way.

Patricians vs. Plebeians

Tradition tells us that, in the first half of the fifth century B.C., the plebeians rebelled at patrician dominance and left Rome in protest. In order to keep the economy of the city from collapsing, a concession was granted the plebs in the establishment of the office of tribune. This official represented the plebs as the consuls represented all of the Roman people. His person was inviolate, and he could intercede in many ways on behalf of his constituents. At a later period, the office of tribune became the most powerful in local politics.

THE TWELVE TABLES

In the middle of the fifth century B.C. (the traditional date is 450), a board of ten eminent Romans was set up to write a constitution. The result, which comes down to us in fragmentary form, does not, as tradition suggests, indicate an exhaustive study of Greek constitutions. It is a rudimentary if logical law code, known as the Law of the Twelve Tables. One provision sought to prevent the plebeians from entering the ruling clique, by prohibiting intermarriage between the classes. Other laws dealt with property rights and legal status. Since it extremely antagonized the plebs, the marriage prohibition was abrogated in 445 B.C., when the Canuleian Law was passed permitting intermarriage.

THE TRIUMPH OF THE PLEBS

For obscure reasons, the consulship was abolished in 444 B.C. It was replaced by the imperium of three or six military tribunes (no relation to the plebeian tribunes) appointed by the senate. Not before 400 B.C. were plebeians able to hold this office. In 367 B.C., the Licinian-Sextian Laws were passed, reestablishing the consulship. They also included a limitation on the size of estates. They provided that one of the consuls be a plebeian, but as if in fear of too much democracy too soon, the newly established praetorship was strictly patrician. By the end of the fourth century B.C., however, the major offices were available to the plebs. Still, the plebeian assembly was treated in a second-class way, and the result was another secession of the plebs. Then the Hortensian Law (287 B.C.) was passed. This gave *plebiscites*, or measures passed by the plebeian assembly, the force of law binding on all Romans. (Roman historical sources are very vague in distinguishing between the tribal assembly, which included all Romans, and the one containing only plebeians. Much scholarly debate has been carried on concerning whether two different assemblies did in fact exist.)

Religious Offices

As it had been in the monarchy, religion during the early Republic was closely connected with the state. Religious ceremonies so pervaded all aspects of government, and law was so tied to religion, that in due time the public cults became little more than an agency of the state. Romans then turned elsewhere for solace. Religious officials continued from the monarchy included the *flamines*, who were appointed to serve individual gods, and the *pontifices*, who were in charge of state cults and were well versed in law. The head of the College of Pontifices was the *pontifex maximus*, who held office for life. Appointed by him was the *rex sacrorum* or "King of Sacrifices," who inherited the functions of the king in the same way that the *archon basileus* in Athens got both his title and his religious functions from the deposed monarch.

THE DUEL WITH CARTHAGE

During the Pyrrhic War, Rome had briefly become an ally of Carthage. But after Rome's annexation of southern Italy, it became clear that the powers had nothing in common but rivalry. Carthage, founded in the ninth century B.C. as a colony of the Phoenician city Tyre, had become the major power in the western Mediterranean and would tolerate no competitor. The resulting Punic Wars destroyed Carthage and made Rome the master of the West.

The First Punic War

The First Punic War (264–241 B.C.) illustrated how adaptable the Romans had become to new conditions, for, starting from scratch, they created a navy to defeat the Carthaginian fleet.

THE CAUSES

The immediate cause of the war came from the Mamertines, pirates of Campanian origin who had been settled in Messana (Messina) by Agathocles of Syracuse as a bulwark against the Carthaginians. Because of their continued plundering, the Mamertines were about to be destroyed by their former patron, Syracuse, now under the leadership of Hiero. In desperation, they sought help from both Rome and Carthage. Carthage responded first and sent a garrison, while the Roman senate pondered the latest developments, not desiring to intervene because of the earlier treaty with Carthage. The *comitia tributa*, on the other hand, wanted to check Carthage. After vigorous debate, the *comitia tributa* decided to send Roman troops to the area in order to get the Carthaginians out of that strategic part of Sicily and help the Mamertines in the process. Thus, hostilities began.

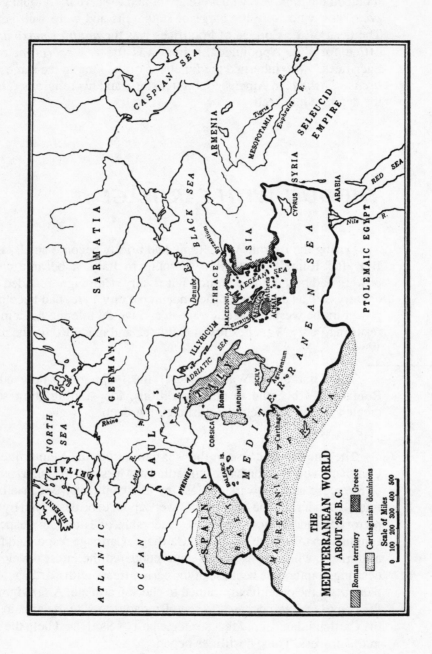

THE MEDITERRANEAN WORLD
ABOUT 265 B.C.

THE WAR

In the first phase of the fighting, the Mamertines decided that they were pro-Roman after all, and ejected the Carthaginian troops. The Carthaginians and their Syracusan allies, having failed to recapture Messana, were then defeated by the Romans. The Syracusans switched allegiance to Rome after the Roman army was greatly reinforced. The result was outstanding military success on land, but none at sea. It became apparent that Rome, up to now an inland power, had great need of a navy, for Carthage excelled in war at sea. Thereupon, a Roman fleet of 120 ships, *quinquiremes* (having five banks of oars), was built (260 B.C.) with the assistance of the south Italian Greeks. Each boat had a grapple that could be hooked onto an enemy ship to bring it close. Then a gangway was brought down and the sailors became soldiers and fought on the Carthaginian ships as if they were land areas. Thus, Rome had become a naval power, and the consul Gaius Duilius was its first admiral.

Victories were won off Mylae (260 B.C.) and Economus (256 B.C.) in Sicily, but a campaign against Carthage ended in a fiasco, due to the blundering of the consul Marcus Atilius Regulus (256–255 B.C.). The low point of the war was reached when, after its return to Sicilian waters and its conquest of the important city of Panormus (Palermo) in 254 B.C., the Roman fleet was defeated and then destroyed by storms. However, the Romans managed to rebuild their fleet and began to besiege Lilybaeum, the chief Carthaginian city in western Sicily. In 242 B.C., the Romans succeeded in destroying a Carthaginian fleet, thereby cutting off the city. The following year, a peace treaty was signed.

Besides a handsome indemnity, Rome acquired control of the island of Sicily, which was eventually organized to become the first Roman province. Carthage was considerably weakened, and its sphere of influence was greatly reduced.

Intermission

By now, Rome had become involved in many areas, and the period between the Punic Wars (241–219 B.C.) was far from peaceful. Incursions by Gallic tribes, including the Boii and the Insubres, were stopped by Roman conquest (225–222 B.C.). In order to protect its Adriatic interests, Rome had put Demetrius of Pharos in charge of the Illyrian region, but he switched allegiance to the king of Macedonia, Antigonus Doson, and his successor Philip V. Although Rome's intervention (First and Second Illyrian Wars, 225–222 B.C. and 220–219 B.C.) and establishment of an Illyrian protectorate was considered by Philip a clear infringement of his sphere of influence, Macedonia was for the moment occupied elsewhere. In 227 B.C., Rome annexed Corsica and Sardinia.

The Second Punic War

The Second Punic War (218–201 B.C.) completely broke the power of Carthage and made Rome the only power in the West. The territory acquired from the war brought Roman influence into every corner of the western Mediterranean.

THE CAUSES

One of the general causes of the war was the undying desire of the Carthaginian Barca dynasty for revenge on Rome. Another was the natural wish of Carthage to regain her lost influence. The immediate cause, however, was the city of Saguntum in Spain. In 226 B.C., Rome and Carthage had agreed that the Ebro River would divide the Roman sphere of influence in the north from that of the Carthaginians in the south. Saguntum lay to the south of this boundary; yet, it had somehow made a defense treaty with Rome. When the Carthaginians began to harass Saguntum, it appealed to Rome. In 218 B.C., the city was captured by the Carthaginians under the command of Hannibal Barca, because Rome had sent no help. Encouraged, Hannibal saw the opportunity to rid Spain entirely of the Romans and crossed the Ebro River into Roman territory. War was then declared.

THE WAR

Hannibal's plan was bold and ingenious: he would not battle the Romans in Spain, but he would attack Italy and crush his enemy by detaching the allied and confederate Italian states. His first task was to avoid battle with the approaching Roman armies, under Publius Cornelius Scipio. He easily managed this because Scipio was diverted by an insurrection of Gauls. Hannibal then crossed the Alps with about forty thousand men and a goodly number of elephants. The rigors of the crossing, however, caused the loss of half the troops. Meanwhile, Scipio returned to Italy and, together with an army headed by Tiberius Sempronius Longus, met Hannibal at Trebia. The result was disaster for the Romans (218 B.C.). Although Hannibal had miscalculated and none of the Roman allies came to his side, he was still master of the situation. In 217 B.C., he utterly destroyed a large army under Gaius Flaminius at Trasimene, and then he continued southward.

In the meantime, the dismayed population of Rome made Quintus Fabius Maximus dictator to cope with the situation. Fabius, having seen the uselessness of fighting Hannibal in open warfare, resorted to guerrilla tactics. Unfortunately, this policy was abandoned in 216 B.C., and a Roman army of more than fifty thousand was decimated by Hannibal at Cannae. The Romans were in a state of shock, and many Campanian cities, whose loyalty to Rome was by no means unequivocal, allied themselves with the Carthaginians. Still, the Romans remained obdurate and were able to defend their city successfully, thanks to its excellent fortifications (211 B.C.). It appears, however, that Hannibal did not actually intend to capture the city but that his purpose in attacking it was to divert Roman troops from Capua. In the same year, Syracuse revolted, and Rome recaptured it. Meanwhile, Hannibal's brother, Hasdrubal, who had been left in charge of Spain, fared badly against the Romans. In 208 B.C., Hasdrubal left the Iberian peninsula, and the following year he was in Italy with an army of thirty thousand going to help his brother, whose resources were declining as he devastated the Italian countryside. But before he could join the forces of Hannibal, Hasdrubal was defeated at Metaurus (207 B.C.).

After the younger Scipio (later called Africanus) completed the expulsion of the Carthaginians from Spain (206 B.C.), he proceeded to meet them on their own soil. Only then did Hannibal leave Italy and return to Africa. The battle fought at Zama in 202 B.C. was won by the Romans and their allies, the Numidians, who were glad to be rid of their Carthaginian neighbors. The peace treaty was signed the following year.

RESULTS OF THE WAR

As a result of the Second Punic War, Carthage lost all of its territory with the exception of the city itself and its vicinity. Most of the Carthaginian fleet and arms were surrendered, and an enormous indemnity paid. In short, Carthage was reduced to a vassal city of Rome. The lands of Italy were devastated, with ensuing ruin of the small farmer class. The large estates of the nobles absorbed the bankrupt farms, while the landless migrated to Rome to look for work, often in vain.

In 197 B.C., Spain was divided into two areas, which now entered the growing roster of Roman provinces.

CONQUEST OF THE GREEK EAST

With the conquest of major portions of the Hellenistic territory, Rome became a world power. The culture of the conquered was fused with that of the Romans, and within one hundred years it had become the standard of civilization in the ancient world.

The First and Second Macedonian Wars

The First Macedonian War (215–206 B.C.) was the inevitable outcome of conflict between Rome and Macedonia after the establishment of a Roman protectorate over the Illyrian coast. This war was actually a chapter of the Second Punic War. Philip V of Macedon made a treaty with Carthage and took advantage of Hannibal's invasion of Italy to try to recover Macedonia's position in Illyria. The subsequent peace pact (205 B.C.) had little effect, for Philip and Antiochus III of the Seleucid Empire had dreams of reestablishing their domains to the size they had reached during the early Hellenistic period. Antiochus proceeded to seize Palestine from Ptolemaic Egypt, now in a weak, somnolent state, while Philip seized certain cities of Asia Minor (203–202 B.C.). Rhodes and Pergamum, small independent states between two giants, appealed to Rome for aid and did not meet deaf ears, since the Romans were ready to pounce on Macedonia. War was declared (200 B.C.), and the Roman army entered the Greek world. In 197 B.C., the armies of Philip were defeated at Cynoscephale under the leadership of the philhellene general Titus Quinctius Flamininus.

Flamininus was greeted by most Greeks as the savior of their homeland, but in a short while it became evident that the Romans had their own plans. Besides, the rivalry of the two leagues of city-states, the Aetolian and Achaean, helped break the spell of Roman liberation. The influence of Macedonia had now been destroyed in Greece, but peace did not arrive for a long time.

The War with Antiochus III

After the war with Philip, the Romans had deliberately provoked Antiochus III by declaring his subjects in Asia Minor free of Seleucid rule. Several years of negotiations failed, and Antiochus was ready for hostilities. In the meantime, the Aetolian League and Sparta seized territory and joined with Antiochus in alliance (195 B.C.). Rome had crushed the allies on the Greek mainland by 190 B.C. and defeated the forces of Antiochus at Magnesia in 189 B.C. To the Achaean League and to Macedonia, who had remained loyal to Rome, went additional territory; but the Aetolian League was severely crippled. The Seleucid Empire lost the western part of Asia Minor, which was divided between the Roman allies, Rhodes and Pergamum.

The Third and Fourth Macedonian Wars and Subsequent Events

Although Perseus, son of Philip V, was intent on reviving his kingdom at Rome's expense, the direct cause of the Third Macedonian War (171–168 B.C.) was antipathy between Macedonia and Pergamum, Rome's staunch ally. The Romans entered the fray, and in 168 B.C. an army under Lucius Aemilius Paullus defeated the forces of Perseus at Pydna. The terms of peace were very harsh, dividing Macedonia into four separate republics. Paranoia seemed to dictate Rome's attitude, and allies as well as enemies were treated hostilely.

The East was by no means a slave to Rome's wishes and, indeed, plans were afoot in the Seleucid Empire—now ruled by Antiochus IV—and Macedonia to recoup their recent losses in prestige and land. In Macedonia, a pretender to the throne began and ended the Fourth Macedonian War (149–148 B.C.). Another battle at Pydna terminated the independence of Macedonia and, in 148 B.C., it became the first Roman province in the East. It had become clear that, as had been the case with Italian territories, Rome could not interfere in Hellenic affairs without outright incorporation of the area. The Achaean League grew restive and, in a brief revolt (147–146 B.C.), succeeded in completely undermining Greek independence. In 146 B.C., Corinth was completely destroyed by the Roman commander Lucius Mummius as an object lesson. Greece was left without even the dignity of its own governor; it was controlled by the governor of Macedonia. However, those cities such as Athens, which had remained loyal to Rome, were treated as Roman allies.

The Third Punic War

The West was by no means untroubled at mid-century. King Massinissa of Numidia, who had been richly rewarded for his aid to Rome in the Second Punic War, had designs on the remaining Carthaginian trading cities. Because Carthage was unable to defend itself without permission from Rome, the Numidians overran all of its possessions and threatened the city itself. Since the Romans were pro-Numidian and the senate group led by Cato the Elder was virulently anti-Carthaginian, no decision was forthcoming. Carthage decided to defend itself (150 B.C.); but when Rome entered the conflict on the Numidian side, the city's days were numbered. It fell in 146 B.C. and was utterly destroyed; afterward, its ground was salted.

THE PROVINCES

The vast wealth that entered Rome from its conquests created a desire for more of the same, which influenced in unfortunate ways the type of government imposed on the newly won areas. Although the provincial system had much to recommend it, it was from the start a means of acquiring riches at the expense of the provincials. It was not reformed until the time of Augustus.

The Provincial Charter

In a sense, the government of a province was an outgrowth of the earlier Roman system of alliances. After a charter for a prospective province had been drawn up by its military conqueror and a delegation of senators, the results usually followed the same general outlines. There were three types of relationship between city-state and Rome. The most nearly autonomous in all but foreign relations was the "free and allied city" *(civitas libera et foederata)*; this position was usually a reward for friendship toward Rome. A not-so-free, but still relatively desirable, status was that of the "free and immune city" *(civitas libera et immunis)*. The communities in this group were free and exempt from taxes, but their status could change at the whim of the senate. Finally there was the taxpaying, unfree city, called a *civitas stipendiaria*, which was ruled directly by the resident governor. All provincial natural resources were of course controlled by Rome, and Roman colonies, consisting of Roman citizens set within the province, were considered extensions of the capital itself. In all cases, Rome had control of foreign policy.

The Governors

At first, the praetors were governors, but it became apparent that the number of praetors could not be increased indefinitely to match the increase in provinces. Thus, ex-consuls and ex-praetors were allotted provinces, which they ruled with an iron fist. Since it was very difficult for provincials to appeal abuses of the governor and his staff, corruption infested all levels of administration. Tax collectors would receive contracts from the Roman government and would badger the population into paying higher amounts, most of which went into their own pockets.

CULTURE OF THE MIDDLE REPUBLIC

Although the Etruscans had contributed greatly to Rome's early culture and had transmitted many of the advantages of Greek civilization, life in the early Republic was far from enlightened. The native genius was not attuned to poetry and art as was that of Greece. Instead, the Roman aptitudes were for religion, law, and technology. At the time of the conquest of the Greek cities in the south of Italy, and especially after the annexation of Greece, the tide of Hellenism flooded a not-always-receptive Rome.

Literature

The most primitive of Roman poetry, called Saturnian verse, had a cryptic meter that has defied analysis. Drama was limited to slapstick skits, and literary prose was altogether missing. In the third century B.C., all of this changed. In order to let Roman schoolboys glimpse into the world of Homer, the south Italian and former slave, Livius Andronicus (ca. 284–204 B.C.) translated the *Odyssey* into the native Saturnian verse. Gnaeus Naevius (ca. 270–201 B.C.) composed the first Roman epic, taking as his subject the First Punic War *(De Bello Punico)*. Naevius also wrote plays of the three types then in vogue: those based on Hellenistic New Comedy *(fabulae palliatae)*, those dealing with Roman comic situations *(fabulae togatae)*, and those based on Roman history *(fabulae praetextatae)*. Like Livius Andronicus, Gnaeus Naevius composed his works in the native Saturnian verse. Quintus Ennius (239–169 B.C.) was the first to adapt dactylic hexameter to the Latin language in his *Annals*, an epic of early Rome. He also wrote a goodly number of plays, some based on Athenian tragedy of the fifth century B.C..

The earliest example of Roman historical prose was, ironically enough, in Greek, for the writer, Quintus Fabius Pictor (fl. ca. 200 B.C.), felt not erroneously that Latin was as yet an inadequate vehicle for the subject; he also wanted the newly absorbed Magna Graecia to understand Roman ways. Typifying the early Roman mentality was the senator Marcus Porcius Cato (234–149 B.C.). Cato was an uncompromising traditionalist and an avowed Hellenophobe, in opposition to the avant-garde circle of the Scipios who helped the diffusion and acceptance of Greek culture. The major distinction of Cato's *On Agriculture* is that it is the oldest surviving prose work in Latin.

The greatest writers of the middle Republic were easily Titus Maccius Plautus (ca. 259–184 B.C.) and Publius Terentius Afer (Terence, ca. 195–159 B.C.). The surviving twenty-one plays of Plautus, a native of Umbria, are fresh and often uproariously funny comedies based loosely on Hellenistic New Comedy. The plays of Terence, who a second-century B.C. biographer stated was born in Carthage, adhere more closely to Greek originals. His style is highly polished, but the plays are not funny; indeed, they are melodramas with happy endings.

Art

Architecture was well developed by the second century B.C. Hellenistic externals, such as the shape of columns, capitals, and sculptural decorations, were grafted onto buildings of native form—for example, temples on high podia. Tufa and travertine were still used extensively in the construction of buildings, and cement was just beginning to be utilized. Arches, spurned by the Greeks, became a means of support and decoration. The *basilica* was a new type of market building with an indoor forum. The foremost example was the Basilica Aemilia (179 B.C.) in the Forum.

Figured painting, found mainly in tombs, showed battles and other historical scenes. Portrait sculpture was foremost of the visual arts. Developed from the wax masks of ancestors, the portrait busts had an almost painful realism.

Religion and Philosophy

As the externals of Roman buildings were Hellenized, so were the outward trappings of the gods. Jupiter and Zeus, Minerva and Athena, Juno and Hera, were so closely identified that in mythological terms they became synonymous. However, the traditional Roman ceremonies continued virtually unchanged.

Although Greek philosophy met with a very hostile reception from the traditionalists, by the middle of the second century B.C. it had found an enduring place in Roman life. Stoicism, which was popularized by Panaetius (185–109 B.C.), was particularly close to Roman ideals.

*T*he Middle Republic witnessed the rise of Rome to the position of a major power in the Mediterranean. It was a painful adolescence for the Republic, as it had to turn back external threats to its security. During the Late Republic things would be different. Rome would increase in strength despite herself, but the Republic would pass from young adulthood into the decline of old age due to social and political turmoil.

Selected Readings

Alfoedi, A. *Early Rome and the Latins* (1965)
Astin, A. E. *Cato the Censor* (1978)
Banti, L. *The Etruscan Cities and Their Culture* (1973)
Bloch, Raymond. *The Etruscans* (1958)
———. *The Origins of Rome* (1960)
Boren, H. C. *The Gracchi* (1968)
Brea, L. B. *Sicily before the Greeks* (1966)
Cristofani, M. *The Etruscans: A New Investigation* (1979)
Gjerstad, E. *Early Rome.* 2 vols. (1953–56)
Pallottino, M. *The Etruscans* (1974)
———. *Art of the Etruscans* (1955)
———. *Etruscan Painting* (1952)
Richter, G. M. A. *Ancient Italy* (1955)
Scullard, H. H. *Roman Politics (220–150 B.C.)* (1953)
———. *A History of the Roman World, 753–146* (1961)
———. *Scipio Africanus in the Second Punic War* (1930)

11

Stresses on the Roman Republic

133–27 B.C. Late Roman Republic

133 Kingdom of Pergamum willed to Rome

133 Tiberius Gracchus elected tribune

123 Gaius Gracchus elected tribune

121 Romans subdue Gallic Allobroges and Arvernii

116 Senate divides Numidia between Jugurtha and Adherbal

107 Gaius Marius elected consul

106–43 Marcus Tullius Cicero—orator and politician

105 Romans defeat Jugurtha

105 Cimbri and Teutones defeat Romans at Arausio

104–100 Marius consul

102–44 Julius Caesar—statesman and historian

102 Germanic tribes defeated at Aquae Sextiae

101 Germanic tribes defeated at Vercellae

95–55 Lucretius—philosophical poet

90–88 Social War

88 Complete citizenship granted to all Roman allies

88 Sulla consul

87 Cinna consul

87–85 Sulla fights Mithridates in East (First Mithdratic War)

86 Marius dies

86 Athens besieged and taken by Rome

85–54 Catullus—lyric poet

83   Sulla lands at Brundisium

82   Battle of Colline Gate—Sulla dictator for life

81   Pompey receives appellation, "the Great"

79   Sulla retires

*T*he Roman Republic, later looked back on as a Golden Age by such Silver Age writers as Juvenal and Tacitus in the last third of the second century B.C., had become a stage for violence. The "good life" of the earlier Republic was gone, and stresses between the various classes of Roman society had reached a breaking point.

THE ESTATES

As we have seen, the early Italian was, generally speaking, a farmer who had a small plot of land that, in good times, could support him and his family. As Rome became the dominant power on the Italian peninsula, ever-increasing numbers of veterans had to be compensated for their services by allotments of land. An additional and far more acute pressure on the small landowner was the senatorial class. Since the nobility of the classical world did not engage in trade or in any demeaning labor, the road to wealth was provided by vast landholdings worked by armies of slaves. The system of the *latifundia*, or super-estates, proved so profitable that the small-scale landowner was squeezed out. The *latifundia* absorbed with little expense to themselves an ever-increasing number of bankrupt holdings. What had been a trickle of emigration from the farms to the city became a torrent, and Rome was faced with a mob of unemployed, unskilled ex-farmers who could not or would not work. The problem grew to severe proportions during and after the Punic Wars, for vast tracts of land were devastated during Hannibal's invasion of Italy. Paradoxically, although the great estates were badly damaged, their owners came out of the wars with more land and wealth than before, because they gained possession of the smaller farms that had been ruined as economic units.

By far the largest source of land for the *latifundia*, however, were the *ager publicus* (public land). When Rome had begun the conquest of Italy, much land (often a third) of a conquered territory was taken over directly by the state. Members of the nobility, known as *possessores*, were granted a large amount of this property. In 367 B.C., the Licinian-Sextian Laws stated that a holding could not exceed 500 *iugera* (approximately 320 acres). In addition, the tenant had to pay a sum to the government as rent. Neither stipulation was heeded by the senatorial class in the second century B.C.

PATRICIANS AND PLEBEIANS

It has been noted that many of the problems of the early Republic revolved around the conflict between patricians and plebeians. As time went on, the plebeians gained the power to elect officials and to convene their own council. The distinction between the two classes gradually began to fade, although differences of income always remained important. Still, it must not be forgotten that the Roman was by nature the most conservative of men. The mystique of the patrician families and clans, such as the Claudii, the Cornelii, and the Julii, remained undiminished, and their quasi-divine origins were taken for granted. Hence, the senate was dominated by the same small group that had ruled it since the beginning of the Republic. Nevertheless, the lower orders had a toehold, so to speak, in governmental control: the *tribal assembly*, which voted according to tribe and not wealth as did the *centuriate assembly*, could ideally be a tool of the majority. More important was the creation at an early date of the office of *plebeian tribune*. This magistrate's person was inviolate, and he was able to veto any proposal of his colleagues. He could also introduce measures before the senate. Since there were ten plebeian tribunes, if the senatorial class could contrive to have one elected, it could control popular legislation.

FOREIGN ENTANGLEMENTS

In addition to the concentration of more and more land and power in the hands of the few and its corollary of the growing urban mob, the overseas expansion of Rome had reached enormous proportions. The First Punic War had brought the first nonpeninsular province, Sicily; and, by the last third of the second century B.C., Rome was mistress of Spain, Italy, the area of Carthage, much of the Balkan peninsula, and the kingdom of Pergamum.

The growth of the Roman Empire had always been haphazard. Perhaps because of a basic feeling of insecurity due to the ever-present power of the Etruscans, the early Romans had made defense treaties with surrounding peoples. Eventually, it became militarily necessary to absorb these territories. When this expanded Rome came into contact with new peoples the process repeated itself. As a result, ever-growing concentric masses of land became associated with the city on the Tiber. Although the Italian lands had become thoroughly Romanized, the senate had no desire to grant their peoples the rights of full citizenship and thus dilute its own base of power. This disparity brought about a potentially explosive situation. Further, Rome's entry into Africa involved her in the affairs of the kingdom of Numidia, and her entry into Asia gave rise to conflicts with the kingdom of Pontus. Thus, the period from 133 to 78 B.C. saw great social and political conflict, both at home and abroad, which eventually led to the dissolution of the Roman Republic.

THE AGE OF THE GRACCHI

The revolutionary programs of the Gracchi brothers to bring the benefits of empire to all classes in Rome led to a violent reaction of the senatorial class and the assassination of both Tiberius and Gaius Gracchus.

The Reforms of Tiberius Gracchus

Tiberius Gracchus was the grandson on his mother's side of Scipio Africanus. His father was also a member of the senatorial class (although the origins of his family were plebeian). This lineage was to prove a distinct advantage in Tiberius' public career. As a youth, he was educated by Greek philosophers in the most advanced way for that period; as a result, he had little love for the ruling senatorial establishment. In 133 B.C., after having been a *quaestor* in Spain, he was elected tribune of the people, and he immediately settled upon a program with which he hoped to reduce senatorial power and at the same time rebuild the class of small farmers who had been nearly wiped out. He thereby planned to restore the citizen army of the early Republic. Under this program, the maximum allowance of public land to an individual was to be the 500 iugera permitted by the laws of 367 B.C., with additional allowances for each of two sons. A commission of three men was set up to redistribute the land. However, by this time it would have taken a computer to disentangle private land from public. The prospect of diminished wealth frightened the senate into action. They saw to it that a tribune of that year, Octavius, should veto any bill which Tiberius would bring before the *Tribal Assembly* to enforce the findings of the commission. Tiberius Gracchus was outraged at such a setback for what he considered the popular will, and he had Octavius removed from office. This action had no legal basis. It provoked a powerful reaction in the constitutionally minded senators and added fuel to their hatred of Tiberius. The senate had provided meager funds for the land commission, but a windfall occurred when Attalus III of Pergamum died and left his entire treasury, as well as the lands of his kingdom, to the Roman people. Tiberius carried a plebiscite (a measure passed by the *Concilium Plebis*) which bypassed the senate, allowing the commission to use part of this money for resettling small farmers throughout Italy.

The point of no return in the deteriorating relationship between Tiberius and the senatorial class was reached when, contrary to precedent, Tiberius announced that he would run again for the tribuneship (for the year 132 B.C.). At this point, even his allies in the senate turned against him, and on election day Tiberius was assassinated by a group of senators. With the unconstitutional acts of Tiberius and the murderous reaction of the senate, the myth of a harmonious society led by an enlightened upper class was shattered.

The Reforms of Gaius Gracchus

With experience in the land commission of his brother Tiberius as a base from which to work, Gaius Gracchus was well qualified to continue popular reform when he was elected tribune in 123 B.C. The program of Gaius was broader and less utopian than that of his brother and, as a result, it had the support of the affluent *equestrian* class, which controlled the commerce of Rome. In order to bolster and augment the agrarian reforms of 133 B.C., Gaius introduced legislation that reorganized tax collection in the newly organized province of Asia (formerly the kingdom of Pergamum). Instead of direct collection, contracts were now to be auctioned to companies of *equestrians*. Thus, the infamous system of tax farming, which had begun in Sicily, spread. In addition to such lucrative contracts, the *equestrians* were granted control of courts trying provincial governors and their officials. They also got the contracts for public works. In order to win over the poor, Gaius entered upon a scheme for distributing cheap grain, much of which was obtained as taxes from Corsica, Sardinia, and Sicily. To gain the goodwill of the dispossessed small farmer, Gaius advocated the settling of Roman citizens as colonists in Italy and overseas. One provision, the resettlement of Carthage as the colony Junonia, particularly irked the sanctimonious senators, for Carthaginian soil had been cursed and salted twenty-three years before; it mattered little that the new settlement was to be outside the benighted area.

By the time Gaius took office, legislation had been passed permitting a tribune to succeed himself, and he was reelected for the year 122 B.C. Although he seemed to have much support for his programs, opposition among all classes was growing quite rapidly. One scheme intended to unify Italy into a nation positively alienated a great number of Romans; this was Gaius' plan of conferring citizenship upon all Italians. Further, a fellow tribune, Marcus Livius Drusus, one-upped Gaius by such mass-appeal devices as proposing twelve new colonies instead of three, and all of those to be in Italy. As a sop to the Italian allies, Drusus suggested that they be exempt from corporal punishment while in military service to Rome. Other reforms included a provincial road system and the replacement of senators by *equestrians* in extortion courts.

In 121 B.C., after Gaius had made an unsuccessful attempt for a third term as tribune, rioting ensued between the pro- and the anti-Gracchan forces. The senate declared martial law, and the consul Gaius Opimius was given supreme command. Gaius Gracchus and many of his followers were killed. The resulting rift between the *populares*, or supporters of the Gracchan reforms, and the conservative *optimates*, or supporters of the senatorial class, grew as time went on and led to more than one civil war.

DEVELOPMENTS IN GAUL AND NORTH AFRICA

External conditions as well were becoming a source of alarm. As a result of foreign intervention, Rome now possessed a new province in southern Gaul, and became involved in a seemingly endless war in North Africa.

Gallic Invasions   The city of Massilia (Marseilles), which had helped Rome during the Second Punic War, asked the senate for aid against Celtic invaders (125 B.C.). In 122 B.C., the Roman armies established Aquae Sextiae (Aix) as a bridgehead in southern Gaul, and by 121 B.C. they had succeeded in subduing the two major Gallic tribes, the Allobroges and the Arvernii. To protect its interests, Rome organized the area around Massilia into a province, calling it Gallia Narbonensis. The Greek port city of Massilia maintained its independence.

Jugurtha

North Africa had been a potential trouble spot since the Third Punic War because of the ambivalent position of the client kingdom of Numidia. During the last war against the Carthaginians, the Numidian king, Massinissa, had helped the Romans. However, when he died in 148 B.C., and when the area of Carthage became the Roman province of Africa, eastward expansion of the kingdom was checked. Massinissa's son, Micipsa, nonetheless remained a faithful ally of Rome. Before his death, he had adopted his nephew, Jugurtha, and made him co-heir with his own two sons, Adherbal and Hiempsal. Although the kingdom was split among the three, Jugurtha had an almost fanatical ambition to be the sole ruler. After having Hiempsal assassinated and forcing Adherbal to flee, he brought his case before the Roman senate in 116 B.C. The senate's decision was not unaffected by Jugurtha's bribes. As a result, the larger part of the kingdom went to him, although Adherbal got Cirta, the major city. This was not enough for Jugurtha, and he took Cirta after a difficult siege, killing all of the inhabitants, including some Italian businessmen. Public opinion in Rome was outraged; the *equestrians* were shocked at the death of their fellow merchants, and the popular party was appalled at the bribery in the senate that had led to it. As a result, in 111 B.C. a Roman army under the consul Lucius Calpurnius Bestia was sent to Numidia. However, Jugurtha was very shrewd, and he made a peace favorable to himself. When war was renewed, Jugurtha's position continued to strengthen, and he defeated the next Roman army. Even the superior leadership of the consul Quintus Caecilius Metellus in 109 B.C. could not secure victory for the Romans.

THE ASCENDANCY OF THE POPULARES: GAIUS MARIUS

The advent of Gaius Marius brought an end to the Numidian campaign and introduced, on a great scale, the element of opportunism into Roman policies.

The End of the Numidian Campaign

It remained for Gaius Marius, a member of the popular party, to find a solution for the Numidian situation. Marius had gained most of his support from the *equestrians*, although subsequent events showed that he was not above deserting his supporters when he thought his career required it. While a *legate* for Metellus in Africa, he worked against his commander; and as a result of failure of the Numidian campaign, Marius was elected consul in

107 B.C. He then took over command of the war against Jugurtha, which had become even more exasperating to the Romans because the Numidian king had allied himself with his father-in-law, Bocchus, king of Mauretania. Despite the military setbacks of the Romans, Marius' *quaestor*, Lucius Cornelius Sulla, was able to persuade Bocchus to betray Jugurtha. The Numidian king was brought back to Rome a prisoner and subsequently strangled. Thus, in 105 B.C., the African struggle was finished.

Defeat of the Cimbri and the Teutones

As the hero of the hour, Marius was elected consul for the unprecedented tenure of five terms for the years 104–100 B.C. Trouble had broken out in Gaul again, and the Romans suffered an ignoble defeat that proved as traumatic as the invasion of the Gauls in the fourth century B.C. The Germanic tribes of the Cimbri and Teutones had won a decisive victory in 105 B.C. at Arausio (Orange) in Gallia Narbonensis. Luckily for the Romans, they chose not to invade Italy at that time. Under the leadership of Marius, these tribes were finally crushed at Aquae Sextiae in 102 B.C. and at Vercellae the following year.

Party Politics in Rome

Marius now had an army that was loyal to him rather than to the senate and the Roman people, for it had been recruited on the basis of the rewards of land and loot it could get in war, with little of the patriotism of earlier times. Property was no longer a qualification for serving in the army. In order to obtain land for his soldiers, Marius allied himself with the leaders of the lower classes, Lucius Apuleius Saturninus and Gaius Servilius Glaucia. The senatorial party was joined by the *equestrians* in opposition to these measures, which in their eyes were too radical. Marius thereupon changed sides, for it appears that his first loyalty was to the merchant class. In the ensuing riots, Saturninus and Glaucia were murdered. Having lost the major buttresses of his power—his veterans and the *populares*—Marius left Rome.

THE SOCIAL WAR

The Roman allies *(socii)* in Italy were far from content with their lot. Although they had fought with the Romans and were becoming assimilated in language and customs, the senate had succeeded in keeping the Italians at a second- or third-rate status. Marcus Livius Drusus (the son of Gaius Gracchus' opponent), who was tribune in 91 B.C., forced through a program of legislation that included, among other provisions, full citizenship for the allies. The senate abrogated this measure. Civil strife again broke out, and

Drusus was murdered. Thereupon, a large number of Italians *(socii)* revolted and set up a new federal nation, with its capital at Corfinium, renamed Italia. A new federal senate was established, and two leaders with *imperium* were chosen. Indeed, even new coinage was issued. In order to keep the rest of the Italians from joining this nation, Rome had to act quickly. Under the leadership of Marius and Sulla, in the north and south respectively, the Romans were able to hold their own; but it was not until Rome offered concessions that the war showed signs of diminishing. The first step was the *Lex Julia* of 90 B.C., which bequeathed full citizenship to those allies who had remained loyal. Eventually, in 88 B.C., complete citizenship was granted to all of the Italian cities when they reaffirmed their loyalty to Rome. As a result of this settlement, Italy became a truly unified nation that, in later centuries, was to become the core of the Roman world.

THE ASCENDANCY OF SULLA

The excesses of the *populares* were followed by the repressive policies of Sulla, who succeeded in restoring oligarchic rule to Rome.

The Inroads of Mithridates

While the Romans were occupied with internal events, the situation in the East was deteriorating rapidly. Although the Hellenistic kingdom of the Seleucids had crumbled, Rome was involved in other struggles and was not in a position to supervise the area. Consequently, pirates ravaged the seas and *equestrian* tax collectors ravaged the communities. Mithridates, ruler of the Black Sea kingdom of Pontus, saw that events had transpired to his advantage. He thought that perhaps he could rule supreme in the East and rid the area of the noxious Romans. By 88 B.C., where Mithridates did not win by force of arms, he was aided by local Greek governments, for to them he seemed a savior from the *equestrian* extortions.

Sulla and the Populares

Lucius Cornelius Sulla, who in 88 B.C. had been a consul on the side of the *optimates*, met with obstacles to his program from the popular party and the *comitia tributa*. Hence, he resorted to military capture of Rome with an army loyal to him that he had commanded in the Social War. His enemies were disposed of, and Marius was forced into exile. One of the two consuls for the following year (87 B.C.) was Lucius Cornelius Cinna. He swore loyalty to Sulla, who thereupon went off to the East to subdue Mithridates. Meanwhile, Cinna abrogated his allegiance to Sulla and was outlawed by the senate. He joined forces with the aged Marius, and together they took Rome, massacring their political enemies. Cinna held the consulship from 87 to 84 B.C. Marius was to have been his colleague for the year 86 B.C., but he died almost immediately after entering office.

Sulla's Campaign Against Mithridates

Cinna sought to deprive Sulla of his command in the East. Due to his machinations, Flavius Fimbria was sent to Asia Minor with a rival army in 86 B.C., but it joined forces with Sulla, whose successes were growing daily. Athens was besieged and taken in 86 B.C., and other cities chafing under the yoke of Mithridates were ready to revolt. Finally, in 85 B.C., peace was arranged under Roman terms. Mithridates had to pay damages and give up all of the territories which he had conquered. The Greek cities in the province of Asia were harshly punished. They were forced to pay a large indemnity, which put them in long-term debt, and Roman soldiers in the region were given freedom to enrich themselves at Greek expense. The East did not recover from this spoilage for many generations.

Sulla's Dictatorship

When Sulla journeyed back to Italy in 83 B.C., he was met by a combined force of *populares* and new Italian citizens, who after much dispute had finally been distributed for voting purposes among the nonurban tribes. Cinna was killed by his own troops while preparing to oppose Sulla's landing at Brundisium in 83 B.C. After a savage civil war, which was concluded at Rome by the Battle at the Colline Gate in 82 B.C., Sulla was the dominant figure in Italy, and in an unprecedented move he became dictator for life.

The new master of Rome followed a conservative *optimate* philosophy, and he wished to turn back the clock to at least the third century B.C. After a bloody proscription of the popular leaders, he set about reorganizing the state. In order to curtail the power of the masses, the tribunate was crippled. Not only were the tribunes prohibited from entering the senate after their tenure in office, but they were forbidden to introduce legislation before the *comitia tributa*. The senate, which had declined in numbers as a result of constant civil strife and the proscriptions of both Marius and Sulla, was enlarged by three hundred new members, mostly from the upper stratum of *equestrians*. In addition, all *quaestors* were made senators upon completion of their terms. Sulla, true to his past-oriented philosophy, considered older men to be automatically wiser. He thus set minimum age limits for holding office: 30 for a *quaestor*, 40 for a praetor, and 42 for a consul. The number of praetors was increased to eight, and they presided over criminal courts with only senators acting as jurors. After terms in office, the praetors as well as the consuls were assigned provinces overseas. The senate allocated the provinces and the governors were greatly restrained in their activities. These magistrates could not be reelected to office for a period of ten years. In addition, to placate those who had fought for him in his campaigns, Sulla sent out colonies of his veterans.

When, in 79 B.C., he felt that his work had been satisfactorily accomplished, Sulla retired to his villa in Campania, where he met a natural death the following year. The Roman Republic had been salvaged for the time being, but the cost in lives and wealth had been enormous. Enduring peace would not come until the Republic was nothing more than a fondly remembered legend.

The years from 138 to 78 B.C. were violent, but the worst was yet to come. The optimates and the populares demonstrated that they could not peacefully work out political differences. In the end, Republican liberty, and disorder, were replaced by dictatorial stability and a lack of freedom.

Selected Readings

Botsford, G. W. *The Roman Assemblies* (1919)
Broughton, G. W. *The Magistrates of the Roman Republic* (1951–52)
Carney, T. F. *A Biography of C. Marius* (1962)
Clay, D. *Lucretius and Epicurus* (1984)
Cowell, F. R. *Cicero and the Roman Republic* (1948)
Gruen, E. S. *The Last Generation of the Roman Republic* (1974)
Hill, H. *The Roman Middle Class in the Republican Period* (1955)
Marsh, F. B. *A History of the Roman World, 146–30 B.C.* (1962)
Sherwin, A. N. *Roman Foreign Policy in the East, 168 B.C. to 1 A.D.* (1984)
Smith, R. E. *The Failure of the Roman Republic* (1955)
Sydenham, E. A. *Roman Republican Coinage* (1952)
Thiel, J. H. *Studies on the History of Roman Sea Power in Republican Times* (1946)

12

The Final Stage of the Roman Republic

77–71 B.C.	Pompey fights Sertorius in Spain
74	Bithynia bequeathed to Rome
73–71	Slave revolt under Spartacus put down by Crassus
71	Lucullus tries to restore Asia Minor
70	Pompey and Crassus consuls
70	Cicero prosecutes Gaius Verres
70–19	Vergil—author of the *Aeneid*
67	Gabinian Law—Pompey in command of the Mediterranean
66	Manilian Law—Pompey in command of the East
65	Pompey defeats Mithridates
65–8	Horace—poet
63	Syria becomes a Roman province
63	Catilinarian plot
63	Cicero consul
62	Pompey returns in triumph from the East
60	First Triumvirate—Caesar, Pompey, and Crassus
59	Caesar consul
59 B.C.–A.D. 29	Livy—historian
58	Clodius tribune
58–57	Cicero exiled
56	Caesar conquers all three Gauls
56	Conference of Triumvirate at Luca
53	Crassus killed

52   Caesar defeats Vercingetorix

52   Pompey sole consul

49–45   Civil War

49   Caesar crosses Rubicon

48   Caesar defeats Pompey at Pharsalus

44   Caesar dictator for life

44   Caesar assassinated

43   Second Triumvirate—Octavian, Antony, and Lepidus

43 B.C.–A.D. 17   Ovid—poet

42   Battle of Philippi

37   Octavian receives partial tribunican power

31   Battle of Actium

30   Egypt becomes a Roman province

*T*he late Roman Republic is amazing in the richness of its cross-currents and diverse personalities. Its history is largely that of self-seeking, larger-than-life figures, who ended by destroying the Republic.

THE RISE OF POMPEY

The rise of Pompey (Gnaeus Pompeius, 106–48 B.C.) was phenomenal, especially during Sulla's administration, and his knack for changing political sides without seeming to change made him popular with all groups. His great ambition was to enter the senatorial class from the *equestrian* order. From vanity, he prevailed upon Sulla to give him the title Magnus ("the Great") after 81 B.C. Following the death of Sulla in 78 B.C., Marcus Aemillus Lepidus, who became consul, wished to institute by force an intensive program of reform in the style of the *populares*. Pompey saw that it was to his advantage to ally himself with the senatorial faction, and with his aid Lepidus was crushed.

Meanwhile, conditions in Spain were in a state of chaos. Quintus Sertorius, who had been governor of Nearer Spain in 83 B.C., decided to establish a separatist regime of his own in that province with the aid of Romans and natives alike. He foiled attempts by such generals as Metellus Pius to subdue him (79–78 B.C.), but he was gradually worn out by the tactics of Pompey, who had received the proconsular *imperium* for this purpose. Sertorius died in 71 B.C., after unsuccessfully trying to combine with King Mithridates of Pontus in an East-West coalition against Rome. Pompey's prestige was now at a high point.

THE RISE OF CRASSUS

Marcus Licinius Crassus (ca. 112–53 B.C.), like Pompey, was an ex-henchman of Sulla's. His unscrupulous ways not only furthered his career, but also made him fabulously wealthy. One of his methods of accruing riches was to buy a burning property for a pittance and then send his own firemen to put out the flames; he thus acquired prime land at very low prices. During the time Pompey was in Spain, a slave revolt led by the gladiator slave Spartacus was raging in southern Italy (73 B.C.). It took several Roman armies and two years to put down the revolt, but Crassus finally succeeded. Crassus was a peer to Pompey in vanity, and he did not wish to share this moment of triumph with his would-be rival. Pompey, however, entered the fray and crucified six thousand fugitive slaves on the Appian Way.

Two facts became clear at this point: first, that both men had either to subdue their egotism and join forces, or else battle it out; and second, that it was now popular to defy Sulla's constitution. Together, Pompey and Crassus were elected consuls in 70 B.C., and they became the strongest anti-Sullans. The tribunate and censorship were restored, and senatorial power was once again curtailed.

THE RISE OF CICERO AND
THE TRIAL OF VERRES

Marcus Tullius Cicero was born at Arpinum in 106 B.C. After a good education in Rome and abroad, he began his legal career. He risked his life in 80 B.C. by opposing one of Sulla's protégés. It was Cicero's fondest desire to be accepted into the inner circle of the senatorial class, although he was a newcomer of provincial *equestrian* stock. His whole career was geared to that aim. He finally won acceptance and parity with the chief lawyer of the day, Quintus Hortensius Hortalus, in the trial of Gaius Verres (70 B.C.).

Verres was typical of the breed of Roman governors who entered a province and administered it in such a way that at the end of his tenure in office he and his cronies had become millionaires. When he returned to Rome, the scandalized Cicero prosecuted him. Cicero's evidence was so unequivocal that Verres was forced to flee to Massilia, but the *Orations against Verres* were nonetheless published; they give an insight into the depth of provincial corruption. By 66 B.C., Cicero held the praetorship, and his star had joined the firmament of the late Republic.

WAR IN THE EAST (THE THIRD MITHRIDATIC WAR)

Mithridates of Pontus seemed indestructible; every time he seemed headed for oblivion, he made a rebound. Sulla's victory did not long hinder Mithridates' plans for expansion and when, in 74 B.C., the Asiatic kingdom of Bithynia was bequeathed to Rome by its last King, Nicomedes, he occupied that country. However, the Roman army under Lucius Licinius Lucullus pushed him back, and he fled to his son-in-law Tigranes, king of Armenia. With the situation under control by 71 B.C., Lucullus took on the unenviable task of repairing the finances of the cities of Asia Minor that had been shattered by the extremely harsh exactions of Sulla as punishment for their friendly attitude toward Mithridates. Thereby, Lucullus incurred the hostility of the *equestrian* class, which had been making an enormous profit at farming taxes and exacting its own levies in the area. In addition, Lucullus' army, which he drove relentlessly, was on the brink of mutiny by the time he pursued Mithridates into Armenia (69 B.C.). The *equestrians* managed to pluck the fruit of victory from his hands in 66 B.C., when they relieved him of his command.

POMPEY'S TRIUMPHS AGAINST PIRATES AND MITHRIDATES

Pompey desired ever more glory, and his eyes were turned eastward. His first opportunity came during the attacks of Cilician pirates, who were preventing normal sea commerce. Indeed, they were so bold as to attack Ostia, the port of Rome. In 67 B.C., one of the tribunes, Aulus Gabinius, came forth with a solution to the problem: an extraordinary law giving Pompey absolute command of the waters of the Mediterranean and the land to the extent of fifty miles from the sea. In addition, Pompey would have vast powers for financing his campaign against the pirates. The senate balked at giving an ex-Sullan, now a pro-*equestrian* semi-*popularis,* such powers. Cicero, however, persuaded them to accept the Gabinian proposal.

Pompey did his job admirably, and the following year another tribune, Gaius Manilius, proposed giving him absolute control of the East as well as the generalship of Lucullus. Once again the senate balked, and once again Cicero, now praetor, defended Pompey's interests. The combination of absolute power *(imperium)* over sea and land gave to Pompey, constitutionally, the dominance that others had previously sought to seize by force.

Tigranes of Armenia saw that his kingdom would come to pieces at the onslaught of the Romans if he maintained his ties to Mithridates. In 65 B.C., therefore, he allied himself with Pompey. Mithridates meanwhile fled to his dependent cities in the Crimea, where he died. So ended the career of the last emulator of Alexander the Great. Pompey reorganized the entire Near East, an achievement that gave Rome additional provinces and gave him a permanent base of operations.

In 63 B.C., Syria, which had been in a state of decadence since the death of Antiochus IV (163 B.C.), became a Roman province. Rome now controlled all Asia Minor, with Armenia as a buffer state between its domains and those of the Parthian Empire.

THE RISE OF JULIUS CAESAR

Gaius Julius Caesar (ca. 101–44 B.C.) was the youngest ruler of the late Republic. His lineage was impeccable, although his clan (the *Julii*) had seen better days. He was the nephew, through the marriage of his mother's sister

Julia, of Marius, and he was Cinna's son-in-law. Caesar ascended the ladder of offices as a *popularis,* and by 65 B.C. had become *aedile.* Unfortunately, that office entailed enormous expenses for public games; Caesar had to borrow more and more money, and his fortunes became tied to those of multimillionaire Crassus. Consequently, while Pompey was in the East, there were power realignments in Rome.

THE CATILINARIAN PLOT

Lucius Sergius Catilina (Catiline) was a very unstable man whose talents were used to his own and the Republic's detriment. A noble whose family's financial status had dwindled, he became an adventurer of the most unscrupulous sort, always seeking new roads to easy riches. He took a not-inconsequential part in the Sullan proscriptions, and in his duties abroad he was notorious for his corrupt practices. When he was prevented from running for the consulship in 66 B.C., he plotted fruitlessly to murder the consuls who eventually took office. When he did run for the year 63 B.C. with the support of Caesar and Crassus, he was defeated by Cicero. He thereupon organized a conspiracy.

By his program of remission of debts, Catiline seemed to be a champion of the popular cause, and as a result he got aid from various anti-senatorial quarters. The size of the plot was exaggerated by Cicero, but if it had not been nipped in the bud, much disorder would have undoubtedly resulted. Cicero knew of the conspiracy and finally exposed it, with the aid of a delegation of Allobroges (Gauls) whom Catiline was trying to involve in the plot. Cicero then arrested the conspirators in Rome, and those who had massed in Etruria fled to the north, where they were joined by Catiline. They were subsequently defeated and Catiline was killed in battle, but the leaders in the capital had to be confronted. In a fit of rage, Cicero convened a special session of the senate to try them; he desired nothing less than their execution. This of course would have required regular judicial proceedings in order to be legal. Caesar was against execution, but after Marcus Porcius Cato, whose views were worthy of his second-century B.C. ancestor, gave an impassioned speech in favor of the death sentence, that verdict held sway. Within five years, Cicero would pay dearly for his decision.

THE FIRST TRIUMVIRATE: CAESAR, POMPEY, AND CRASSUS

After an interrupted praetorship in 62 B.C. and duty in Further Spain as governor, Caesar returned to Rome in 60 B.C. to run for the consulship for the following year. Because he was unpopular with the senatorial class, he foresaw difficulties. Pompey, who had returned from the East in triumph in 62 B.C., disbanded his army, probably in the hope that this action would increase his political influence among the *optimates,* and also because he had always been a constitutionalist. Unfortunately, Pompey had many enemies in the senate, including Cato and Lucullus, who prevented the passage of the land bill for his veterans and other measures that he requested. As a result, Pompey joined forces with Caesar and Crassus in an extralegal personal coalition called the First Triumvirate.

Caesar as Consul

The Triumvirate was strong enough to get its way, and in 59 B.C. Caesar was duly elected consul. He immediately set forth on a program designed to fulfill the requirements of his partner Pompey. The bill for parceling out land to the veterans of the Eastern wars was predictably blocked in the senate, and Caesar brought it before the *comitia tributa.* There too his ambitions were thwarted until he applied intimidation in the form of Pompey's veterans. After that, all Caesar's legislation had smooth sailing. To further cement his alliance with Pompey, Caesar gave him his daughter Julia in marriage.

Following Caesar's consulship, the *optimates* tried to sabotage his hopes of gaining an important provincial governorship, where he could raise an army and threaten their hegemony. However, the harmless province of forests and paths of Italy that they had offered him was changed, under pressure, to a profitable five-year tenure in Illyricum and Cisalpine Gaul. Upon the death of the governor of Transalpine Gaul, Caesar was given that province also.

Clodius

In the meantime, it was necessary for the Triumvirate to consolidate its position and rid Rome of its real and potential enemies. Publius Clodius and his sister, Clodia, were members of the fast-moving youth of the mid-first century B.C., who demonstrated by their actions that the traditions of the moralistic early Romans were far from alive—and who were consequently attacked in Cicero's speeches. Clodius chafed at being a patrician and, with the aid of Julius Caesar, he became a plebeian through a fictitious adoption. Besides the gratifying achievement of shocking the *optimates* by this move, Clodius was now able to enter the tribuneship, an office which he held in 58 B.C.

Despite the fact that Cicero had been an ardent adherent of Pompey, he had found it politically inexpedient to work with the Triumvirate. Clodius, who carried on a vendetta against Cicero, now managed to have a law passed exiling those who had put Roman citizens to death without a court trial, as Cicero had done in putting down the Catilinarian conspiracy. Cicero went into exile until 57 B.C., when Pompey had him recalled. Cato was sent off to Cyprus as governor, and consuls subservient to the Triumvirate were elected for the following year.

Caesar's Conquest of Gaul

Caesar was now ready to leave for his Gallic provinces, which were inhabited by a variety of peoples. In the southwest (Aquitaine) were Iberians, in the center of what is now France were Celts, and in the north were the Belgae of Germanic extraction. All of these groups were divided into tribes, which sometimes fought with one another. Therefore, most of the Celtic group had been the Aedui, but they were defeated by the Germanic Suebi headed by Ariovistus. In a surprising move, the Roman senate had withdrawn its friendship from the Aedui and bestowed it on their conquerors. The Suebi proved unworthy of the honor and began harassing the Gauls.

Another source of trouble were the Celtic Helvetii in what is now Switzerland. When they threatened the Roman province of Narbonensis, Caesar had his work cut out for him. With the help of the Aedui, he defeated the Helvetii and the Suebi, and then he conquered a coalition of Belgic tribes. In 56 B.C., Caesar was able to say that all three Gauls had been conquered.

The Crisis of 56 B.C.

Crassus and Pompey, who at best had been nonhostile rivals, now began to regain their old feelings of dislike for each other. Clodius had overplayed his hand, and Pompey had turned against him. Street gangs in the guise of political clubs appear to have been terrorizing the city; especially aggressive were the factions headed by Clodius and his rival, Titus Annius Milo, Pompey's new ally.

The situation did not appeal to Caesar, who thought that only the *optimates* would gain by this state of chaos. Accordingly, he called Pompey and Crassus to a conference at Luca in northern Italy, which brought about an uneasy rapprochement among the Triumvirate (56 B.C.). It was decided that Pompey and Crassus would become consuls for the year 55 B.C. Thereafter, for five years, Pompey would control Spain; Crassus, Syria; and Caesar, Gaul. Caesar went back to his province, while Crassus and Pompey returned to seize the consulships.

The Final Subjugation of Gaul

Following further victories in Gaul, Caesar crossed over into Britain. After a brief reconnaissance (55 B.C.), he made the gesture of conquering Britain (54 B.C.), which was not truly subdued until the time of Claudius. The Gauls once again revolted, and once again Caesar triumphed (53 B.C.). In 52 B.C., however, he met with a serious obstacle—Vercingetorix, who came close to being a Gallic national leader. For a time, Vercingetorix was able, by guerrilla tactics, to hold his own against Caesar's armies, but he was finally besieged at the fortress of Alesia and crushed. Caesar's power was now too enormous for either Pompey or the *optimates,* and plans were made to bring about his downfall. In 54 B.C., the death of Julia ended the personal tie between Pompey and Caesar.

The End of the Triumvirate

The final break between Pompey and Caesar occurred at the death of Crassus. Crassus had gone off to his province in the East, but his abilities as a general were worse than indifferent. His adversary was Parthia, a kingdom in western Asia which, having begun a great expansion under the Arsacid dynasty in the third century B.C., had now supplanted the Seleucids as the great power of the Middle East. Crassus' lust for military glory met with tragedy for himself and his army; his troops were ambushed near Carrhae (53 B.C.), and he was killed. Thus, with the buffer of Crassus removed, Pompey and Caesar faced each other as antagonists.

CONFLICT BETWEEN POMPEY AND CAESAR

Pompey was the only member of the Triumvirate who remained in Italy after the Luca conference. Hence he was in a position to consolidate his alliances. The gang-fighting continued and, in 52 B.C., Milo killed Clodius, whose unruly adherents used the Curia (Senate House) as his funeral pyre. The small clique of senators who controlled that august body, and whose loyalty to the past was greater than toward Rome itself, decided that Pompey was, after all, the person to eliminate Caesar and restore the Republic. So long as Caesar had an army, it would be impossible to harm him. In 50 B.C., however, his tenure in Gaul would expire, and it would then be feasible to prosecute him for an assortment of illegalities.

In the meantime, no consuls had been elected for 52 B.C. hence Pompey, who had held extraordinary powers in the past, was now put in the unusual position of being sole consul. Pompey thwarted Caesar's plan to run for the consulship for 49 B.C., which, by giving him continuity in office, would have obviated his prosecution as a private citizen. A law was passed that a candidate for the highest office in the state must himself be present to stand for election.

A stalemate developed during the years 51–50 B.C. Caesar offered to give up his troops if Pompey did the same. However, the pro-Pompey faction forced through resolutions ordering Caesar to give up his army and step down from his expired office, or be declared an outlaw. Pompey's commands had been renewed and strengthened, so that he at least was abiding by the letter of the law. When the tribunes Marcus Antonius (Mark Antony) and Quintus Cassius tried to block this turn of events, they were forced to flee, and they joined Caesar at the banks of the Rubicon River, dividing Cisalpine Gaul from Italy.

THE CIVIL WAR

In 49 B.C., Caesar crossed the Rubicon and immediately met with friendship in the Italian municipalities, to whom Pompey represented the entrenched nobility. The *optimates* had no great love for Pompey; they had used him only as a temporary expedient. Caesar's lenient treatment of friend and foe alike endeared him to the Italians, and within the year he had control of all of Italy. He also ensured the continuance of the grain supply by gaining control of Sardinia, Sicily, and Africa. Then he defeated Pompey's forces at Ilerda in Spain. On his return to Italy, Caesar was made dictator.

Pompey's Flight to the East and Subsequent Events

Pompey fled to the East, where he had built up a military establishment loyal to him. Caesar, lacking ships, could not immediately pursue him. In 48 B.C., Caesar managed to get an army to Epirus, but it was unable to defeat the forces of Pompey. The next theater of action was near the town of Pharsalus in Thessaly, where the armies of Caesar won a complete victory (48 B.C.). It was now only a matter of time before Caesar cleared out Pompey's allies. Pompey fled to Egypt, where he was assassinated on order of the teenaged Ptolemy XIII.

The situation in Egypt was far from settled, for Cleopatra and her brother-husband were involved in a dynastic squabble. Caesar, siding with Cleopatra, defeated Ptolemy XIII and married her off to a younger brother, Ptolemy XIV. Meanwhile, in Asia Minor, Pharnaces, son of Mithridates, had decided it was high time to emulate his father and reconquer Asia. In 47 B.C., Caesar arrived at Zela, observed the situation, and conquered *(Veni, vidi, vici)* Pharnaces. On returning to Italy, Caesar had just enough time to bring order to the city before he departed for Africa.

The Final Defeat of the Optimates

Since the *optimates* had believed that Pompey was their tool, the civil war in their eyes was fought between the aristocratic virtues of the Republic (themselves) and the destructive forces of the *populares* (Caesar). With the help of King Juba of Numidia, they made a last stand at Thapsus in North Africa (46 B.C.), where they were defeated by the Caesarian forces. The demise of the semilegendary early Republican virtues was symbolized by Cato's suicide. The last effort of the *optimate* forces under Pompey's sons was defeated at Munda in Spain in 45 B.C.

CAESAR'S DICTATORSHIP

In 45 B.C., Caesar was made dictator for ten years, and a year later he became dictator for life. The powers that were at his command surpassed even those of Pompey at his acme; yet he did not abolish the rotted structure of the Republic. During his tenure in office, Caesar reformed much of Roman life, but his highhanded methods earned him the enmity of the traditionalists.

The Basis of Caesar's Power

Extended dictatorship did not have roots in Roman tradition, for during the early Republic the office was a temporary one, sanctioned only during severe emergencies. Sulla used this institution as the major prop of his power and thus converted it into a tyranny in the Greek sense. Caesar followed in Sulla's footsteps, but added some quasi-constitutional twists. He was a permanent *imperator,* or a general in a perpetual state of triumph. His body was inviolate, for although he did not have the full powers of the tribuneship, he had its sacrosanctity, and he could convoke the popular assembly *(comitia tributa).*

Caesar's prestige was such that he was honored with the title *pater patriae* ("father of the fatherland"), and he was always first to speak in the senate. Because he had taken over the censor's powers, he could also revise the senate rolls. In addition, although he would not be deified in life, a temple was built to his Clemency, and the month Quintilis was renamed July in his honor. In short, Caesar had a variety of powers through which he developed a mystique of personality always backed by the military. He laid the basis for future emperors, although the idea of monarchy as such, with its associated regalia, seems to have been repugnant to Caesar as well as to Roman tradition.

Caesar's Reforms

The reforms of Caesar were in the economic, social, and political areas. Because the grain dole had spread to an overly large number of people, Caesar decreased this number by having the recipients checked. The traditional lunar calendar had become so inaccurate that festivals could no longer be held at the proper season. As a result, Caesar adopted the solar calendar of an Alexandrian astronomer. An intensive program of colonization was begun, and many municipalities were founded in Narbonensis, Spain, Africa, and Asia. In addition, the admission of many provincials to citizenship helped lay the groundwork for the Romanization of the empire.

The Assassination of Caesar

The tenets of Cato lived on in the minds of certain members of the senatorial clique, and a plot was hatched to assassinate Caesar and restore the Republic. The conspirators' narrow views could not foretell that the elimination of Caesar would bring yet more strife and the final eradication of the Republic, since a government based on a small segment of a city was not capable of dealing with the problems of a world empire. On the Ides (fifteenth) of March, 44 B.C., the plot reached fruition, and Caesar was stabbed in the Senate House. Involved in the conspiracy were Gaius Cassius, Marcus Junius Brutus, and Decimus Junius Brutus, among others. Sextus Pompeius, who had fled after the Battle of Munda (45 B.C.), stood waiting in the wings.

THE END OF THE REPUBLIC

The heirs of Caesar, Mark Antony, and Octavius (soon to be Octavian), did not feel much love for each other, but together with Lepidus they formed the Second Triumvirate. In due course, conflict arose between Octavian and Antony, which ended in the absolute triumph of Octavian and the establishment of the *principate*.

The Rise of Mark Antony

Marcus Antonius (Mark Antony, ca. 82–30 B.C.), who had shared the consulship with Caesar, saw himself as the sole heir of the dictator. But he thought it prudent not to antagonize the senators while he was getting his bearings, and so they accepted Caesar's program in return for Antony's letting the assassins remain free. At Caesar's funeral, however, Antony read the dead leader's will, which he had gotten by devious means, and so enflamed the public against the murderers that a riot ensued. Nevertheless, the leaders of the assassination managed to flee. The will stated that Gaius Octavius (b. 63 B.C.), a grandnephew of Caesar, was to be his posthumously adopted son. Antony, of course, did not think that the sickly youth of eighteen would be much of a threat. Besides, Octavius was in Epirus, where Caesar had sent him for military training.

Antony knew, as Caesar had known, that having a good province to govern after one's consulship was an excellent way to build a base of power. Following the assassination, he managed by force and guile to get Gaul and Cisalpine Gaul transferred to him. Unfortunately, the latter was already under the command of Decimus Brutus.

The Arrival of Octavius

Octavius meanwhile arrived in Rome to claim his inheritance and to avenge himself on the assassins of his uncle. At first, he was treated casually, but when he managed to raise an army, attitudes changed. Mark Antony had decided the time was right to seize Cisalpine Gaul from Decimus, and besieged him at Mutina (Modena) in northern Italy. Octavius, desiring recognition, led a senatorial army which relieved the city, but Antony fled (43 B.C.). Octavius was shortly after disenchanted with the senate when it refused him a triumph, and he threatened that body with his troops. Almost immediately, he was acclaimed son of Caesar, and his name became Gaius Julius Caesar Octavianus (Octavian). He was also made consul. At this time, it seemed to be to his advantage to reconcile himself with Antony. Thus, in 43 B.C. was born the Second Triumvirate, which included Antony, Octavian, and Caesar's Master of the Horse, Marcus Aemilius Lepidus, the junior member.

The Second Triumvirate

The Second Triumvirate showed its cards openly, for it was set up by law and each member had full consular powers for five years (the *Lex Titia*, 43 B.C.). Agreements were made concerning proscriptions, and although Octavian was not opposed to Cicero, he sacrificed him to the wrath of Antony. Ostensibly, the aim of the Triumvirate was to avenge Caesar's death, thereby restoring the Republic. In truth, however, it helped Antony and Octavian to establish major bases of power. In 42 B.C., Antony and Octavian pursued the conspirators to Macedonia, where, after their defeat at Philippi, Marcus Brutus and Cassius killed themselves.

Antony vs. Octavian

Antony had now obtained the East as well as Gaul and held the strongest position in the Triumvirate. Octavian had control of Italy and the rest of the West, while Lepidus served mainly as a buffer. Antony and Octavian were drifting further apart. After the Philippi campaign, Antony remained in the East to strengthen his position, and eventually went to Egypt with Cleopatra (40 B.C.).

Following a seemingly successful reconciliation in which Octavian's sister Octavia married Antony, the alliance began to deteriorate again. Antony returned to Egypt and appeared to be overly impressed by the power and trappings of the Hellenistic monarchs. Octavian, meanwhile, was launching a major propaganda offensive which denigrated Antony as desiring to build his own empire and make himself king. In contrast, Octavian suddenly appeared as the defender and restorer of all Republican virtues. The result was predictable warfare: Antony and Cleopatra sent a fleet against Italy (32 B.C.), but it was met by Octavian's navy off Cape Actium in Greece (31 B.C.) and destroyed. The victory of Octavian, and the pursuit of Antony and Cleopatra to Egypt and their consequent suicides, resulted in the creation of that uniquely Roman form of government, the *principate* (which will be discussed in the next chapter), as well as in the assimilation of grain-rich Egypt into the Roman system of provinces.

THE CULTURE OF THE LATE REPUBLIC

The late Republic excelled in all fields of the arts: architecture, painting, sculpture, poetry, and prose. The Hellenic forms of writing had long been absorbed and were now second nature to Roman poets and rhetoricians. In the plastic arts, Rome had created its own language of visual experience.

Literature

Two giants in poetry—Catullus and Lucretius—and three in prose—Varro, Cicero, and Caesar—have survived from the late Republic. The diversity and excellence in their styles, varying not only from author to author, but even within the works of each author, indicate the maturity that literature had attained during this period.

VERSE

Gaius Valerius Catullus (84–54 B.C.), who was born in northern Italy, went to Rome at about the age of eighteen. His short life was made painful because of his love affair with "Lesbia," identified as Clodia, sister of Clodius. This liaison inspired some of his best poetry. He wrote in a variety of meters derived from all periods of Greek poetry, but was especially influenced by the lyrics of the Alexandrian school. Many of his poems have a satirical cast, others a lyrical one.

Titus Lucretius Carus (ca. 95–55 B.C.) wrote a masterpiece of Epicurean literature, *De Rerum Natura* ("On the Nature of Things"), in epic form (dactylic hexameters in six books). It deals with most aspects of life and the universe, for in Lucretius' view he who understands all things need have no fear of death. Many of Lucretius' scientific theories, such as those of atoms and evolution, seem surprisingly modern.

PROSE

Marcus Terentius Varro (116–27 B.C.) was a giant in the field of philology and possessed an enormous library. Among his major works are *De Lingua Latina* ("On the Latin Language"), which deals with the origins and uses of Latin words, and *De Re Rustica* ("On Country Matters"), which discusses the proper form of agriculture.

Cicero's enormous output of works can be divided into several categories, the most important of which are the *Orations,* written in the middle style of rhetoric, between the simple Attic and the flamboyant Asianic. In addition, there are the *Letters,* written in a relatively informal style, and works on rhetoric. In his philosophical writings, Cicero was eclectic, but tended toward Stoicism. Cicero also wrote some poetry, but it lacked inspiration.

Caesar was an excellent historian. His works (*The Commentaries*) are divided into *De Bello Gallico* ("On the Gallic War") and *De Bello Civili* ("On the Civil War"). These works have been considered perfect models of the Roman Attic style. Despite the fact that he was writing of his own victories, Caesar was both objective and accurate.

Art

The form of painting inherited from the Hellenistic period, known as the First Pompeiian Style, in which mock masonry of encrusted exotic stones was represented in colored plaster, gave way, in about 65 B.C., to the Second Pompeiian Style. In the new genre, the wall was made to vanish in a series of architectural and mythological vistas.

Sculpture continued to be extremely realistic in portraiture, while monumental copies of Greek masterpieces were increasingly used for the newly evolved Roman buildings.

New forms of architecture were created that made considerable use of arches and the beginning of niched wall surfaces, in, for example, the Forum of Julius Caesar begun in 51 B.C. A new type of theater, freestanding rather than part of a hillside, was also created; the first permanent one is the Theater of Pompey in Rome (55 B.C.).

The first years of the principate *were full of promise. Stability and peace were provided by a strong ruler. However, some of Augustus successors were not up to the task, and the Romans lost stability and security as well as liberty.*

Selected Readings

Adcock, F. E. *Caesar as a Man of Letters* (1956)

Arnold, W. T. *The Roman System of Provincial Administration* (1909)

Beard, M. and Crawford, M. H. *Rome in the Late Republic* (1983)

Boissier, G. *Cicero and His Friends* (1987)

Fowler, W. W. *Social Life at Rome in the Age of Cicero* (1964)

Frank, Tenney. *Catullus and Horace* (1928)

Frankel, E. *Horace* (1957)

Gelzer, M. *Caesar: Politician and Statesman* (1968)

Hill, Herbert. *The Roman Middle Class in the Republican Period* (1952)

Leach, J. *Pompey the Great* (1978)

Marshall, B. A. *Crassus: A Political Biography* (1976)

Taylor, L. R. *Party Politics in the Age of Caesar* (1949)

Sihler, E. G. *Cicero of Arpinum* (1933)

Yavetz, Z. *Julius Caesar and His Public Image* (1984)

13

The Principate and the Early Empire

28 B.C.	Octavian receives the title, "princeps"
27	Octavian receives the title, Augustus
27 B.C.–A.D. 284	The *principate*
27 B.C.–A.D. 14	Augustus
23	Augustus receives highest power in the state *(maius imperium)*
20	Rome and Parthia define spheres of influence
6	Birth of Jesus Christ
A.D. 9	Arminius destroys three Roman legions in Teutoburg Forest
14	Augustus dies
14–37	Tiberius
19	Germanicus dies
23	Sejanus head of Praetorian Guard
23–79	Pliny the Elder—natural historian
35–95	Quintilian—rhetorician
37	Tiberius dies
37–41	Caligula
39–65	Lucan—writer of epics
40–104	Martial—epigrammist
41–54	Claudius
43	Conquest of Britain
45–95	Statius—writer of epics
50–120	Plutarch—biographer
50–130	Juvenal—satirist

54–68 Nero

56–120 Tacitus—historian

62–113 Pliny the Younger—epistles

64 Great fire in Rome

68 Insurrection of Vindex

68–69 Galba, Otho, Vitellius

69–79 Vespasian

70–140 Suetonius—historian

70 Titus destroys Jerusalem

79–81 Titus

79 Eruption of Vesuvius destroys Pompeii and Herculaneum

81–96 Domitian

*T*he dynasty begun by Augustus ended with the death of Nero. During that time, despite the vagaries of reigns such as those of Caligula and Nero, peace and prosperity were established in the Roman world. This Pax Romana was further implemented by the first two Flavians.

THE BEGINNING OF THE PAX ROMANA

The Battle of Actium can be said to represent the last stand of the Hellenistic and Roman Republican worlds and the beginning of the amalgam of Greco-Roman civilization. Universal peace was symbolized in 29 B.C., when Octavian closed the doors of the Temple of Janus, traditionally kept open in time of war. The lacerating wounds of the late Republic would now have an opportunity to heal.

Octavian as Augustus

In 28 B.C., a grateful senate bestowed upon Octavian the title *princeps,* which made him the "First Citizen" of the Republic and "more equal" than other Romans. Thus, the heir of Julius Caesar was now armed with two of the basic props for his future rule: the all-important tribunician power and a state of perpetual triumph *(imperator).* He had, in addition, a vast amount of wealth and the absolute loyalty of the army. However, the Romans loved legal fiction, and the new Caesar followed the letter of the law exactly by receiving all of his powers from the senate and the people. Hence, the true secret of Octavian's aims was not obvious to the senators, who believed that at long last the Republic would be restored. Not only was Gaius Julius Caesar Octavianus the first citizen, but there was something superhuman about his aspect. Thus, it seemed fitting to bestow upon him a title to indicate this closeness to the gods. In 27 B.C., the highest honor was given to the *princeps:* he would now be known as Augustus. As his adoptive father had given his name to the month of July, so now the month of Sextilis became August. In the East, Augustus became a living god and, in the Italian municipalities, a college of priests known as *augustales* was founded.

Real power supported honorific titles, for in the same year, 27 B.C., Augustus got direct command (proconsular *imperium*) over the crucial provinces of the Gauls, the Spains, Egypt, and Syria. Finally, in 23 B.C., Augustus was given the last word in all provincial administration, the *maius imperium.* These powers were theoretically not in excess of those granted during the Republic, and were accordingly renewed over the years by an acquiescent senate. To complete the spectrum of powers, which were Republican only in their separation, in 12 B.C. Augustus became *pontifex maximus.* As "chief priest," he was able to restore and consolidate the state cult as yet another bulwark of his rule.

The Reforms of Augustus

Augustus thoroughly changed many aspects of Roman life with his all-encompassing reforms. The state was saved and would remain intact until the disasters of the third century A.D.

POLITICAL AND SOCIAL REFORMS

In the first years of his rule, Octavian had held the consulship and, consequently, possessed the powers of censor. This allowed him to delete any name he wished from the rolls of the senate, an authority that he exercised three times during his reign. In addition, he increased the size of the senatorial class, since the reigns of terror of Marius and Sulla and the civil wars of the first century B.C. had greatly depopulated this group. This also gave him control of the senate. To further strengthen the patrician class, Augustus passed a series of puritanical laws forbidding luxurious and loose living. Bachelors were so discouraged that many married to avoid the high taxes (18–17 B.C.).

After Augustus relinquished the consulship, the candidates for this, as well as for lower offices, had to be approved by him before election in the *comitia.* As during the Republic, the progression in office began with the *quaestorship,* although the *princeps* could intercede to advance a favorite. Augustus created a new official, the *urban prefect,* who took charge of the courts and the new military organization (the *urban cohorts*) within the city. He divided Rome into fourteen regions, subdivided into 265 *vici,* or wards. A prefect selected from the *equestrian* order headed a department of *vigiles,* who combined the duties of firemen and policemen. In addition, the grain dole was controlled by registration of the recipients.

RELIGIOUS REFORMS

Roman public worship had none of the mystery and little of the comfort provided by less official and pompous religions. Even in earlier periods, the worship of Jupiter, Juno, and Minerva had not filled the Romans with awe. Thus, the state cults had fallen into disuse. Augustus revitalized official religion by rebuilding temples (among them, that of Jupiter Optimus Maximus) and making ceremonies more solemn and impressive. He also tried to revive belief in a variety of gods, including the deified Romulus (Quirinus) and Venus, from whom the Julian clan was said to have sprung.

MILITARY REFORMS

The Praetorian Guard, comprising nine cohorts (about a thousand each), was posted outside Rome to protect Augustus. There was also a large regular army. Although the *princeps* tried to have completely Roman (or at least Italian) legions, this proved impossible, and soldiers were drawn from provincial communities. In any case, they soon identified with the area in which they were stationed and had offspring by local women (a soldier was not allowed to marry during this period). Romanization thus spread to remote areas. The process was furthered by the settling of colonies of veterans throughout the empire. Agrippa (63–12 B.C.), who had commanded the victorious fleet at Actium, remained the right-hand man of Augustus during the early part of his reign. He controlled the armies and established a permanent navy with bases at Ravenna and Misenum.

NEW PROVINCES

During the *principate* of Augustus, Rome conquered large areas of land. Galatia, annexed in 25 B.C., rounded out provinces in central Asia Minor. A diplomatic triumph of Augustus was an agreement reached with Parthia in 20 B.C., defining respective spheres of influence. Spain was completely conquered in 19 B.C. By A.D. 4, a whole new tier of provinces had been added, including Rhaetia, Noricum, Pannonia, Illyricum, and Moesia, and extending from Provence to the Black Sea and from the Alps and Dalmatia to the Danube. In addition, the Romans crossed the Rhine frontier in Batavia, occupying a generous slice of western Germany, although it was soon lost. It was the fondest wish of Augustus to extend the Danube-Rhine frontier to the Elbe. However, in A.D. 9 a German revolt led by Arminius (Hermann) succeeded in destroying three legions under Varus in the Teutoburg Forest. It was clear that Roman power had been overextended; and Augustus, pondering the loss of the legions and their standards, abandoned his ambitions across the Rhine and Danube.

PROVINCIAL REFORM

The administration of the provinces was regularized and thoroughly cleansed. It was now virtually impossible for master extortioners, such as Verres in the late Republic, to become provincial governors. Each of the imperial and senatorial provinces, with the exception of Egypt, had a governor selected from the senate. Usually a province in a strategically crucial position was imperial (under the direct control of the emperor and garrisoned with Roman legions). Settled and Romanized areas were senatorial (under the direct control of the senate). The first checks upon the ruler of a province were a *quaestor* and *legates* who accompanied him; they were responsible to Augustus and the senate. As a further inducement to honesty, for the first time the governors received salaries. If temptation proved too great, the senate tried cases of malfeasance. Egypt was governed by a *legate* from the *equestrian* order appointed directly by Augustus. The *equestrians* were further enlisted as procurators in the provinces, and were placed in charge of tax collection.

The Establishment of the Julio-Claudian Dynasty

The only child of Augustus was Julia, born to Scribonia, whom he divorced to marry Livia. Livia had two sons, Drusus and Tiberius, by her first husband, Tiberius Claudius Nero. Augustus appears to have distrusted his stepsons, and designated as his heir Marcellus, the son of his sister, Octavia. In order to consolidate the Julian succession in 25 B.C., Marcellus was obliged to marry Julia. To the great sorrow of Augustus, Marcellus died two years later. Agrippa, who had been the factotum of the empire, was now groomed for the role of successor. Inevitably, he was married to Julia in 21 B.C. and, in 18 B.C., he was given the proconsular *imperium* and the tribunician power. Unfortunately, Agrippa died in 12 B.C. Tiberius then married Julia, and the sons of Julia and Agrippa, Gaius and Lucius Caesar, became the heirs-designate. By A.D. 4, both boys were dead, Julia had been exiled by Augustus for alleged adultery, and Tiberius had gone off to Rhodes. Despite some misgivings, Augustus could not fail to see his stepson's outstanding qualities. Tiberius and Drusus had commanded the Illyrian legions from 13 to 9 B.C. Drusus died, but Tiberius went on to get tribunician power for several years. Finally, in A.D. 4, he was adopted by Augustus, and within a few years shared with his stepfather the responsibilities of government. Since to a Roman, a legally adopted son was as good as one born to the family, Tiberius was accepted as the rightful heir. Thus, when Augustus died in A.D. 14, the succession of the Julio-Claudians was assured.

CULTURE DURING THE AUGUSTAN AGE

The efflorescence of literature, painting, sculpture, and architecture that began during the first century B.C. continued undiminished during the *principate* of Augustus. Indeed, it can be said that the arts reached an apogee during this period. Maecenas, the most trusted adviser of Augustus, supported talented writers, among them Vergil and Horace.

Vergil

Publius Vergilius Maro (70–19 B.C.) was born near Mantua in northern Italy. His rural background greatly affected his outlook, and he described the countryside lovingly in his *Eclogues,* or *Bucolics* (49–37 B.C.), and in his *Georgics* (36–29 B.C.). Vergil appears to have been convinced of the Messianic aspect of Augustus' reign without much prodding from Maecenas or the *princeps,* and he eagerly undertook the composition of the *Aeneid* (29–19 B.C.). The work is an epic of the highest caliber, although derived to some extent from Homer's *Odyssey* and *Iliad.* The first six books deal with the adventures of the Trojan prince Aeneas after the destruction of his city in the Trojan War. After much wandering, and having incurred the everlasting hatred of the Carthaginians, Aeneas arrives in Italy, where it is fated that his descendants will create the greatest of all empires. In the sixth book, Aeneas descends to the underworld and meets his dead father, who tells him of Rome's future greatness and of the founding of the Julian clan by Aeneas' son, Iulus. The last six books deal with Aeneas' settlement in Italy and conflicts with native peoples. The entire epic is pervaded with a sense of mission and an optimistic world view which is extremely rare in Roman literature and thought; the common belief was that the past was best. The *Aeneid* became the classic work of Roman verse for future generations.

Horace

Quintus Horace Flaccus (65–8 B.C.) was born in southern Italy. He was a more independent spirit than Vergil and was sometimes irritated by Maecenas and Augustus. Among his lyric works are the *Epodes,* and the *Odes.* The *Epistles* describe in dactylic hexameter vignettes of everyday life. The tone is mild and mellow, for Horace was an eclectic Epicurean who enjoyed what pleasures came his way.

The Elegiac Poets

Propertius (ca. 50 B.C.–ca. 15 B.C.) and Tibullus (ca. 48–19 B.C.) wrote love poems in elegiac couplets (a line of pentameter following one of hexameter).

The most famous of this group of poets is Ovid (43 B.C.–A.D. 17), who wrote advice for the lovelorn in the *Art of Love* and the *Remedies of Love.* In the *Metamorphoses,* he made from Greek mythology a continuous epic in hexameters, with Roman stories appended. The *Fasti* deals with Roman festivals and is an excellent source for early Roman legends. The overtly erotic tone of Ovid's works about love incurred Augustus' displeasure. Supposed indiscretions between the poet and Julia finally roused the *princeps* to action, and Ovid was exiled to Tomi on the Black Sea, where he died.

Livy

Titus Livius (59 B.C.–A.D. 29) was born in Patavium (Padua). Although his prose style is rather opaque, his *History* (covering the period from the foundation of Rome until 9 B.C.) was the first major historical work written in Latin. It is especially valuable for its delineation of early Roman history.

Art

The realism of late Republican reliefs and portraits was tempered in the Augustan period by classicism. Augustus founded a new Golden Age, and thus had to identify with the most golden of past ages, fifth-century B.C. Athens. A statue found in Livia's villa near Prima Porta shows the *princeps* in full armor in an orator's pose. The style is idealized, and the stance follows the canon of Polycleitus. The screen for the Altar of Peace, dedicated in 9 B.C., represents the family of Augustus together with allegorical figures, all in idealized classical style.

Architecture developed greatly during the reign of Augustus. His Forum, dedicated to Mars the Avenger, is an exemplar of urban planning; a symmetrical axiality offers sudden surprising vistas. Public works such as the naval installations at Misenum were also of the highest caliber.

In painting, the Second Pompeiian Style, which attempted to represent real architectural vistas on walls in order to delight the eye and expand the room, was replaced around 10 B.C. by the flat and delicate Third Pompeiian Style. The new style specialized in representing attenuated Egyptian fancies.

THE JULIO-CLAUDIANS

Much has been written about the profligate nature of the Julio-Claudian emperors, but it must be remembered that a consolidation of the *principate* and an expansion of the empire also took place at this time.

Tiberius

The succession of Tiberius (42 B.C.–A.D. 37) was remarkably smooth. Having already deified Augustus, the senate and the Roman people gave his successor all of the necessary honors and powers of *princeps*. The fiction of the Roman Republic was gradually dying out, as evidenced by the fact that the *imperium* of Tiberius did not have to be renewed every few years, as had that of Augustus, but endured until his death. Tiberius' relationship with the senate was not as easy as had been that of his adoptive father, for he lacked the latter's charisma. Further trouble for the new emperor was forthcoming in the magnetic personality of his nephew, Germanicus. In A.D. 13, Germanicus had been sent to Germany to quell a revolt of the troops, and his star began to shine a bit too brightly for Tiberius' comfort. After several indecisive battles in the northern regions, Germanicus was transferred to supreme command of the East, where the Parthians were a perpetual threat. Having restored stability and established Armenia as a buffer state (A.D. 18), Germanicus illegally entered Egypt (which was the special domain of the emperor). The paranoia of Tiberius and the enmity of Piso, then governor of Syria, may have been the direct causes of Germanicus' death in A.D. 19.

More difficulties were at hand for Tiberius when, in A.D. 23, he selected the *praetorian prefect* Sejanus as his right-hand man. Sejanus was not a loyal Agrippa or Maecenas, but a self-seeking adventurer who betrayed the very people who helped him achieve power. In A.D. 26, Tiberius, beset by feelings of persecution, fled Rome for Capreae (Capri). The reins of government were in the hands of Sejanus, whose recklessness caused the deaths of Germanicus' widow, Agrippina, and his sons, Nero and Drusus, not to mention the poisoning of the emperor's own son Drusus. Finally, in A.D. 31, Sejanus' reign of terror was ended when he was tried and executed for conspiracy.

Tiberius was growing old in his self-imposed exile, and his heirs were dead. As a last resort, he appointed Gaius, youngest son of Germanicus, and Tiberius Gemellus, his own grandson, as co-heirs. Gaius was known as Caligula ("Bootkins") because, as mascot of the troops during Germanicus' campaigns, he had worn miniature boots. Although Tiberius died morose and bitter, he left behind him an empire that had consolidated the advances achieved during the reign of Augustus. Plans for the conquest of Germany had been abandoned, but Cappadocia in Asia Minor was added to the provinces.

Caligula

In A.D. 37, the senate ruled that Caligula (A.D. 12–41) was the sole heir to the throne. The new emperor adopted Tiberius Gemellus but very shortly after ordered him murdered. Caligula, although untutored in the arts of government and acting like a spoiled child, was saintly during his first year of office compared to his subsequent behavior. Apparently, his personality changed after a stroke. Mere mortal deeds were not to be his, for he thought himself to be the equal of Jupiter, if not that of the Father of the Gods himself. Caligula's attempt to foist his divinity upon his subjects resulted in riots in Judaea and assassination attempts at home. In foreign affairs, the emperor may have contemplated expansion, but nothing was accomplished until the next reign. Caligula was finally killed in January A.D. 41. He was succeeded by his uncle, Claudius.

Claudius

Claudius (10 B.C.–A.D. 54), the younger brother of Germanicus, had been consistently rejected as successor to the purple because of his introverted, scholarly nature. It appeared, indeed, that he had no desire to rule. Nonetheless, upon being pressed into service by the Praetorian Guard as a foil against any senatorial attempt at restoring the Republic, he began to take his new occupation seriously. Since the new emperor was well versed in the history of the Roman nation, he realized the desirability of continuing many Republican traditions and deferring often to the senate. At the same time, since the empire was becoming more and more complex, a permanent civil service was a necessity. Claudius established four departments administered by Greek freedmen of ministerial rank: correspondence *(ab epistulis)*, finances *(a rationibus)*, petitions *(a libellis)*, and judicial matters *(a cognitionibus)*. Claudius also furthered a program of vital public works, including a port basin at Ostia.

Expansion of the empire continued. Most of southern Britain was taken in A.D. 43, and Mauretania, which bad been in a state of civil war due to the assassination of its king, was divided into two provinces by A.D. 44. In order to bring peace to the strategically vital Hellespont, Thrace was added to the system of provinces in A.D. 46.

Claudius was particularly unfortunate in his choice of wives. Messalina, his spouse upon his accession, was not only quite liberal in bestowing her favors, but plotted against Claudius with one of her paramours, Gaius Silius, a member of the senatorial class. When the emperor discovered this, he had his wife executed. They had two children, Octavia and Britannicus, who was designated as heir. The next wife of Claudius, his niece (daughter of Germanicus) Agrippina, proved more fatal than Messalina. She had a son whom she induced Claudius to adopt as Nero Claudius Caesar; he succeeded Britannicus as heir apparent. Tradition has it that, in A.D. 54, Agrippina gave Claudius a delectable dish of poisonous mushrooms, thereby dispatching him to the Elysian Fields.

Nero

Nero (A.D. 37–68) had been tutored by the Stoic philosopher, Seneca, but he was not fit to rule. When he became emperor at the age of sixteen in A.D. 54, his mother Agrippina tried to dominate him, and the *praetorian prefect* Burrus succeeded. Thereafter, Nero's burning passion was to eliminate his mother. First he had Britannicus murdered, and then, after many futile attempts, he had Agrippina assassinated. He divorced his wife, Octavia, sister of Britannicus, and married the opportunistic Poppaea Sabina. At about the same time (A.D. 62), Burrus died and Seneca was eliminated. The new *praetorian prefect,* Tigellinus, interested only in his own advancement, encouraged Nero's most flagrant excesses. Besides his profligate side, there were Nero's "artistic" facets, including his determination to be the greatest opera singer in the Greco-Roman world. He terrorized the aristocracy for money and was generally considered the harshest of tyrants. The negative opinion was increased manyfold after the great fire of A.D. 64, which is said to have destroyed one-fourth of Rome. Nero, who had been taking the waters at Antium when he heard the news, rushed to Rome, perhaps, as some say, to comfort the homeless populace, but mainly to crystallize his own plans for urban renewal. It was not enough for him to live on the Palatine; he had to have a colossal establishment that included forests, lakes, and pavilions. The space made itself available conveniently enough with the great fire, and Nero built his fabled Golden House. According to Suetonius, when it was finished he said, "At last I have begun to live like a human being." In order to detract from his extravagances, Nero blamed the Christians for igniting the city, and they thus faced their first major persecution. In A.D. 65, the senatorial class revolted, but were quashed with the help of Tigellinus. Other conspiracies were also nipped in the bud.

In the provinces, the empire faced several crises. King Vologeses I of Parthia put his candidate on the throne of Armenia (A.D. 54). The general Corbulo succeeded in winning back that area for Rome by A.D. 63, but, having incurred the jealousy of Nero, he was forced to commit suicide. In Gaul, the native prince Vindex started an insurrection (A.D. 68). Meanwhile Galba, governor of Hispanic Tarraconensis, declared himself emperor, and there was an insurrection under Macer in Africa. Nero killed himself in A.D. 68 to avoid being taken by his enemies. Suetonius relates that he said with his last breath, "How great an artist dies with me."

ANARCHY: THE FOUR EMPERORS

The death of Nero brought the line of the Julio-Claudians to an end, and the forces of chaos that had been lurking beneath the surface of the empire emerged. The problem was an old one that can be traced back to the time when Marius first hired mercenaries. These troops were loyal to none save the person who hired them. When the interests of the state coincided with those of the most powerful leader, all was well, but when the state began to experience storms and several leaders claimed the emperorship, the general with the strongest military following prevailed. The senate was obligated to approve the new ruler. Thus, Tacitus stated correctly in the case of the acclamation of Galba: "The secret of empire has been revealed; emperors can be made elsewhere than in Rome."

Vindex, whose revolt had been primarily against Nero, favored Galba. His revolt was put down and he himself was executed, but by A.D. 69 Galba had gained support of the Praetorian Guard. He accomplished almost nothing during his short tenure as emperor except the nomination of a senatorial successor, Piso. Meanwhile, Vitellius, in command of the Upper German armies, was acclaimed emperor, while in Rome Galba and Piso were executed, and Otho, the current spouse of Poppaea Sabina, was enthroned. After invading Italy and defeating Otho's forces, Vitellius became sole emperor, but he proved so unpopular that the situation was far from settled. It remained for Titus Flavius Vespasianus (Vespasian) to bring back peace and to establish a new dynasty.

THE FLAVIANS

Under the first two Flavians, Vespasian (A.D. 9–79) and Titus (A.D. 34–81), the Roman world recovered from the excesses of Nero's reign and the chaos of the year A.D. 69. Indeed, so firm a base was established that even the tyrannical Domitian's fifteen-year rule did not seriously impair peace and prosperity.

Vespasian

The situation in Judaea had long been explosive, for not only did the Jews desire to remain free from outside influence, but they were divided among themselves. Caligula had precipitated a revolt by insisting that his divinity be worshiped in Jerusalem. In A.D. 66, Nero sent Vespasian and his son, Titus, to quell continuing unrest, and the Flavians met with increased success. When Vitellius was killed after a brief tenure in office, the senate conferred the purple on Vespasian. This was actually only a coming to terms with a *fait accompli*, for Vespasian had already been acclaimed *imperator* by the legions of Egypt and Judaea.

The task ahead was of extreme difficulty, for the empire was all but bankrupt, the senate had again dwindled in number, revolt was raging in the Rhine area and in Judaea, and the composition of the legions was far from desirable. Vespasian left Titus in charge of subduing the Jews. In A.D. 70, he destroyed Jerusalem and returned to Rome in triumph. At about the same time, the situation in Gaul and Batavia was brought back to normal. Civilis, a prince of the Batavii, who had begun an insurrection, was defeated by the Roman general Cerealis.

With the borders calm at last, it was essential to find a method to keep them that way. The legions were reorganized to the number of twenty-eight, consisting of soldiers from various places rather than one locality. In addition, the Roman officer corps received tours of duty in different areas in order that they not identify too closely with one locality. The Praetorian Guard was completely reorganized, with Titus as its chief.

In order to restore shattered finances, Vespasian had to have money very quickly. He revamped the entire fiscal structure by raising taxes, by revoking privileges from non-taxpaying cities, and by being parsimonious with the money thus collected. Not only was the empire restored to solvency, but a magnificent program of public works was undertaken. So that the Flavians might be considered public-spirited citizens, and not Oriental tyrants like Nero, the great lake in the center of the Golden House complex was filled in, and the area was returned to the people of Rome in the form of the Flavian Amphitheater, or Colosseum, as it was later called. The temple of Jupiter Optimus Maximus was rebuilt. The senate was replenished with provincials, as well as Italians and Romans. The relationship of Vespasian to the senate was generally good, for, like Augustus, he theoretically deferred most of his actions to that body. Although there were several plots against him, they were quashed.

Not only was the empire consolidated internally; there was some modest expansion. By A.D. 72, the client kingdom of Commagene was joined to the province of Syria, and Lesser Armenia was incorporated as a province. When Vespasian died in A.D. 79, there was no problem of succession, for Titus, who had been co-regent with his father, was extremely popular. Vespasian, meanwhile, joined the roster of the deified emperors: Julius Caesar, Augustus, and Claudius.

Titus and Domitian

Titus was a celebrity as well as a ruler, and to the Romans during his brief reign (A.D. 79–81), he could do no wrong. After the disastrous eruption of Vesuvius, which covered Pompeii with volcanic ash and Herculaneum with molten lava, his noble behavior further endeared him to the populace. During the year A.D. 80, Rome suffered a fire and plague. Titus died of the plague, and he was afterward deified.

Vespasian's other son, Domitian (A.D. 51–96), was not of such exemplary character as his brother. Like Caligula and Nero, he had suffered various traumas before he became ruler, having been all but ignored by his charismatic father and brother. As with Caligula and Nero, Domitian's reign seems to divide into sections; during the first part he was a fairly moderate ruler, but during the second part paranoia, delusions of divinity, and subsequent tyranny set in.

The program of public works was continued and the civil service strengthened by replacing freedmen with *equestrians*. After a revolt by the general Saturninus in A.D. 88, Domitian cowed the senate completely and entered many *equestrians* in its rolls. Then he began a cat-and-mouse game with the senators that resulted in the death of many. The Rhine-Danube frontier was strengthened, but successes in Britain were cut short by Domitian's irrational recall of the governor, Agricola. The terror became so great that the emperor was assassinated in A.D. 96. Not only was Domitian not deified, but all traces of him were ordered destroyed, inscriptions erased, and statues defaced.

Rome was about to enter its Silver Age. The empire would reach its point of maximum expansion, the arts would flourish, and stability and security were the order of the day. The Silver Age would end with the accession of another tyrant to the imperial throne. Although he was eventually deposed, others took his place.

Selected Readings

Abbott, F. F. and Johnson, A. C. *Municipal Administration in the Roman Empire* (1926)

Boethius, Axel. *The Golden House of Nero: Some Aspects of Roman Architecture* (1960)

Bowersock, G. W. *Augustus and the Greek World* (1966)

Brion, Marcel. *Pompeii and Herculaneum* (1960)

Brogan, O. K. *Roman Gaul* (1953)

Buchan, John. *Augustus* (1937)

Campbell, J. B. *The Emperor and the Roman Army* (1984)

Crook, J. *Consilium Principis: Imperial Councillors* (1955)

Earl, D. *The Age of Augustus* (1968)

Garnsey, P. D. A. and Saller, R., *The Early Principate* (1982)

Griffin, Miriam. *Nero, the End of a Dynasty* (1984)

Hammond, Mason. *Augustan Principate in Theory and Practice* (1968)

Jones, A. H. M. *Augustus* (1970)

Lovick, B. *Tiberius the Politician* (1976)

Mackail, J. W. *Virgil and His Meaning to the World of Today* (1963)

Marsh, F. B. *Founding of the Roman Empire* (1927)

———. *The Reign of Tiberius* (1931)

Millar, F. and Segal, E. (eds.). *Caesar Augustus* (1984)

Rowell, H. T. *Rome in the Augustan Age* (1962)

Salmon, E. T. *A History of the Roman World, 30 B.C.–A.D. 138* (1927)

Seager, R. *Tiberius* (1972)

Starr, Chester. G. *The Roman Empire, 27 B.C.–A.D. 476: A Study in Survival* (1982)

Taylor, L. R. *Divinity of the Roman Emperor* (1931)

Wright, F. A. *Marcus Agrippa* (1937)

14

The Height of Roman Expansion

A.D. 96–98	Nerva
98–117	Trajan
114–117	Parthian War
115	Ctesiphon falls to Trajan
117–138	Hadrian
120–200	Lucian—author of cynical satirical works
fl. 121–151	Claudius Ptolemy—astronomer
125–180	Apuleius—satirical novelist
129–199	Galen—physician
130	Praetors' edicts codified
132	Jerusalem refounded as Aelia Capitolina
138–161	Antoninus Pius
161–180	Marcus Aurelius
168	Germanic barbarians pushed back from Italy

During the time between the accession of Nerva and the death of Marcus Aurelius, the Roman Empire witnessed its greatest material prosperity. The young sapling that Augustus had planted, and that had grown despite attempts at stunting it by Caligula, Nero, and Domitian, now reached its maximal height and full summer foliage.

FIVE GOOD EMPERORS

The key to the success of the reigns of Nerva, Trajan, Hadrian, Antoninus Pius, and Marcus Aurelius was the smooth functioning of the balance between the senate and the emperor. In addition, the system of adopting as successor a man suitable to rule was an everlasting credit to all of these men except Marcus Aurelius. However, despite peace, well-being, and the efflorescence of Silver Age culture, this period suffered a spiritual malaise and witnessed the beginning of the growth of mystery religions and superstition.

Nerva

Nerva (A.D. 30–98) was a kindly old aristocrat when, in 96, he was declared emperor by the senate. The wounds of Domitian's reign still smarted and the resulting reaction was toward tolerant rule. In this benign atmosphere, various programs of public assistance were promulgated, including the *alimenta,* or food relief for needy children. The army, however, resented the nonmartial Nerva. Hence, perhaps to prevent a repetition of the events of the year A.D. 69, Nerva designated Marcus Ulpius Trajanus (Trajan), a most able general, as successor. After his death in 98, Nerva was deified.

Trajan

The accession of Trajan (A.D. 53–117) was unprecedented. Unlike the Julio-Claudian and Flavian methods of succession, Trajan was unrelated to his predecessor and adoptive father. In addition, he had been born in Spain, and it will be recalled that it was only during the reign of Claudius that a goodly number of provincials was admitted to the senate. But times had changed, and the new emperor met with almost universal approval.

Nerva's policy of government aid to the poor and infirm through the *alimenta* program continued and was extended by Trajan. Many of the cities outside of Rome were in severe financial straits. In the West the governments of *duo-* or *quattuor-virs* (equivalent to consuls) and *decurions* (provincial senators), and in the East the local continuations of Hellenic forms of government, were unable to pay for the lavish public works constructed under previous emperors. Trajan provided aid and financial exemptions to these areas. Pliny the Younger was dispatched as *legate* to reestablish finances in the province of Bithynia, and his correspondence with Trajan, which has been preserved, gives an important insight into the problems of the period.

The military problems that Trajan encountered abroad were many, for Nerva had all but ignored the provinces. Several regions, including the eastern Danube area and the frontier with Parthia, required special attention. The provinces of Upper and Lower Moesia had been particularly vulnerable to attack from tribes on the north shore of the Danube. Domitian had made a treaty of alliance with the Dacian king, Decebalus. Decebalus, however,

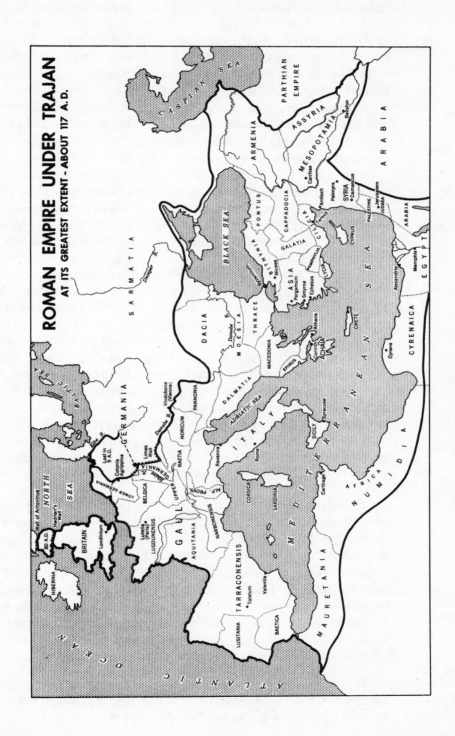

ROMAN EMPIRE UNDER TRAJAN
AT ITS GREATEST EXTENT – ABOUT 117 A.D.

ignored his obligations to the empire and gradually began to threaten the Roman boundaries. This situation was intolerable to Trajan, and during the years 101–102 he invaded Dacia and captured the capital, Sarmizegethusa. Decebalus became a client king, a position most distasteful to him, for he wished to organize an empire in the eastern Danube region. He attacked the Roman outposts and invaded the territory of the Iazyges, allies of Rome. In 106, Trajan again crossed into Dacia and captured Sarmizegethusa, which he made into a Roman colony. After Decebalus killed himself, Dacia became a province. Not only was the new acquisition of crucial strategic importance, but it had extensive gold deposits.

The spheres of influence of Rome and Parthia had never been fully settled. The Romans could not forget the ignoble defeat of Crassus at Carrhae in 53 B.C. In addition, the borders between Roman and Parthian domains had never been stabilized, although the treaty between Nero and Vologeses had affirmed Armenia as a buffer state and provided that the choice of the Armenian king had to meet with Rome's approval. In 110, Osroes (Chosroes), king of Parthia, deposed the ruler of Armenia and put a Parthian on the throne in his stead. Trajan then began his invasion of the East (114). Victories practically fell into the laps of the Romans, and Trajan soon conquered Armenia, Assyria, and Mesopotamia. Thus, for the first time, the Fertile Crescent was controlled by the Colossus of the West. In 115, Ctesiphon, the capital of Parthia, was taken, but by this time the Romans had overextended themselves, and the Parthians were regaining strength. Following revolts in Assyria and Mesopotamia, Trajan was able to reconquer portions of those regions. However, the Eastern situation was far from calm, for there was a massive revolt of the Jews that could not be fully controlled until the reign of Hadrian. On his way home from the East in 117, Trajan died, and Hadrian, a member of the imperial household, became emperor. Trajan joined the deified emperors.

Hadrian

Hadrian (A.D. 76–138) was apparently never adopted by Trajan as had been customary during the administrations of the better emperors. Gossipy contemporaries imply dislike of Hadrian by Trajan, a liaison between Hadrian and Trajan's wife, Plotina, and the subsequent poisoning of that emperor. These stories appear to be malicious fabrications of Hadrian's enemies. After all, Hadrian had been Trajan's ward since boyhood and had been recently entrusted with important offices. The probable truth is that Trajan was so occupied with his military campaigns that he had little time to think about a successor.

CONSOLIDATION OF THE EMPIRE

Hadrian's character was quite different from that of his predecessor. Although he too had been born in Spain, he was educated in Hellenic culture, and was consequently inclined towards all things Greek. He was a general, to be sure, but his entire approach was scholarly. This did not increase his popularity with some members of the senate who continued to cherish old family traditions. Even as late as the second century A.D., when Roman and Hellenistic culture had fused, there were quite a few latter-day Catos. Besides, it was known that Hadrian's approach was not that of further conquest, but of consolidation, for he had learned from Trajan's experiences how precarious was the Roman hold on Armenia and the eastern Fertile Crescent. This policy did not appeal to many militaristically patriotic members of the senate. Consequently, before Hadrian returned to Rome from the East, there were already the beginnings of an ugly conspiracy. Four generals of consular rank planned a coup (118). In Hadrian's absence, they were condemned to death by the senate. It is interesting to note that, although it had always been illegal to execute Roman citizens without the proper trial, such murders happened often and with little comment during the reigns of Nero and Domitian. However, once an atmosphere of freedom returned, the emperor was copiously blamed for the smallest excess even if he was not directly responsible. It was thus an uphill battle for Hadrian, first to gain popularity, and then to maintain it. Still, his generosity to the populace in tax matters and his double gift to the armies did not meet with disfavor.

GOVERNMENT REFORMS

Hadrian reformed the government in Rome by tightening and expanding the civil service, completing the replacement of freedmen by paid *equestrians*. In addition, he took judicial matters away from the senate by dividing all of Italy outside of Rome into four districts, each headed by a former consul appointed by the emperor. Hadrian's most important contribution to government was the promulgation of a law code based on the past edicts of praetors. This was completed by Salvius Julianus in A.D. 130.

FOREIGN AFFAIRS

Hadrian traveled extensively, and he thus got a very clear picture of conditions throughout the empire. Since the emperor's aim was consolidation of defensible territories, he made a treaty with Osroes (Chosroes), king of Parthia, restoring most of the Mesopotamian lands to him. Armenia was removed from the system of provinces and once more became a client kingdom. A wall was built across Britain to protect the Romanized part of the island from incursions of northern barbarians. The frontiers of Germany and Dacia were also strengthened. In A.D. 132, continued uneasiness in Judaea broke out in revolt. Jerusalem had lain in ruins since its destruction by the Flavians. Hadrian decided to rebuild it as a Roman colony (Aelia Capitolina) dedicated to the Capitoline Jupiter, whose temple he ordered built on the site of the great temple of the Jews. Only after much bloodshed, and the virtual elimination of the Jews from Palestine, was the ensuing revolt suppressed.

CULTURAL LIFE

In many ways, Hadrian was a leader of the intellectual and spiritual life of his period. He was eclectic, choosing bits and pieces from past and present, from Egypt to Greece. This variety is exemplified by the villa that he had built for himself below Tibur (Tivoli). The daring architecture was strictly Roman, but the various sections of the villa complex were named after famous places of the ancient world and included works of art from them. The spiritual homeland of Hadrian was Athens, on which he lavished an extensive building program. He also entered the Eleusinian Mysteries.

ARRANGEMENT FOR THE SUCCESSION

In order to avoid any doubt about succession, Hadrian adopted Lucius Aelius in 136, and then retired to his villa. When Aelius died in 138, Hadrian adopted a well-loved member of the senatorial class, Antoninus Pius, who in turn adopted Aelius' son, Lucius Verus, and Antoninus' wife's nephew, Marcus Aurelius. Hadrian died in 138 and was deified.

Antoninus Pius

Antoninus (A.D. 86–161) was an exemplary product of the senate, and was loved by the people. Unlike Hadrian, he remained in Rome, and he sought to centralize the administration even more than had his predecessor. He eliminated the four judicial districts of Italy, returning trials to the control of praetors.

Although there were pockets of unrest, the empire reached, perhaps, its height of prosperity and peace. Roman Britain was extended northward and was secured by the Antonine Wall. Antoninus died in 161 at the age of seventy-five and was deified by universal acclaim.

Marcus Aurelius

Hadrian did not spare expense or restrict scope in the education of the young Marcus Aurelius (A.D. 121–180). Accordingly, Marcus was well versed in Greek culture. As his guiding philosophy, he chose Stoicism, which was most germane to the Roman character, and he wrote down his Stoic precepts in the *Meditations*.

If the Greco-Roman world had been an entity unto itself, the millennium might have arrived under Marcus. Unfortunately, the process of migrating peoples, which had begun at the dawn of history and had slowed down during the reigns of Hadrian and Antoninus, began regaining momentum. In addition, Parthia, under the aggressive rule of Vologeses III, began threatening Armenia once more.

Upon his accession in 161, Marcus bade the senate acclaim his adoptive brother, Lucius Verus, as his co-Augustus. (All emperors were called Augustus at the time.) It was not a felicitous choice, for Verus was quite unsuitable for office. When the Parthians invaded Armenia, Verus was sent east with an army. The day was won, however, by other generals, including Avidius Cassius, who not only conquered Mesopotamia, but in 165 took the Parthian capital, Ctesiphon. Armenia again became a client state, and Avidius remained in Mesopotamia to insure Roman hegemony of the region. The main contribution of Lucius Verus was the bringing back with him to Rome of a disastrous plague. He died in 169.

In 166, the Germanic tribes not only breached the Danube defenses but pushed as far south as Aquilea on the Adriatic Sea. It became clear to Marcus that, if Rome were to survive, the land of these people (the Quadi, Marcomanni, and Iazyges) would have to be annexed, as Dacia had been, thus considerably shortening the eastern Danube frontier. After ridding Italy of the barbarians in 168, Marcus Aurelius fought the Quadi and Marcomanni in the Danube region. He had almost succeeded in making the area into a province in 175 when alarming news reached him: Avidius Cassius, commander in the East, upon hearing a false report that Marcus was dead, had declared himself *princeps*. Marcus Aurelius departed for the East and, when the troops learned that the emperor was alive after all, they killed Avidius. Meanwhile, however, the Romans had lost their overwhelming superiority in the Danube region. Consequently, instead of annexing the Quadian and Marcomannic lands (modern eastern Hungary and Czechoslovakia), the Romans established a demilitarized zone, about five miles wide. Meanwhile, large numbers of Romanized settlers along the border had been killed during the wars. In order to repopulate the territory and to defend it properly, Marcus brought in Germanic peoples. Thus began a slow process of barbarization of the border areas that was to lead to untold difficulties in the third century and later.

The greatest mistake that Marcus Aurelius made was the appointment of his son, Commodus, as co-Augustus. In his defense, it might be said that he was sufficiently shaken by the attempted usurpation of Avidius Cassius to want to establish a hereditary *principate;* also, his predecessors had left no sons. In addition, Marcus Aurelius was hardly ever at Rome and thus had little opportunity to learn the true character of his son. Still, he should have known better, for Commodus wanted nothing more than to be a Herculean gladiator. Marcus Aurelius returned to the front in 177, when the Quadi and Iazyges broke their word and again invaded Roman territory. Victory was near, but in 180 Marcus Aurelius died; he was deified. With him ended all hope of an enlightened, benign and peaceful *principate*. The future was to be bleak, indeed.

CULTURE DURING THE SILVER AGE

The Silver Age of Romano-Hellenistic culture can be said to extend from the reign of Tiberius through that of Marcus Aurelius. In many ways, it was a continuation of the Golden Age civilization of the Augustan period, but in the literary field there appears to have been a change toward a more rhetorical style, and in the visual arts spectacular theatrical effects predominated. It was an age of satire, pedantry, and precious eclecticism, of vertiginous architectural paintings and astounding forums, palaces, and baths.

Literature

Although verse was successfully utilized in Martial's and Juvenal's satires, this was primarily an age of prose. A parallel might be cited with Athens, where during the Golden Age verse was the dominant form of literature, but after the Peloponnesian War and the Sophistic revolution, prose with a strong rhetorical bias was the major form of expression.

SENECA

Seneca (Lucius Annaeus Seneca, ca. 4 B.C.–A.D. 65) was born in Spain. After a thorough training in rhetoric and philosophy, he began his copious output of literary works. Because he was connected with Burrus, he became Nero's tutor and he had the fondest hopes of creating a new Alexander the Great. Unfortunately, this was not to be, and, indeed, in A.D. 65, when Seneca got involved in a conspiracy, the emperor forced him to commit suicide. He died in Stoic fashion. There are extant many of Seneca's works, and they fall into three main categories. The ethical and philosophical works, which include the *Dialogues* and *Epistles,* are based on Seneca's own version of Stoicism. The epigrammatic and satirical works include *The Pumpkinification of Claudius.* The tragedies are in rhetorical verse, and extremely bloody. A simple comparison of the Medeas of Euripides and of Seneca will indicate that the latter was probably never meant to be performed but was read aloud in a salon of *literati.*

RHETORIC

Quintilian (ca. A.D. 35–95) wrote several influential works on rhetoric. His *Oratorical Instruction* delineates the ideal education for the future orator. Since the free speech of the late Republic had become superfluous, when not curtailed, during the *principate* oratory became a sterile pedantic exercise of one-upmanship in rarefied literary circles.

THE EPIC

Rhetoric pervaded all forms of writing, with unfortunate results in the area of epic literature. Lucan's (A.D. 39–65) *Civil War,* which deals with the struggle between Caesar and Pompey, seems artificial when compared with

Vergil's *Aeneid*. The *Thebaid* (recounting the struggle between the brothers Eteocles and Polynices) of Statius (ca. A.D. 45–95) is replete with tortured mythological references.

SATIRE

One of the most flourishing genres during the Silver Age was satire. The *Epigrams* of Martial (ca. A.D. 40–104) are devastating in their very simplicity. (In order to protect himself, Martial used fictitious names.) The sixteen *Satires* of Juvenal (ca. A.D. 50–130), composed in hexameters, give a fascinating if paranoiac view of life in contemporary Rome. Legacy hunters, fortune tellers, and even Augustus himself all fall under caustic scrutiny. In the East, Lucian of Samosata (ca. A.D. 120–200) wrote cynical satirical works in Greek. The *True History* is an ancient forerunner of Swift and the *Dialogues* spare no one; especially satirized are the hallowed Olympian gods.

THE NOVEL

Closely related to satire are the novels of Petronius Arbiter (d. A.D. 66), *The Satyricon*, and of Apuleius (ca. A.D. 125–180), *The Golden Ass*. *The Satyricon* tells of the erratic and erotic misadventures of three young men. The main body of the extant novel deals with the fantastically vulgar feast of the parvenu Trimalchio and his low-class wife, Fortunata. *The Golden Ass*, an expansion of a satire by Lucian, describes the miraculous transformation of one Lucius into an ass and his subsequent adventures.

HISTORY AND BIOGRAPHY

Tacitus (ca. A.D. 56–120) was the greatest Roman historian. In his *Annals* and *Histories*, he described and analyzed the early empire. His style was very spare and he was capable of demolishing an emperor with an understatement of a few words. Suetonius (ca. A.D. 70–140) wrote *The Twelve Caesars*. Although he had access to records, he invariably chose the most sensational accounts and wrote them in tabloid style. In the Greek East, Plutarch (ca. A.D. 50–120) wrote his *Lives*, in which famous Greeks and Romans were compared and contrasted.

BELLES LETTRES

The correspondence of Pliny the Younger (ca. A.D. 62–113) provides important insight into his period. *The Attic Nights* of Aulus Gellius (ca. A.D. 123–165) is a potpourri of history and literary criticism, which relishes archaic authors in particular—regardless of merit.

SCIENCE

Pliny the Elder (A.D. 23–79) included useful fact and fanciful fiction in his *Natural History*. In the Greek East, Claudius Ptolemy (fl. A.D. 121–151) wrote copious works on astronomy and geography, and Galen (ca. A.D.

129–199) wrote texts on medicine. Despite the importance of their work, both Ptolemy and Galen transmitted fallacies, the geocentric theory of the universe and the noncirculation of the blood, which plagued Europe until as late as the seventeenth century.

Art

During the Silver Age, there was an increase in the spectacular and the magnificent in all branches of the visual arts. Technical virtuosity reached a zenith.

PAINTING

The Fourth Pompeiian Style, which came into evidence during the reign of Nero, featured an overwhelming architectural wall decoration in painting and stucco relief. Planes appear to project and recede; columns and rich gilt decoration, sphinxes, and trophies almost seem to fall onto the head of the viewer. After Nero's reign, the designs were more subdued, and artists picked elements of the first three Pompeiian styles.

SCULPTURE

Official sculpture during the Julio-Claudian era continued the classicism of Augustus, but during the period of the Flavians a new realism came into being. Drill work was used, especially in the elaborate hairdos of ladies, which are worthy of the eighteenth century. A less flamboyant type of portrait sculpture appeared during the Antonine period. Eyeballs were now incised, with resulting increased expression. Because of changes in burial customs in the middle of the second century, sarcophagi tended to replace cinerary urns. Their larger surface areas gave rise to complex mythological and heroic compositions that became more elaborate with the passage of time.

ARCHITECTURE

As architectonic skill increased, buildings became more exciting. The Golden House of Nero, the Colosseum, the Domitianic Palaces, the Imperial Forums, and Hadrian's Villa are but a few examples of the Roman architects' virtuosity. The plane wall was shunned and surfaces began to curve, project, and recede. These buildings delight the observer with their orderly axiality and surprising effects. Not only are they pleasing to the eye but, having been built by Romans, most of them were quite practical—as for example, the Trajanic hexagonal harbor basin at Portus and the apartment blocks at Ostia.

SOCIAL AND ECONOMIC LIFE

With the incorporation of the Mediterranean region into the Roman Empire, there resulted a flowering in commerce. Pirates had been eliminated from the seas, and a multitude of ships tied together the main ports of the area. Of all the great cities of the empire, Rome took the most and contributed the least. Luxury products, such as marble from Greece and even silks from China (by caravan routes across Asia), found their way into the great homes of the capital. Shipping was controlled by corporations (whose offices can still be seen today in the ruins of the port of Ostia), although the imperial government took charge of grain shipments.

Social Life

Despite the massacres of Nero and Domitian, senatorial families in Rome and their provincial copies, the *decurions,* remained the center of imperial life. As during the Republic, the great were surrounded by clients who attended their patrons in political and social gatherings and who were given means of sustenance in return. The entourage of a wealthy Roman included freedmen (freed slaves), who by law were still tied to their former masters, and free-born citizens who wanted to better their positions.

Besides the vast number of unemployed in the capital who were supported by the government, there were many free workers who led unobtrusive lives. They were either descendants of slaves from all over the empire or of the original artisan stratum in the population. If a slave were manumitted and then married a freed woman, the children of this marriage were completely free. For mutual protection, common religious beliefs, and burial, workers banded together in guilds *(collegia).* Thus, Roman society was highly institutionalized during the empire. With the advent of chaotic conditions during the third century, society would become increasingly more rigid.

Industry

Industry was not highly developed, by modern standards. The typical industry was a small workshop, although the government controlled sizable segments of the construction industry, which were maintained on a relatively large scale. Certain regions specialized in specific products. Thus, Arretium (Arezzo) was renowned for its relief pottery, Gaul for textiles, and Greece for statuary. As a result of the enduring peace, the most common source of slaves, war captives, disappeared. In addition, there were many manumissions during the early years of the empire. Hence, the number of slaves employed in industry decreased.

Agriculture

The small free farmer was even rarer than he had been during the Republic. Large estates belonging to the emperor or rich senators, or (in the East) those of temples, were managed by supervisors. Tilling the soil were tenant farmers *(coloni),* who became increasingly obligated to the land-owners. Although serfs worked some of the Eastern estates, the use of slave labor in agriculture declined as in industry.

THE GROWTH OF ROMAN LAW

Because the Romans had a more structured outlook than the Greeks, it is no surprise that they developed law to a fine art. The earliest Roman law was based on the Twelve Tables, interpreted by priests such as the *pontifex maximus*. In addition, private individuals *(iuris prudentes)* defined what was legal for their patrons, and this eventually entered the larger body of Roman law. When praetors were elected, it was customary for them to issue an edict proclaiming their interpretation of existing laws. These edicts were finally codified in the *Edictum Perpetuum* in about the year 130. Roman civil as well as criminal law was based on reason and logic, and by the Antonine period many irrational elements had been eliminated. The jurist Gaius (born during Hadrian's reign) even recognized a natural law *(ius gentium)* that affected Romans and foreigners alike. Under Justinian in the sixth century A.D., Roman law was definitively codified, and thus it was passed on to medieval Europe.

With the death of Marcus Aurelius, his son, Commodus, became emperor. He may be likened to Nero, and like that infamous emperor of the Julio-Claudian line, he met a violent end. The events of 69 A.D. were repeated, and the Roman world changed for the worse.

Selected Readings

Berger, A. *Encyclopedic Dictionary of Roman Law* (1953)
Duncan-Jones, R. *The Economy of the Roman Empire* (1974)
Farquharson, A. S. L. *Marcus Aurelius* (1952)
Ferguson, J. *The Religions of the Roman Empire* (1970)
Hammond, M. *The Antonine Monarchy* (1959)
Henderson, B. W. *The Life and Principate of the Emperor Hadrian, A.D. 76–138* (1923)
Huettl, W. *Antoninus Pius.* 2 vols. (1933–36)
Jones, A. H. M. *The Cities of the Eastern Roman Provinces* (1937)
Lepper, F. A. *Trajan's Parthian War* (1948)
Macdonald, W. *The Architecture of the Roman Empire* (1969)
Magie, D. *Roman Rule in Asia Minor.* 2 vols. (1950)
Meiggs, R. *Roman Ostia* (1960)
Millar, F. *The Roman Empire and Its Neighbors* (1967)

Nash, E. *Roman Towns* (1949)

Perowne, Stewart. *Hadrian* (1960)

Rostovtzeff, M. I. *Social and Economic History of the Roman Empire.* 2 vols. (1957)

Sedgwick, H. D. *Marcus Aurelius: A Biography* (1921)

Webster, G. *The Roman Imperial Army* (1969)

15

The Beginning of the Empire's Dissolution

A.D. 180–192 Commodus

192 Pertinax and Didius Julianus

193–211 Septimius Severus

195–199 War with Parthia

205–270 Plotinus—Neoplatonist

211–212 Geta

211–217 Caracalla

212 *Constitutio Antoniniana*—all residents of empire citizens

217–218 Macrinus

218–222 Elagabalus

222–235 Alexander Severus

227 Sassanian dynasty begun in Persia

230–233 War with the Sassanians

232–305 Porphyry—Neoplatonist

235 Maximinus Thrax acclaimed emperor

235–284 Period of the "Barracks Emperors"

250 Christians persecuted

253–268 Gallienus

259 Valerian taken prisoner by Sassanians

270–275 Aurelian

271 Wall built around Rome

272 Reconquest of Palmyra from Queen Zenobia

273 Reconquest of Gaul from Tetricus

The period from the death of Marcus Aurelius to the accession of Diocletian marks one of the most abysmal eras in the history of the ancient world. If the Roman state had maintained the resilience of the early principate, *Septimius Severus might have put the empire back in shape as the Flavians had done after the disastrous year,* A.D. *69. Unfortunately, some essential element had evaporated. The new breed of third-century leaders were more often than not selfish military men. When conditions began to improve under Aurelian, there was no question of restoring the second-century version of the* principate, *much less the Republic. Only a repressive tyranny could bring back a semblance of unity.*

COMMODUS

Although young Commodus (A.D. 161–192) presumably was called on to share in the responsibilities of government by his father, Marcus Aurelius, he never took them seriously. In 177, he was made co-Augustus, and he even graced one of the Danubian campaigns with his presence. However, after the death of Marcus in 180, the true character of the new emperor made itself evident. In order to avoid further disturbance of his acted-out fantasies, Commodus decided to settle the deteriorating situation in the Danube region in a most disgraceful fashion: he abandoned all of the gains made by Marcus, thus leaving the Danube as the northern boundary of the empire. In addition, he bribed the Germanic tribes into peaceful behavior with large amounts of money. Commodus was to be found neither in the palaces nor the Senate House, but in the arena. As Nero had thought that he was the greatest singer in the world, so the son of Marcus Aurelius sincerely believed himself to be the best gladiator, Hercules incarnate. This irresponsible approach to government so alienated the senate and the Roman people that the reign of Commodus could not end in any but a violent way. In 192, he entered upon the consulship dressed as a gladiator. This was the last straw; Commodus was assassinated.

ANARCHY

The same destructive forces that had brought the Roman world to the brink of collapse in the year 69 and had been constantly simmering below the surface saw the light of day again in 192. The key to power was the military, and the key to the military was money. Whoever gave the most remunerative gift to the soldiers obtained office.

The first in this line to hold the purple was Pertinax. Although he had been acclaimed by the Praetorian Guard after promising them a huge sum of money, he never paid his debt. In addition, although he claimed to have restored the *principate,* Pertinax compounded the graft already present. Wholly unpopular, he was killed after three months in office.

This sheerly financial approach to officeholding became painfully patent when the emperorship was auctioned to a wealthy senator, Didius Julianus. He, too, was thoroughly unpopular. Again, rival army leaders fought for the throne. The legions of Syria raised the governor of that region, Pescennius Niger, to the purple, and he began making military inroads in the East. Simultaneously, the governor of Upper Pannonia, Septimius Severus, saw his opportunity and had himself acclaimed emperor by his troops (193). He marched on Rome, using the "martyrdom" of Pertinax as an excuse to take over power. Meanwhile, Didius Julianus had been executed. Upon his arrival in Rome, Septimius deified Pertinax and dissolved the Praetorian Guard; he thought it wise to police Italy with troops of his own choice. Clodius Albinus, then governor of Britain, also had imperial ambitions, but Septimius calmed him down by making him a "Caesar." (At this time, the term *Caesar* referred to the emperor's heir, who did not have a real share in imperial power. As has been seen previously, the Augustus was either the emperor himself, or else his heir-designate with whom he shared power.)

THE SEVERANS

The Severans were the only enduring dynasty in the third century. They ruled until 235. They were like the Flavians in that they came after a period of chaos. But Septimius was the only Severan worthy of the title of emperor; the rest were either bloodthirsty men, such as Caracalla, or inept youths, such as Elagabalus.

Septimius Severus

Septimius Severus (146–211) was born in Leptis Magna in North Africa. He had received adequate civil and military experience for the *imperium*. However, he had to wipe out all opposition before he could be firmly ensconced on the throne. Septimius' campaigns in the East to destroy Pescennius Niger resulted in Roman destruction of several cities, including Byzantium, which had supported him. The resourceful Niger had also made an alliance with Vologeses IV, king of Parthia. This proved to be a mistake for both parties, since the Parthian dynasty was in a state of semicollapse, which was hastened by Septimius' defeat of Pescennius Niger in 194 at Issus.

Before moving on to the West, where Clodius Albinus, not satisfied with his appellation of Caesar, had declared himself emperor, Septimius tried to satisfy the Roman longing for stability and security. Since the Antonine period was looked back upon as a Golden Age, and since Marcus Aurelius was regarded as the last of the good legitimate emperors, Septimius, in Roman legal fiction at its most ludicrous, declared himself "adopted" by the deified Marcus. Also, to secure succession, the eldest son of Septimius, Caracalla (Marcus Aurelius Antoninus), was made a Caesar.

The forces of Septimius defeated Albinus at Lugdunum (Lyons) in 197, and the city was destroyed as punishment for its complicity. Then Septimius once again went to the East, where the Parthians had invaded Roman territory. After a decisive victory and the destruction of Ctesiphon, Septimius succeeded where even the august Trajan had failed: the entire rich eastern Fertile Crescent became the Roman province of Mesopotamia.

On return to Rome in 202, Septimius began his program of reforms, aimed at reducing the senatorial class, feeding the lower classes, and above all supporting the army. The senate was decimated by the execution of Septimius' enemies, and refilled with provincials. The *praetorian prefect* got important new judicial powers and was put in charge of grain distribution. In addition, free services to the poor were established. The codification and rationalization of law continued under the stewardship of the jurist Papinian. No means of obtaining money was left untapped, and all municipalities were held responsible for handing over their taxes. As a result, Rome, Leptis Magna, and other cities were rebuilt in magnificent fashion. The army was increased in size, got a lion's share of the bounty, and was granted additional privileges such as the right to marry while stationed abroad. Borders were refortified, and breached defenses repaired.

Despite the obviously evil disposition of Caracalla, Septimius designated him co-Augustus and, therefore, heir in 198. In the Antonine fashion, the younger brother, Geta, was made Caesar that year and Augustus (co-heir) in 209. The two brothers had a distinct dislike for each other despite the pleas of their mother, Julia Domna (who presided over the most prestigious literary salon of the day). After Septimius died in 211 while campaigning against the

Caledonians in Britain, open hostilities broke out between Caracalla and Geta.

Caracalla

Shortly after becoming co-emperor, Caracalla (188–217) killed Geta and had every remembrance of him erased from inscriptions and statues. In 212, in order to receive taxes to which only Roman citizens were subject, Caracalla decreed that all free inhabitants of the empire would thenceforth be Roman citizens (the *Constitutio Antoniniana*). The emperor then endowed the legions with large amounts of money to ensure their loyalty and thus to secure the borders. However, Caracalla was deeply hated, and in 217 he was assassinated by Macrinus, the *praetorian prefect,* who then became emperor. Macrinus, however, was much disliked by the senate, for he was a member of the *equestrian* class and cared very little for senatorial niceties. He also alienated the troops who had been loyal to him, because he did not proffer them their promised pay increase.

Elagabalus (Heliogabalus)

The family of Septimius' widow, Julia Domna, was very clannish and ambitious. Her sister, Julia Maesa, who had fled home to Syria after the assassination of Caracalla, began to plot to restore her family to the purple. She claimed her teenage grandson, Bassianus (priest of the god Elagabalus, whose name he adopted), as the rightful heir of the Severans. The Eastern legions were loyal to her, and by 218 Macrinus was dead and Elagabalus (202–222) was on the throne. He made his cousin, Alexander, his heir to ensure succession. Bassanius' four-year reign was marked by a continual religious orgy that shocked even the case-hardened Romans of the third century. In addition, his irresponsibility in government was too much for all concerned, and the emperor-priest was killed at the age of twenty.

Alexander Severus

The new emperor, Alexander Severus (208–235), was dominated by his grandmother, Julia Maesa, and then by his mother, Julia Mamaea. He was not overly popular, for the Romans considered him a foreigner. Nonetheless, a liaison was established between the emperor and the senate by a group of senators serving in a council of legal advisers.

The borders were once again in danger, especially those in Mesopotamia. The weak Parthian Empire was overthrown in 224 and a new dynasty, the Sassanians, founded by the Persian Ardasbir, was established (227). The Sassanians were extremely militaristic, fancying themselves successors of the Achaemenids, and thus pressures built up in Mesopotamia. Meanwhile, the Germanic Alemanni were spreading unrest in the north. Alexander was not very militarily minded, and, as a result, he alienated the troops. He was murdered in a revolt of the army, and the governor of Pannonia, Maximinus Thrax (the Thracian), was acclaimed emperor (235). Thus began the period of what has been sometimes called the "Barracks Emperors." Hardly any died a natural death. There was not, and at this time there could not be, a

Vespasian, or even a Septimius Severus, to save the day. Rome was destined to endure its greatest agony yet.

CHAOS (235–284)

With no stable ruler, and with barbarians breaking through its border defenses, Rome celebrated the millennium of its foundation. Ironically, the moment occurred during the reign of the not overly civilized Philippus Arabs (the Arab) (244–249). Germanic tribes, such as the Visigoths (West Goths) and the Franks, invaded the empire. The new Sassanian Empire, on seeing that Rome was in disarray, made great inroads in the East. The lowest ebb was reached when the emperor Valerian (253–260) was taken prisoner by the Sassanian king, Shapur (Sapor) I. At the same time, Gaul declared its independence under the rule of Postumus (259), and Palmyra became an independent kingdom in the East in the process of defending itself against the Sassanians. It appeared that the end had come. But a latent resiliency made itself felt, and under Gallienus (253–268), Claudius (II) Gothicus (268–270), and Aurelian (270–275), recovery began. In 271, a wall was built around Rome to secure it from attack. This was the first fortification around the capital since the fourth century B.C. Aurelian succeeded in reconquering Gaul, then (273) ruled by Tetricus; and Palmyra, ontrolled by Queen Zenobia (272). However, the bloodthirsty traditions of the army continued, and Aurelian was assassinated. It was not until the reign of Diocletian, who became emperor in 284, that the ruined economic, financial, and political institutions of the Roman Empire were recast and strengthened. This reformation gave the ancient world more than a century of survival. But it was a changed world; absolutism, not enlightened rule, was its climate.

CULTURAL AND RELIGIOUS LIFE

During the third century, literature was not the vital force it had been in earlier times. The visual arts portrayed graphically the agony of the period. A religious or mystical-philosophical seeking pervaded all aspects of life from the lower to the highest classes.

Art

Painting and sculpture became more expressive. Intense *Weltschmerz,* rather than idealizing calm or intelligent preoccupation, was the dominant mode. Vast tangled compositions appeared on sarcophagi, replete with much otherworldly symbolism. The running drill and extensive undercutting heightened the supernatural effects and conveyed an almost abstract sense of patterned light and shade.

Religion and Philosophy

Mystery religions had been present in Roman life since the early Republic, but it was not until the Antonine period that there was a great proliferation of these cults. Despite the material prosperity of the second century, the populace craved immortality and a deeper feeling of belonging to the universal order. The icy state cult, with its legalistic formulas and its shadowy afterlife, did not fill this need, nor did most of the philosophies inherited from Hellenic culture. When conditions worsened during the third century, adherents of the older mystery cults, the new mystical philosophy, and Christianity multiplied even more. Astrology became a vital force. If life was evil, there must be some place in the thereafter where man could find peace.

CYBELE

Cybele was a fertility goddess imported from Asia Minor. Her cult revolved mainly around the mournful death of her consort, Attis, and his joyous resurrection in the spring. In commemoration of this event, some adherents indulged in self-mutilation. The cult was Romanized in 205 B.C., but it did not gain wide currency until the reign of Claudius. In the second and third centuries A.D., it acquired astrological accoutrements.

ISIS AND SERAPIS

Isis and her consort, Serapis, of hybrid Egyptian and Hellenistic origins, were a supernatural pair similar to Cybele and Attis. The death and resurrection of Serapis took place in the fall, in accordance with the Egyptian floodtime. Rites such as baptism and periodic cleansing were aimed at endowing the adherent with such spiritual purity as to assure his immortality.

MITHRAISM

The Persian cult of Mithra proved most popular among the soldiers. It was based on a Persian dualism: the forces of good constantly battling those of evil. The god Mithra, by sacrificing a sacred bull, saves mankind. The initiate was baptized in bull's blood and worshiped at services in underground chapels. If he succeeded in purifying himself, he went to heaven; sinners burned in hell.

NEOPLATONISM

By the third century A.D., the traditional Greco-Roman combinations and permutations of Platonism, Stoicism, and Epicureanism offered little solace for the mind obsessed by the mysteries of the cosmos. The thinking man's answer to the exotic cults was Neoplatonism, which, although based on the doctrines of Plato and Pythagoras, involved preterphilosophical ecstasies. Neoplatonists believed that the pervading universal force is the One, which the soul may reach in an ecstatic revelation. Thus, it differed from Plato's theory that the Ideal can be reached only through the utmost efforts in reason and philosophy. The leading Neoplatonists were Plotinus (205–270), Porphyry (232–305), and Iamblicus (250–325).

CHRISTIANITY

The organization of Christianity begun by St. Paul made the new religion not only acceptable to Greeks and Romans, but formed it into an actively proselytizing creed. In addition, Christianity began to build an excellent structure to weather the increasing intolerance. The basic appeal of Christianity was similar to that of the mystery religions, in its teaching of personal immortality and an afterlife as the reward of faith and good deeds. Christ's vernal death and resurrection resembled in some aspects those of Attis and Serapis, although he differed from them in having had a historical existence. The exclusive monotheism of the Christians, however, was in the Judaic tradition. It precluded certain patriotic obeisances to such state deities as Jupiter and the deified emperors. For Romans, to whom this worship had become nothing more than a pledge of allegiance, this seemed an unreasonable attitude. When scapegoats were demanded, for example, after the fire of A.D. 64, the Christians proved to be easy targets. Tighter organization and necessary secrecy of services brought more persecution. Finally, the ever-increasing number and influence of its adherents resulted in terrible bloodbaths. Under Decius (ca. 250) and Diocletian (303), the persecutions were to reach high points of ferocity.

*T*he Roman Empire was dying, and the final blows were not only inflicted from without, but from within as well. Various rulers had to fight foreign invasions and suppress rebellious generals. The empire was able to linger on, but the end was coming.

Selected Readings

Baynes, N. H. *The Early Church and Social Life* (1927)
Birley, A. *Septimius Severus* (1971)
Boak, A. E. R. *Manpower Shortage and the Fall of the Roman Empire in the West* (1955)
Bolin, S. *State and Currency in the Roman Empire to 300* A.D. (1958)
Chessman, G. L. *The Auxilia of the Roman Imperial Army* (1914)
Owen, Francis. *The Germanic People* (1960)
Parker, H. M. *A History of the Roman World, A.D. 138–337* (1958)
Perowne, Stewart. *Caesar and Saints* (1962)
Pistorius, P. V. *Plotinus and Neoplatonism* (1952)
Starr, C. G. *The Roman Imperial Navy* (1959)
Webster, G. *The Roman Imperial Army* (1969)

16

Reconstruction and Fall of the Empire

A.D. 284–305 Diocletian

286–305 Maximian

293 Tetrarchy founded—Galerius and Constantius Chlorus Caesars

301 Edict of Maximum Prices

303–311 Christians persecuted

312 Battle of Mulvian Bridge

313 Edict of Milan

324 Licinius killed

324–337 Constantine Sole Emperor

325 First Ecumenical Council at Nicaea

330 Constantinople ready for occupancy

330–400 Ammianus Marcellinus—historian

335–420 St. Jerome

337–340 Constantine II

337–350 Constans

337–361 Constantius3

340–402 Symmachus—writer of epistles

350 Constans killed

354–430 St. Augustine

360–363 Julian The Apostate

363–364 Jovian

364–378 Valens

367–383 Gratian

370–405	Claudian—poet
378	Valens killed at Battle of Adrianople
379–395	Theodosius I
382	Altar of Victory removed from Senate House
391	Paganism proscribed by Theodosius
395	Empire divided: Arcadius in East, Honorius in West
400	Macrobius writes *Saturnalia*
408–450	Theodosius II Emperor of the East
410	Visigoths under Alaric sack Rome
429	Vandals invade Africa
438	Theodosian Law Code
453	Attila dies
455	Vandals sack Rome
475–476	Romulus Augustulus, last Emperor of the West
476	Odovacar The Goth rules Italy as king
488	Ostrogoths under Theodoric invade Italy
527–565	Justinian, Eastern Emperor
529–534	Law Code of Justinian
554	Justinian temporarily recovers parts of West

*T*he Roman Empire was rescued at the eleventh hour by a Dalmatian soldier named Diocletian. In addition to calking the leaks in the defensive system of the empire, Diocletian began reform of its economic and political structures. Under Constantine and his successors, reforms continued. The external defenses became increasingly difficult to maintain, as barbaric peoples were now migrating rapidly. The bureaucracy kept things in order internally, but most of the population was milked dry by the enormous burden of taxation that went into graft and defense. The Eastern and Western portions of the empire separated in 395. In the fifth century, the Western Empire declined and was finally completely conquered by Germanic peoples. The Eastern Empire endured much longer.

DIOCLETIAN

It would have seemed that the rough soldier acclaimed by his troops in 284 was to be yet another Barracks Emperor. But Diocletian (ca. 245–305) proved shrewder than his predecessors. There were many military problems to resolve before the major economic and political difficulties of the empire could be resolved. Diocletian first disposed of Aper, the *praetorian prefect* who had murdered the previous emperor, Numerian. Next, he defeated Numerian's brother, Carinus (285), and thereby became sole emperor. Diocletian then formulated a series of plans that would officially divide supreme power, thus lessening the chance of rivals coming to the fore and also making the borders more defensible. In addition, Diocletian aimed at separating the military from civil government in order to minimize the political impact of the army.

Maximian, a fellow countryman of the emperor, was first made Caesar, and in 286 became co-Augustus. Maximian took charge of the West, while Diocletian himself commanded the East. Maximian was able to quell a revolt of a Gallic tribe (the Bagudae), but failed to crush an insurrection of Carausius in Britain. He then set up a new capital in Mediolanum (Milan), which was nearer to the troubled border areas than was Rome. Diocletian's Eastern capital, Nicomedia in Bithynia, was chosen for the same reason.

The Tetrarchy

In 293, Diocletian reorganized the imperial elite into a system truly unique in history. It will be recalled that, beginning in the second century A.D., when an emperor wished to designate an heir he had him made a Caesar, and if he wished to share rule with his heir during his lifetime, he made him a co-Augustus. There was, however, no clear system as to the way this succession occurred. Diocletian, having decided that it was strategically necessary to have four imperial rulers, organized the *Tetrarchy*. Diocletian in the East and Maximian in the West continued as the two Augusti. In addition, Galerius became Caesar of Diocletian and Constantius Chlorus became Caesar of Maximian. Each of the two Caesars married the daughter of his Augustus in order to unite the imperial clique into a family. When an Augustus died, his Caesar was to replace him and in turn had to choose another Caesar, presumably on merit. Thus, succession was to be unequivocal and smooth. Each Caesar, though nominally under an Augustus, had supreme command of an area of the empire. Galerius was given the Danube region and Constantius got Britain and Gaul. After 296, Britain was once more controlled by the imperial government, and by 298 all major insurrections had been settled in East and West. The Sassanians temporarily lost their sting after being defeated by the Romans in 298. If frontier trouble arose, the strengthened border garrisons could easily suppress it.

Civil Government

The political reforms of Diocletian were extensive. The haphazard provincial system, based merely on a chronological accretion of territory, had become all but ungovernable. Diocletian reorganized the four major divisions of the empire as *prefectures,* each headed by a *prefect* as civil ruler directly responsible to his Caesar or Augustus. These were in turn divided into *dioceses* ruled by *vicars.* The smallest units, provinces, were subdivisions of the dioceses ruled by governors. The *equestrian* class, because it harbored no particular loyalties to Republican traditions, filled most of these new administrative posts.

Financial Reforms

The stable money of the second century had been so often inflated by alloying its silver content with bronze, that, by the period of Aurelian, the coins were all bronze with a silver wash on them. Diocletian tried to shore up the finances of the empire by restoring silver and gold coinage in 296. However, the gold and silver coins introduced by Diocletian were apparently not great in number, and the inflated bronze issues were still the major currency. In trying to make the older money conform to the new silver and gold issues by reducing them to their intrinsic metallic values, Diocletian brought on a tremendous upsurge in prices. To combat inflation, Diocletian promulgated the Edict of Maximum Prices (301). The government attempted to regulate every aspect of life, employing spies such as the *agentes in rebus,* who reported on administrative operations. But lacking the paraphernalia of modern totalitarian regimes, it had difficulty in enforcing decrees. Under Diocletian, taxes were collected rigorously. Taxes established for landowners were based on units of land and of labor. The small farmers and moderately comfortable middle classes were all but squeezed out of existence.

Court Ceremonial

In order that the government be not only respected but worshipped, a completely new system of emperor-citizen relationships was established. Unlike even the more extreme Julio-Claudians such as Nero, who had been entitled *princeps* (first citizen), the new emperors were *domini* (lords). They wore diadems and purple robes, and subjects had to prostrate themselves in their presence. Diocletian would have had it believed that he was Jupiter's ward, and that Maximian was the protégé of Hercules. In short, the *principate* had been converted into a kingship in all but name, for even now certain aspects of Republican tradition were so strong that the term *rex* (king) could not be uttered in connection with the emperors.

The End of Diocletian's Reign

After a thoroughgoing persecution of the Christians in 303, Diocletian retired in 305 due to ill health. He pressured Maximian into retirement as well. Constantius and Galerius became the new Augusti, while Severus was selected as the new Caesar of the West, and Maximinus Daia, Caesar of the

East. Diocletian died in 313, at which time his life's work seemed to have already been undone.

THE INTERREGNUM

The new arrangement of Tetrarchs made no one happy except Diocletian. Presumably the best men had been selected as Caesars, although it is closer to the truth to say that they had personal ties with one of the new Augusti, Galerius. Constantine, son of Constantius, and Maxentius, son of Maximian, felt cheated. When Constantius died in 306, the army in Britain lost no time in making Constantine Augustus. This did not fit the scheme of things, and by maneuver and compromise, Constantine was finally confirmed as Caesar of the West, replacing Severus, who in turn filled the office of Augustus left by Constantius. The only complication was that Maxentius also wanted to be a Caesar, if not an Augustus.

In a series of moves whereby Maxentius gained control of Italy and the support of his father, Maximian, Severus was killed and Maxentius got his fondest wish: he became an Augustus. There was now one Augustus too many, for Maximian had reappointed himself to that office. To complicate matters further, Maximian allied himself with Constantine, who was then declared Augustus. Meanwhile, Galerius named Licinius to replace Severus as Augustus. It became clear that the Tetrarchy was not working, and the specter of the third century began to haunt the imperial government. After the execution of Maximian by Constantine for disloyalty in 310, and of Galerius in 311, Constantine and Maxentius lined up as the chief contenders for the post of senior Augustus. At the Battle of the Mulvian Bridge (312), Constantine won the day—according to legend because of his adoption of the Christian god as his protector.

CONSTANTINE THE GREAT

Constantine (ca. 274–337) entered Rome in triumph, and was promptly made senior Augustus by the senate, with Licinius as his junior colleague. In 313, he issued the Edict of Milan, which reaffirmed and expanded the provisions of an Edict of Toleration issued by Galerius. Christianity could now stand side by side with paganism in the Roman world. It was inevitable that Constantine and Licinius would first become rivals and then enemies. After open warfare between the two, Licinius went down in defeat and was eventually killed. In 324, all traces of the Tetrarchy vanished, and Constantine became the sole emperor.

Constantinople

Much had to be done to keep the empire from disintegrating. If it had not been for the human factor in general and greed in particular, the Tetrarchy might have been a permanent solution for the problems of government. It must be conceded, however, that it was too rigid and artificial a system. Constantine learned from the successes as well as from the errors of Diocletian. An empire with several administrative centers now seemed to be the only feasible choice. Therefore, in 324 Constantine selected the site of the ancient Megarian colony of Byzantium as a permanent eastern "Rome." The choice was quite felicitous, for the new city guarded the strait between the Black Sea and the Mediterranean, and it was within striking distance of potential and real trouble spots. The city called Constantinople was ready for occupancy in 330. However, Rome itself was always considered the empire's main source of spiritual power. In a sense, there was a subconscious expectancy that, when the present difficulties ended, the mother city would once more become the primary seat of government. Of course, this never happened.

Defense and Government

The armies were strengthened, and a new strategy was employed to maintain stability. Constantine added mobile troops to the defensive system. They were stationed not at frontiers, where garrisons were decreased, but at inland centers. When an insurrection in a province or a breach of the borders took place, troops could easily rush there to restore order. Barbarians were used regularly as officers, as well as in the rank and file.

A vast bureaucracy was built up to handle the far-flung activities of government. Its complexity was awesome, and it controlled all aspects of the Roman citizens' existence. Life became a prison for the hapless majority. The growing bureaucracy ate up taxes; taxes were increased; and graft was rampant. Men were forced to remain in the professions of their fathers. The provincial aristocracy, the *curiales,* were forced to pay the costs of government, and as a result became impoverished. Yet they had to remain *curiales*.

In addition, urban craftsmen were tied to their trades, and tenant farmers *(coloni),* who worked estates owned by the flourishing senatorial class, were soon reduced to the status of serfs.

In contrast to the degraded status of most Roman citizens, the court shone brilliantly. The elaborate ceremonies and forms of etiquette created by Diocletian were further complicated. Everything connected with the emperor became holy. For example, the cabinet of advisers of Constantine was named the *sacrum consistorium.*

Other Changes and Succession

Constantine's desire for control of all aspects of life extended to the area of religion. In 325, when a doctrinal schism occurred among the early Christians, Constantine convoked the First Ecumenical Council at Nicaea.

As was the usual situation in imperial circles during the Roman Empire, succession was a problem. Fortunately, Constantine had an ample supply of sons. After the death of the oldest, Crispus, there remained Constantine II, who took charge of the western regions; Constans, who controlled Italy and the central areas; and Constantius, who ruled the east. All were Caesars. When Constantine died in 337, there was not a little friction among the brothers. On his deathbed, Constantine was baptized, thus truly uniting the emperorship and the Church.

THE ESTABLISHMENT OF CHRISTIANITY

As the Capitoline cult proved inadequate in pervading the emperorship with an aura of divinity, new religions were adopted by Augusti. Thus, both Aurelian and Constantine had identified with the Unconquered Sun. The new world of the absolutist Dominate required a strong dogmatic religion that for Roman citizens could serve as an all-encompassing belief system as well as bring them under the spiritual and political control of the emperor. If any pagan religion had been used for such purposes, its relatively tolerant attitudes toward other cults would surely have hardened to keep out dissent. Constantine saw Christianity, in its unified doctrines, universal appeal, uncompromising monotheism, high moral standards, and superior organization, as the religion of the future. The officers of the Church paralleled those of civil government. Bishops generally exercised spiritual control over dioceses. Metropolitans were bishops of large cities, and could exert influence throughout their prefectures. On the community level, elders or presbyters officiated at services.

As was bound to happen, splits in belief began to appear. One of the basic creeds of Christianity was that of the Trinity. It was accepted as a mysterious truth that the Divinity consisted of three Persons of one substance: the Father, the Son, and the Holy Spirit. The adherents of Arius, trying to apply logic to a mystery, concluded that the Son was not of the same divine substance as the Father. Christianity divided into two hostile camps: the Athanasians and the Arians. Constantine intervened, and in 325 the Council of Nicaea was held. It affirmed the correctness of Athanasius and branded Arianism as heresy. This decision did not settle the matter, for first Arianism and then other schismatic beliefs plagued Christianity. The council did, however, formulate an orthodox position that, unfortunately, resulted in the persecution by Christians of "heretics" who held divergent doctrines.

THE SONS OF CONSTANTINE

Although Constantine II was the oldest of Constantine's three sons, all became Augusti. They now had supreme command over those regions that they had controlled as Caesars. In due course, Constans battled against Constantine II, who in 340 was routed and killed at Aquilea. Constans now had complete control of the West, while Constantius was supreme in the East. However, the armies had their own ambitions, and raised a general, Magnentius, to the rank of Augustus. In 350, Magnentius had Constans killed, but shared supreme power in the West with another usurper, Vetranio. Constantius did not like the turn of events, but his war with the Sassanian king Shapur (Sapor) II prevented him from invading the West. Finally, in 353, he was able to win back the western provinces.

There were hardly any relatives left to become the Caesars of Constantius, for all but two cousins, Gallus and Julian, had been slaughtered after Constantine's death. Gallus was a Caesar briefly, but he was executed in 354. In 355, Julian became Caesar in defense of Gaul. The relationship between Caesar and Augustus was far from cordial. In 360, while Constantius was in the East, Julian was acclaimed Augustus by his troops. Although Constantius was about to overthrow his cousin by military might, he designated Julian as his heir before he died in 361.

JULIAN

Julian (332–363), known as "the Apostate," attempted to revive paganism as the official religion of the Roman state. His creed, however, was a far cry from the Olympian beliefs of the Greeks and the earlier Romans, for it was organized into a church that followed the Christian model, while using Neoplatonic doctrines as a guiding philosophy. It had little appeal, and with the death of Julian, Christianity once more became the state religion.

The western borders had been temporarily settled, and now it was time to terminate the war with Persia. Unfortunately, Julian was killed before victory was secured (363). He was succeeded by the earthy commander Jovian. The Romans retreated and, as a result, lost portions of Mesopotamia and all of Armenia. Jovian died the following year.

THE VALENTINIANS

The border areas were becoming extremely hard to defend, as the western migrations of barbaric peoples increased. The devastating incursions of the Huns brought further chaos, because large groups of Goths fled the Asiatic horde and headed for the empire. In 364, Valentinian, a skilled army officer, was selected emperor. He chose his brother Valens as co-Augustus in charge of the East. Meanwhile, Valens was having a very trying time. The ever-increasing number of Gothic refugees sought and got permission to reside within the borders of the empire. They were supposed to relinquish their arms, but corrupt Roman officials were bribed to look aside. Then the Romans began to harry the Goths. Pillage was the result. Valens tried to push the barbarians out of Roman territory, but he lost his life at the Battle of Hadrianopolis (Adrianople) in 378.

THEODOSIUS I AND HIS SONS

Theodosius I, who became emperor of the East in 379, could not bring a military solution to the Gothic problem. Instead, he made a treaty that allowed the Goths to become a federate people living within and defending the empire. Before Theodosius died in 395, he had put down insurrections and unrest. His sons, Honorius and Arcadius, became Augusti of the West and East, respectively. It was no longer feasible to defend the two parts of the Empire as one, and hence the division begun by Diocletian became a total separation. Neither of the two administrations had jurisdiction in the territory of the other.

THE FALL OF ROME

In 382, a portentous event had taken place in Rome. The Altar of Victory, which had symbolized Rome's military might, was removed from the Senate House because it was considered pagan. To the senatorial class, which, despite the establishment of Christianity, was still steeped in classical traditions, this spelled the end. The world did not have long to wait, for in 410 the Visigoths took Rome. The shock of this event cannot be underestimated, for the spiritual capital of the universe had not been attacked since the beginning of the fourth century B.C. In 455, it was the Vandals' turn to sack Rome. Still, the tenuous thread of imperial authority maintained itself until the year 476, when Romulus Augustulus, the last Roman citizen to hold the purple, was deposed. Odovacar (Odoacer), who succeeded him, was a Goth, and he ruled as king.

By the sixth century, there were an Ostrogothic kingdom in Italy, Burgundian and Frankish kingdoms in Gaul, Suevian and Visigothic kingdoms in Iberia, and a Vandal kingdom in North Africa. During the reign of the Eastern emperor Justinian, some of these territories were temporarily recovered (554) under the able generals Belisarius and Narses.

The East fared much better than the West. By the end of the sixth century, it had been transformed into the Helleno-Christian Byzantine Empire. In a truncated form, it lasted until 1453, when Constantinople fell to the Ottoman Turks.

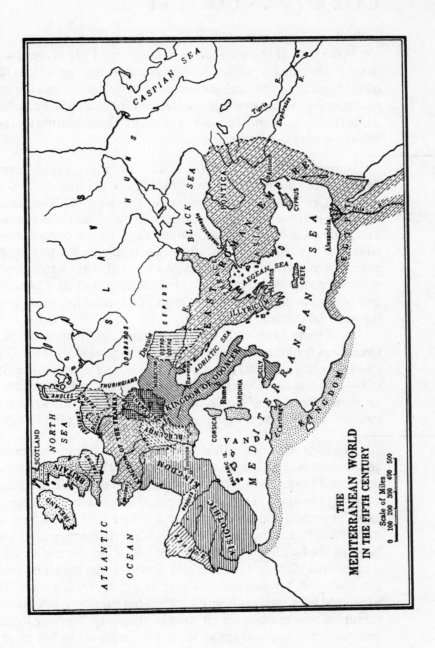

THE
MEDITERRANEAN WORLD
IN THE FIFTH CENTURY

Scale of Miles

0   100   200   300   400   500

LATE ROMAN CULTURE

In the field of literature, the last flowering of pagan creativity took place in the fourth century, while Christian literature reached its first high development. Secular architecture continued to be grandiose and impressive, and a new language in construction was created for churches. Sculpture in general tended to be static, and the faces of portraits painted during this period tended to have staring expressions.

Literature

Ammianus Marcellinus (ca. 330–400), the greatest historian of the period, wrote the history of the empire from the first century A.D. through the reign of Valens, thus continuing the work of Tacitus. Symmachus (ca. 340–402) was a pagan whose epistles defended the classical way of life. The *Saturnalia* of Macrobius (written ca. 400) is a collection of anecdotes, talks, and law which clearly shows the intellectual tastes of the senatorial elite. The superficially Christian Ausonius (d. 395) wrote poems about the beautiful countryside around the Moselle River in Gaul. Claudian (370–405), another pagan plated with a thin layer of Christianity, wrote poems praising the imperial clique.

St. Jerome (335–420) wrote and translated many religious works. As Greek was forgotten in the West, Jerome's translation of the Old Testament into Latin (the Vulgate) proved his most lasting contribution. St. Augustine (354–430) was the major Christian writer at the time of the barbarian attacks on Rome. His *City of God* brought Platonism into the system of Christian thought, and became a keystone of education during the Middle Ages.

Art

The huge mass of the Basilica of Constantine in Rome demonstrates that architecture was still capable of great works. The new churches seem to have developed from a simpler variety of basilica or public meeting hall. It was generally out of the question to use pagan temples for Christian services. The usual procedure was to dismember a temple and reconstruct the elements into a church. The common floor plan was cruciform, with the nave or main body of the building containing three aisles. At the end of the nave was a semicircular niche or apse, in front of which was the altar. When a locality could afford it, brilliant mosaics were used in decorating walls. This medium, which had been used profusely on floors but sparingly on walls during earlier centuries, now reached a high point in virtuosity. The true Roman genius in architecture evaporated in the West, but continued in full force in the areas of Byzantine influence.

The official portraits of the emperors, showing them with stem absolutist stares, indicated that this indeed was a new era. Groups of people on reliefs and paintings were now represented frontally. An otherworldly cast to the subjects' faces distinguished Christian art, which had broken away from the classical mold.

THE LEGACY OF THE ANCIENT WORLD

As the basis of civilization did not die out after the numerous barbarian invasions in Mesopotamia and Greece, so it survived the fall of Rome. As in past times, while the invaders appeared to have destroyed civilization, in reality much of it survived and was added on to by new influences. By the ninth century, Europe was on its way to recovery, and by the twelfth century the full revival of learning had begun. At that time, the composite Germanic-Latin culture of Western Europe was to be enriched by the newly rediscovered treasures of Greek and Roman literature. Even to the present day, the Western world has found a major source of inspiration in the art and writings of the ancients.

Selected Readings

Arnheim, M. T. W. *The Senatorial Aristocracy in the Late Roman Empire* (1972)

Bowersock, G. W. *Julian the Apostate* (1978)

Brown, P. *The World of Late Antiquity* (1971)

Burckhardt, J. *The Age of Constantine the Great* (1956)

Dodds, E. R. *Pagan and Christian in an Age of Anxiety* (1965)

Downey, Glanville. *Constantinople in the Age of Justinian* (1960)

Goffart, Walter. *Barbarians and Romans, A.D. 418–584: The Techniques of Accommodation* (1980)

Jones, A. H. M. *The Latter Roman Empire, 284–602.* 3 vols. (1964)

Macmullen, R. *Constantine* (1970)

———. *Soldier and Civilian in the Latter Roman Empire* (1963)

Momigliano, A. (ed.). *The Conflict between Paganism and Christianity in the Fourth Century* (1963)

Rawson, E. *Intellectual Life in the Late Roman Republic* (1985)

Thompson, E. A. *Romans and Barbarians: The Decline of the Western Empire* (1982)

———. *The Historical Work of Ammianus Marcellinus* (1947)

Walbank, L. W. *The Decline of the Roman Empire in the West* (1953)

Williams, S. *Diocletian and the Roman Recovery* (1985)

Index

A

Abraham, 39
Achaea, 51
Achaean League, 131, 160, 161
Achaeans, 65
Achaemenid dynasty, 46
Acharnians (Aristophanes), 101
Acropolis, 104
Actium, battle of (29 B.C.), 193, 195
Adadnirari II, 42
Adherbal, 171
Aediles, in Roman Republic, 152
Aegean Basin, geography of, 51
Aegina, 84
Aegis III, 131
Aegospotami, 98
Aeneid (Vergil), 197
Aeolians, 62
Aequi, 147, 149
Aeschines, 112
Aeschylus, 99–100
Aetia (Callimachus), 133
Aetolia, 51, 95
Aetolian League, 130–131, 160
Agamemnon, 55
Agamemnon (Aeschylus), 99
Agathocles of Syracuse, 155
Agesilaus, 108
Agricola, 204
Agrippa, 195, 196
Agrippina, 199, 200
Ahab, 40, 41
Ahmose I, 32
Ahura-Mazda, 48
Akhnaton, 34–35, 37
Akkad, 11, 16
Albinus, Clodius, 220, 221
Alcaeus, 75
Alcibiades, 96, 97

Alcmaeonidae, 68
Alcman, 75
Alemanni, 222
Alexander the Great, 111, 113, 116, 121, 180
    character of, 122
    conquests of, 122–123, 125
    early reign of, 121–125
    successors to, 125–126
Alexander IV, 125
Alexandria, 126, 132, 137
Altamira cave paintings, 4
Amasis, 45
Amenemhat I, 27
Amenemhat III, 28
Amenhotep III, 34
Amenhotep IV, 34
Amon, 27, 28, 34
Amon-Re, 27, 28, 128
Amorites, 17, 18–19, 38, 39
Amphipolis, 90, 95
Amphissa, 113
Amyntas II, 111
An, 17
Anabasis (Xenophon), 115
Anacreon of Teos, 75
Anahita, 48
Anaxagoras of Clazomenae, 102
Anaximander, 76
Anaximenes, 76
Andronicus, Livius, 162
Animism, 4
Annals (Tacitus), 163, 213
Antigonid Kingdom, 130
Antigonus II Gonatas, 126, 130
Antigonus III Doson, 130, 157
Antioch, 129, 132, 137
Antiochus I, 126, 129
Antiochus III, 129, 130, 159–160
Antiochus IV, 160, 180

Antipater, 122, 125
Antonius, Marcus (Marc Antony), 185
    in Egypt, 188–189
    versus Octavian, 188–189
    rise of, 187–188
    in 2nd Triumverate, 188
Apelles, 117
Apennines, 141
Aphrodite, 77, 137
Aphrodite of Melos, 137
Apollo, 54, 77, 89
    Oracle of, 112
Apollodorus of Athens, 133
Apollonius of Rhodes, 133
Apuleius, 213
Apulia, 141
Aquilea, 211, 234
Arabian Desert, 11
Arabs, Philippus, 223
Aramaeans, 38–39
Aratus of Sicyon, 131
Arbela, 123
Arbiter, Petronius, 213
Archidamian War, 94–95
Archidamus, 94
Archilochus, 75
Archimedes of Syracuse, 135
Architecture
    in Egypt, 25, 30
    in Greece, 79, 104, 118
    Hellenistic, 137
    Roman, 163, 190, 198, 214
Ardasbir, 222
Areopagus, Council of, 67, 68
Arginusae Islands, 97
Argolid, 51
Argonautica (Apollonius), 133
Argos, 65, 96, 108
Arianism, 234
Arians, 234

Aristagoras, 83
Aristarchus of Samos, 134
Aristarchus of Samothrace, 133
Aristides, 85, 88
Aristippus of Cyrene, 115
Aristophanes, 101, 117
Aristotle, 116–117, 122
Armenia
    and control of Syria, 129
    and Mithridati War, 179
    as Roman province, 180, 199, 201,
        203, 208, 209, 210, 211
Arminius, 195
Arpinum, 178
Arretium, 215
Arrhidaeus, Philip, 125
Art
    Egyptian, 29–30
    in Greece, 77–79, 103–104, 117–118
    Hellenistic, 136–137
    Mycenaean, 54–55
    Roman, 163, 190, 198, 214, 224,
        238
    Sumerian, 18
Artaphernes, 84
Artaxerxes, 108, 113
Artaxerxes II, 108
Artemis, 79
Art of Love (Ovid), 197
Aryans, 19
Asculum, battle of (279 B.C.), 151
Ashur, 18, 41, 42
Ashurbanipal, 42
Ashurnasirpal II, 42
Assyria, 41–42, 208
    administration in, 42, 44
    culture in, 44
Assyrians, 40
Astyages, 47
Athanasians, 234
Athanasius, 234
Athena, 89, 163
Athena Nike, Temple of, 104
Athenian confederacy, second, 108–109,
        110
Athens, 65–66, 121
    under Cleisthenes, 70–71
    in Hellenistic period, 131
    under Pericles, 89–92
    political development in, 66–69
    reforms in, 68–70
Athos peninsula, 85
Atlantis, legend of, 56
Attalus I, 132
Attalus III, 169
Atthides, 115
Attica, 51, 84, 85, 90–91
Attic Nights (Aulus Gellius), 213
Augustulus, Romulus, 236

Aurelius, Marcus, 210–211, 216, 219,
        223
Ausonius, Christian, 238
Australopithecines, 2
Avidius, 211
Ay, 35

B

Babylon, 19, 42, 47
Babylonians, 18–19
    code of Hammurabi in, 19
    culture of, 19
Bacchae (Euripides), 100
Bacchiads, 64
Bacchylides (Pindar), 99
Barracks Emperors, 222–223
Basilica Aemilia, 163
Basilica of Constantine, 238
Bassanius, 222
Bathsheba, 40
Belshazzar, 46, 47
Beneventum, battle of (275 B.C.), 151
Bessus, 123
Bestia, Lucius Calpurnius, 171
Bithynia, 179, 229
Bocchus, 172
Boeotia, 51, 65, 84, 85, 89, 94, 95, 109
Boeotian League, 108, 109, 130
Boii, 157
Brasidas, 95
Britain, Roman rule of, 200
Britannicus, 200
Brundisium, 174
Bruttium, 141
Brutus, Decimus Junius, 187, 188
Brutus, Marcus Junius, 187, 188
Bucolics (Vergil), 197
Burrus, 200, 212
Byblos, 27, 38
Byzandum, 113
Byzantium, Megarian colony of, 232

C

Caelian, 144
Caere, 143
Caesar, Gaius, 196
Caesar, Julius
    assassination of, 187
    and civil war, 185–186
    conflict between Pompey and, 184–
        185
    and conquest of Gaul, 183–184
    as Consul, 182
    and crisis of 56 B.C., 183
    dictatorship of, 186–187
    as historian, 190

Caesar (cont'd)
    reforms of, 187
    rise of, 180–181
Caesar, Lucius, 196
Calah, 42
Caligula, 199, 202
Callicrates, 104
Callimachus of Cyrene, 133
Cambyses, 45, 47
Campania, 141, 150
Canuleian Law, 154
Cape Actium, 189
Cape Artemisium, 85
Capitoline, 144
Cappadocia, 199
Capua, 150
Caracalla (Marcus Aurelius Antoninus),
        220, 221, 222
Carchemish, 38, 42, 46
Carinus, 229
Carneades of Cyrene, 136
Carthage, 38, 161
    defeat of, 87
    and Punic Wars with Rome, 155–159
Carthaginians, 87
Carus, Titus Lucretius, 189
Cassander, 125, 126
Cassius, Avidius, 210–211
Cassius, Gaius, 188
    and assassination of Caesar, 187
Cassius, Quintus, 185
Catilina, Lucius Sergius, 181
Catilinarian conspiracy, 181, 183
Cato, Marcus Porcius, 163, 181, 182,
        183
Cato the Elder, 161, 163
Catullus, Gaius Valerius, 189
Caudine Forks, 150
Cayster River, 44
Censors, in Roman Republic, 152
Centuriate Assembly, in Roman
        Republic, 153
Cerealis, 202
Chadwick, John, 54
Chaeronea, 113
Chalcidian League, 112
Chalcidice, 62, 93, 111
Chalcis, 62
Chaldeans, 40, 42, 46
Chandragupta, 129
Charun, 143–144
Chios, 89
Choephoroi (Aeschylus), 100
Chremonides, 131
Christianity, 225
    establishment of, 233–234
Cicero, Marcus Tullius, 178–179, 183,
        188, 190
Cimbri, 172

Cimmerians, 42, 45
Cimon, 88
Cinna, Lucius Cornelius, 173–174
Cirta, 171
Cisalpine Gaul, 182, 185, 188
City of God (St. Augustine), 238
City states
  in Greece, 61, 62
  of Sumerians, 14–15
Civilis, 202
Civil War (Lucan), 212–213
Claudian, 238
Claudii, 167
Claudius, 200
Claudius (II) Gothicus, 223
Cleisthenes, 65, 70–71
Cleombrotus, 109
Cleomenes, 70
Cleomenes III, 131
Cleon, 94–95
Cleopatra, 185, 188, 189
Clodius, Clodia, 182
Clodius, Publius, 182–183, 184
Clouds (Aristophanes), 101
Cnidus, 108
Cnossus, 51, 52, 53
Colline Gate, battle at (82 B.C.), 174
Colosseum, 214
Commagene, 203
Commentaries (Julius Caesar), 190
Commodus, 216, 219
Communication, 8
Conon, 98, 108
Constans, 234
Constantine, 231, 232–233
Constantine II, 234
Constantinople, 232
Consuls, in Roman Republic, 152
Corbulo, 201
Corcyra, 92, 93
Corfinium, 173
Corinth
  and Corinthian War, 108
  and Dorian invasions, 71
  Gulf of, 92
  Isthmus of, 86
  League of, 113, 121
  and Macedonian War, 111
  as member of Peloponnesian League, 107
  in Mycenaean world, 54
  and Peloponnesian War, 92, 93, 94, 95
  and Syracuse, 62, 111
  tyranny in, 64–65
Corinthian order, 118, 137
Corinthian War, 108
Cornelii, 167
Coronea, battle at, 89

Corsica, 141, 157
Council of Five Hundred, 71, 91
Council of the Areopagus, 89, 91
Crassus, Marcus Licinius, 178, 208
Crete, chronology of, 51–52
Critias, 98
Croesus (Lydians), 45
Cro-Magnon Man, 4
Ctesiphon, 208, 211
Culture. *See specific type*
Cumae, 62, 142
Cunaxa, 108
Cuneiform, 13
Cyaxeres (Medes), 46
Cybele, 224
Cyclades Islands, 51, 56, 57
Cylon, 68
Cynics, 115
Cynoscephale, battle of (197 B.C.), 160
Cyprus, 89
Cypselus, 64–65
Cyrenaics, 115, 135
Cyrene, 62, 126
Cyrus the Persian, 40, 45, 47, 108
Cyzicus, 97

D

Dacia, 207–208, 209
Daia, Maximinus, 230
Damascus, 38, 39, 40, 42
Darius I, 47, 83–84
Darius II, 108
Darius III, 122, 123
Datis, 84
David, 40
Decebalus, 206–207
Decelea, 97
Decimus, 188
Decius, 225
Delian League, 88, 89, 93
De Lingua Latina (Varro), 190
Delos, 51, 56, 84, 88, 131, 132
Delphi, oracle at, 64, 77
Delphic Amphictyony, 112, 130
Demeter, 136
Demetrius I, 132
Demetrius of Phaleron, 125–126
Demetrius of Pharos, 157
Demetrius Pohorcetes, 126
Democracy, in Greece, 70–71, 90–92, 97–98
Democritus, 102
Demosthenes, 95, 112, 114–115
De Rerum Natura (Carus), 189
De Re Rustica (Varro), 190
Description of the Earth (Hecataeus), 76
Destruction of Troy (Polygnotus), 103
Dialogues (Plato), 115

Dialogues (Seneca), 212
Dimini, 51
Diocletian, 225, 229–231
Diogenes, 115
Dionysius I, 110–111
Dionysius II, 111, 116
Dionysus, 136
  theater of, 99
Dioscurides of Samos, 137
Djoser, 26, 30
Domitian, 203–204, 206, 209, 215
Domitianic Palaces, 214
Domna, Julia, 221, 222
Dorian invasions, 57, 59, 71, 142
Doric order, 79, 104
Draco, 68
Drama
  in Greece, 75, 98–101, 117
  Hellenistic, 133–134
Drusus, 196, 199
Drusus, Marcus Livius, 170, 172–173
Dumuzi, 17, 37
Dyscolos (Menander), 133–134

E

Eclogues (Vergil), 197
Economus, 157
Edictum Perpetuum, 216
Egypt, 22
  administration in, 27
  Alexander the Great in, 123
  art in, 29–30
  cult of the dead in, 29
  decline of central authority in, 26
  end of empire in, 35–36
  geography and climate of, 22
  Germanicus entry into, 199
  Hyksos domination of, 28
  literature in, 30
  Ma'at in, 25, 29
  Middle Kingdom in, 27
  New Kingdom in, 32, 34–35
  Old Kingdom in, 24–26
  pharaoh in, 25
  political and social life in, 25–26
  Ptolemaic Kingdom of, 126–128
  pyramids in, 30
  religion in, 25, 28–29
  Saite Kingdom of, 45
  and trade, 27
  unification of, 22, 24
Elagabalus, 222
Elam, 12, 48
Elamites, 17, 18
Elbe, 195
Elements (Euclid), 135
Elijah, 41
Elymians, 62

Empedocles of Acragas, 102
Enki, 17
Enlil, 17
Ennius, Quintus, 162
Epaminondas, 109, 110, 111
Ephialtes, 89
Epicureanism, 135
Epicurus of Athens, 135
Epidamnus, 92
Epidaurus, 118
Epigrams (Martial), 213
Epistles (Horace), 197
Epistles (Seneca), 212
Epodes (Horace), 197
Eratosthenes of Cyrene, 134
Erechtheum, 104
Erechtheus, 77
Eretria, 83, 84
Eridu, 14
Esarhaddon, 42, 45
Esquiline, 144, 145
Eteocles, 213
Etruria, 181
Etruscans, 62, 142–144
Euboea, 84
Euclid of Alexandria, 135
Eumenides (Aeschylus), 100
Eummenes I, 132
Euphrates River, 11, 18
Euripides, 100
Eurybiades, 85
Evagoras (Isocrates), 114
Evans, Arthur, 51
Ezekiel, 41
Ezra, 41

F

Fertile crescent, geography of, 11
Fimbria, Flavius, 174
First Triumvirate, 182–184
Flaccus, Quintus Horace (Horace), 197
Flamininus, Titus Quinctius, 160
Flavian emperors, 202–204
Fortunata, 213
Frogs (Aristophanes), 101

G

Gabinius, Aulus, 180
Gaius, 199, 216
Galatia, 195
Galba, 201, 202
Galen, 213
Galerius, 231
Gallic invasions, 149–150, 170
Gallus, 234
Gaul, 215, 223, 236

Gellius, Aulus, 213
Gelon, 87
Gemellus, Tiberius, 199
Genealogies (Hecataeus), 76
Georgics (Vergil), 197
Germanicus, 199, 200
Geta, 222
Getae, 121
Gilgamesh, 18
Gizeh, 30
Glaucia, Gaius Servilius, 172
Golden Ass (Arbiter), 213
Golden House of Nero, 214
Gordium, 44, 122
Gracchus, Gaius, 169–170
Gracchus, Tiberius, 168–169
Greece. *See also* Athens; Sparta
    Aetolian League in, 130–131
    architecture in, 79, 118
    art in, 103–104, 117–118
    city states in, 61
    colonies of, 62, 64, 90
    culture in, 74–79, 98–104, 114–118
    decline of, 110
    and defeat of Carthage, 87
    democracy in, 90–92, 97–98
    drama in, 98–101, 117
    Hellenistic period. *See* Hellenistic
        Greece
    historical writings in, 75–76,
        101–102, 115
    Ionian revolt in, 82–83
    literature in, 60–61, 74–75, 98–101
    Middle Age in, 59–61
    painting in, 117
    Peloponnesian War in, 92–98
    under Pericles, 89–92, 104
    Persian wars in, 83–87
    philosophy in, 76–77, 102–103,
        115–117
    reawakening and evolution of, 61–65
    religion in, 77–78
    rise of Athenian imperialism, 87–88
    Roman conquest of, 150–151,
        159–161
    sculpture in, 79, 118
    Spartan hegemony, 107–109
    Theban hegemony, 109–110
Gudea, 17
Guti, 17
Gyges, 44

H

Habiru, 39
Hacilar, 7
Hadrian, 208–210
    villa of, 214
Halafian settlements, 7

Halicarnassus, 118
Halys River, 36
Hammurabi, 19
    code of, 19
Hannibal Barca, 158–159
Harmhab, 35
Hasdrubal, 159
Hassuna, 7, 41
Hathor, 29
Hatshepsut, 32, 34
Hatti, 36
Hattusas, 36, 37
Hattusilis II, 35
Hattusilis III, 37
Hebat, 37
Hebrews, 39
    destruction of, 40
    kingdoms of, 40
    land of, 39–40
    religion of, 41
Hecataeus of Miletus, 76
Hecatompylos, 123
Helen, 55
Hellenica (Xenophon), 115
Hellenic League, 130
Hellenistic Greece
    under Alexander the Great, 121–125
    Antigonid kingdom in, 130–131
    birth of kingdoms, 125–126
    culture of, 132–137
    Pergamum in, 132
    Ptolemaic kingdom in, 126, 128
    Rhodes in, 132
    Seleucid kingdom in, 129
Helleno-Christian Byzantine Empire,
    236
Helots, in Sparta, 72, 73, 107
Hera, 77, 163
    Temple of, 79
Heraclea, battle of (280 B.C.), 151
Heracleitus of Ephesus, 77, 102
Hermus River, 44
Hernici, 147, 149
Herodotus, 84, 87, 101, 115
Herophilus of Chalcedon, 134
Hesiod, 74
Hiempsal, 171
Hiero, 155
Hieronymus of Cardia, 133
Himera, battle of (480 B.C.), 87
Hipparchus, 70, 134–135
Hippias, 70, 83–84
Hippocrates, 102
Hippodamus, 137
Hiram, 38, 40
Histiaeus, 83
Histories (Tacitus), 213
Historical writings
    in Greece, 75–76, 101–102, 115

Historical writings (*cont'd*)
  Hellenistic, 133
  Roman, 213
History (Herodotus), 101
History (Livy), 198
History of the Peloponnesian War
  (Thucydides), 101–102
Hittites, 19, 35, 36–37
Homer, 54, 55, 60–61, 75, 116, 122, 133
Homo neanderthalensis, 2
Homo sapiens, 2, 4
Horace (Quintus Horace Flaccus), 197
Hortalus, Quintus Hortensius, 179
Hortensian Law, 154
Horus, 29
Hurrians, 36, 38, 39, 42
Hyksos, 28, 32

I

Iamblicus, 225
Iazyges, 211
Ictinus, 104
Ideograms, 13
Idylls (Theocritus), 133
Iliad (Homer), 54, 55, 60–61, 71, 74,
  75, 133
Ilium, 122
Illyricum, 182, 195
Imperioal Forums, 214
Inanna, 17
India, Alexander the Great in, 123, 125
Insubres, 157
Ionian revolt, 82–83
Ionians, 57
Ionic order, 79
Ipsus, battle of (301 B.C.), 126
Isagoras, 70–71
Isis, 29, 224
Isocrates, 114
Issus, battle of (333 B.C.), 122–123
Italy. *See also* Roman Empire; Roman
    Republic; Rome
  Etruscans in, 142–144
  geography of, 141
  prehistory, 142

J

Jarmo, 7
Jemdet-Nasr, 13
Jeremiah, 41
Jericho, 7, 38
Jerusalem, 40, 46
  Roman control of, 209
Jezebel, 41
Judah, 40
Juba (Numidia), 186

Judaea, 199, 202, 209
Judah, 40, 42, 46
Jugurtha, 171, 172
Julia (daughter of Caesar), 182, 184
Julian ("the Apostate"), 234, 235
Julianus, Didus, 220
Julii, 167
Julio-Claudian emperors, 196, 198–201,
  230
Juno, 146, 163
Jupiter, 146, 163
Justinian, 236
Juvenal, 166, 213

K

Kadesh, 37, 38
Karnak, 35
Kassites, 19
Khafre, 30
Khufu, 30
Kish, 14, 16

L

Lacedaemon, 71
Laconia, 51, 65, 72
Lagash, 16, 17
Lake Regillus, battle of (493 B.C.), 147
Lamachus, 96
Lamian War, 125, 131
Larsa, 14
Lascaux cave paintings, 4
Latifundia, 166–167
Latin League, 147, 149
Latins, 144
Latium, 141
Laurium, 85
Laws
  code of Hammurabi, 19
  Roman, 154, 167, 173, 216
Laws (Plato), 116
Lemnos, 108
Leonidas, 85–86
Lepidus, Marcus Aemilius, 177, 188
Leptis Magna, 221
Lesbos, 89, 94–95
Letters (Cicero), 190
Leucippus of Miletus, 102
Leuctra, battle of (371 B.C.), 109
Lex Julia, 173
Libya, 62
Libyan Desert, 22
Licinian-Sextian Laws, 154, 167
Licinius, 231, 232
Lilybaeum, 157
Linear A language, 53
Linear B writing, 52, 54

Literature
  in Egypt, 30
  in Greece, 60–61, 74–75, 98–101
  Hellenistic, 132–133
  Hittite, 37
  Roman, 162–163, 189, 197–198,
    212–214, 238
  Sumerian, 18
Livia, 196
Livius, Titus (Livy), 144, 198
Longus, Tiberius Sempronius, 158
Lower Egypt, 22, 35–36
Luca conference, 184
Lucan, 212–213
Lucanians, 62, 151
Lucian of Samosata, 213
Lucullus, 179, 180, 182
Lugalzaggesi, 16
Lugdunum, 221
Lyceum School, 116
Lydians, 42, 44–45
Lyric poets, in Greece, 75
Lysander, 97, 98, 107
Lysias, 114
Lysimachus, 125, 126, 129, 132
Lysippus, 118
Lysistrata (Aristophanes), 101

M

Ma'at, concept of, 25, 29
Macedonia, 111, 131
  Celtic (Gallic) invasions of, 126
  under Philip II, 111–113
Macedonian War
  first, 159–160
  fourth, 160–161
  second, 160
  third, 160
Macer, 201
Macrinus, 222
Macrobius, 238
Maesa, Julia, 222
Magdalenian culture, 4
Magi, 48
Magnentius, 234
Mamaea, Julia, 222
Mamertines, 155, 157
Man
  chalcolithic, 7–8
  evolution of, 2
  first modern, 2, 4
  mesolithic, 5
  neolithic, 5, 7, 56, 142
Mandnea, 96
Manetho, 24
Manfinea, 108
Manilius, Gaius, 180
Mantinea, battle of (362 B.C.), 109, 110

Marathon, battle of (490 B.C.), 84
Marcellinus, Ammianus, 238
Marcellus, 196
Marcomanni, 211
Mardonius, 83, 86, 87
Marduk, 19, 42, 46
Mari, 18, 38
Marius, 194
Marius, Gaius, 171–172
Maro, Publius Vergilius (Vergil), 197
Martial, 213
Massilia, 170, 179
Massinissa, 161, 171
Mathematics, Hellenistic, 135
Mauretania, 200
Maxentius, 231
Maximian, 229, 230
Maximum Prices, Edict of, 230
Maximus, Jupiter Optimus, 195
Maximus, Quintus Fabius, 158
Medea (Euripides), 100
Medes, 42, 46, 47
Medicine, in Greece, 102
Mediolanum, 229
Meditations (Marcus Aurelius), 210
Megacles, 68
Megalopolis, 109
Megara, 62, 68, 94, 95
Melian affair, 96
Melos, 96
Memorabilia (Xenophon), 115
Menander of Athens, 133
Menerva, 143
Menes, 24
Menkaure, 30
Merneptah, 35, 39
Mesolithic man, 5
Mesopotamia, 11, 208. *See also civilizations in*
Messalina, 200
Messana, 155, 157
Messene, 109
Messenia, 72
Messenian War
   first, 72
   second, 72–73
   third, 89
Metamorphoses (Ovid), 197
Metaurus, battle of (207 B.C.), 159
Metellus, Quintus Caecilius, 171
Micipsa, 171
Milan, Edict of, 232
Miletus, 62, 83
Milo, 184
Miltiades, 84, 88
Minerva, 146, 163
Minoan civilization, 51–52
   cities in, 52–53
   culture in, 53

Minotaur, 53
Mita, 44
Mitanni, 34, 37, 38, 41
Mithra, 48
Mithraism, 225
Mithridates, 131, 173, 174, 178, 179, 180, 185
Mithridatic War, third, 179
Mnesicles, 104
Moesia, 195, 208
Moses, 39, 41
Mount Carmel, 5
Mousterian culture, 2
Mulvian Bridge, battle of the, 231
Mummius, Lucius, 161
Munda, battle of (45 B.C.), 186, 187
Mutina, 188
Mycenae, 71
Mylae, 157
Myron, 103
Mythopoeic development, 8
Mytilene, 95

N

Nabis, 131
Nabonidus, 46, 47
Nabopolassar, 46
Naevius, Gnaeus, 162
Naram-sin, 16
Narbonensis, Gallia, 170, 172, 187
Narmer, 24
Naucratis, 45, 62
Naupactus, 92
Naxos, 56, 88
Neanderthal man, 2
Neapolis, 150
Nearchus, 123
Nebuchadnezzar, 40, 46
Necho, 45
Neo-Babylonians, 40
Neolithic period, 5, 7, 56, 142
Neoplatonism, 225
Nero, Tiberius Claudius, 196, 199, 200–201, 208, 209, 212, 215, 219, 230
Nerva, 206
Nicaea, Council of, 234
Nicias, Peace of (421 B.C.), 95–96
Nicomedes, 179
Nicomedia, 229
Niger, Pescennius, 220, 221
Nile region. *See also* Egypt
   geography and climate of, 22
Nineveh, 42, 46
Ninhursag, 17
Nippur, 17
Nofium, battle of (407 B.C.), 97
Noricum, 195

Nubia, 27, 34
Numerian, 229
Numidia, 171–172
Numidians, 159

O

Ochlocracy, 117
Octavia, 188, 200
Octavian
   versus Antony, 188–189
   arrival in Rome, 188
   as *Princeps*, 193–194
   reforms under, 194–196
   in 2nd Triumvirate, 188
Octavius, Gaius, 187–188. *See also* Octavian
Odes (Horace), 197
Odovacar (Odoacer), 236
Odyssey (Homer), 55, 60–61, 74, 133
Oedipus at Colonus (Sophocles), 100
Oedipus the King (Sophocles), 100
Olympias, 125
Olympic games, 77–78
Olynthiacs (Demosthenes), 115
Olynthus, 112
On the Origins of Plants (Theophrastus), 134
On the Successors (Hieronymus), 133
Optimates, 170, 186
Orations (Cicero), 190
Oratorical Instruction (Quintilian), 212
Orchomenus, 110
Oresteia trilogy (Aeschylus), 99
Orontes River, 38, 129
Orthagoras (Greek), 65
Osiris, 25, 29, 37
Osroes, 208, 209
Ostia, 180
Ostrogoths, 236
Otho, 202
Ovid, 197

P

Painting. *See also* Art
   in Greece, 103, 117
   Hellenistic, 136–137
   Roman, 190, 198, 214
Palatine, 144
Palestine, 34
Palestinian Natufians, 5
Palmyra, 223
Panaetius, 136, 163
Panegyricus (Isocrates), 114
Pangaeus, Mount, 112
Panion, 128
Pannonia, 195, 222

Panormus, 157
Paris, 55
Paros, 84
Parrhasius, 117
Parthenon, 104
Parthia, 184, 195, 208, 209
Patricians, 167
Paullus, Lucius Aemilius, 160
Pausanias, 87–88
Pax Romana, 193–196
Peace of Callias, 89
Peiraeus, 89
Peisistratus, 69–70
Pelopidas, 109
Peloponnesian League, 73, 94, 96, 107,
    130
Peloponnesian War, 107
Peloponnesus, 51
Pepi II, 26
Perdiccas I, 111, 125
Pergamum, 126, 132, 160
Periander, 64–65
Pericles, 89–92, 104
Perinthus, 113
Persephone, 136
Persepolis, 48
Perseus, 160
Persians, 46
    administration of, 47–48
    culture in, 48
    under Cyrus, 47
    under Darius, 47
    Median Kingdom in, 46–47
    religion in, 48
Persian wars, 83–87
Pertinax, 220
Phalerum, 84
Pharaohs, in Egypt, 25. *See also specific*
Pharnaces, 185
Pharos Lighthouse, 137
Pharsalus, 185
Pheidias, 103
Pheidippides, 84
Philip II, 111, 116, 121
Philip III Arrhidaeus, 125
Philip V, 129, 130, 157, 159
Philippics (Demosthenes), 115
Philippus (Isocrates), 114
Philistines, 39, 40
Philocrates, Peace of (346 B.C.), 112
Philosophy
    in Greece, 76–77, 102–103, 115–117
    Hellenistic, 133, 135–136
    Roman, 163, 212, 225
Philoxenus of Eretria, 136
Phocis, 112
Phoenicians, 38, 142
Phonograms, 13
Phrygians, 42, 44

Pictogram, 13
Pictor, Quintus Fabius, 163
Pindar, 99, 122
Piso, 202
Pithecanthropus erectus, 2
Pittacus, 75
Pius, Antoninus, 210
Pius, Metellus, 177–178
Plague, in Greece, 94
Plataea, 84, 94
    battle of (479 B.C.), 87
Plato, 111, 115–116, 225
Plautus, Titus Maccius, 163
Plebians, 167
Pliny the Elder, 213
Pliny the Younger, 213
Plotina, 208–210
Plotinus, 225
Plutus (Aristophanes), 117
Poetry, Hellenistic, 133
Politics (Aristotle), 117
Polybius of Megalopolis, 133
Polycleitus, 103, 198
Polycrates of Samos, 65, 75
Polygnotus of Thasos, 103
Polynices, 213
Pompeii, 203
Pompeius, Sextus, 187
Pompeius, Gnaeus (Pompey), 182
    conflict between Julius Caesar and,
        184–185
    in first triumvirate, 182–184
    flight of, 185
    rise of, 177–178
    triumph of over pirates and
        Mithridates, 180
Pontus, 173
Populares, 170, 173–174
Porphyry, 225
Porus, 123
Poseidon, 54
Postumus, 223
Potidaea, 62, 93
Pottery
    in Greece, 78, 103
    Neolithic, 7
Praetors, in Roman Republic, 152
Praxiteles, 118, 137
Priam, 55
Priscus, Tarquinius, 146
Propertius, 197
Propylaea, 104
Protagoras of Abdera, 99
Psammeticus I, 45
Ptolemy, Claudius, 213
Ptolemy I, 125, 128
Ptolemy I Soter, 126
Ptolemy II, 126
Ptolemy II Philadelphus, 128

Ptolemy III Euergetes, 128
Ptolemy IV Philopater, 128
Ptolemy XIII, 185
Ptolemy XIV, 185
Pumpkinification of Claudius (Seneca),
    212
Punic War
    first, 155, 157, 167
    second, 158–159, 170
    third, 161, 171
Pydna, battle of (148 B.C.), 160
Pylos, 54, 71, 95
Pyramids, Egyptian, 25, 30
Pyrrhic War, 155
Pyrrhus, 151
Pythagoras, 76, 225
Pythagoreans, 76

Q

Qarqar, 40
Quadi, 211
Quaestors, in Roman Republic, 152
Quintilian, 212
Quirinal, 144, 145

R

Ramses II, 35, 37, 39
Ramses III, 39
Raphia, 128
Raphida, battle of (217 B.C.), 128
Re, 25, 27, 28, 34
Red Sea, 22
Regulus, Marcus Atilius, 157
Rehoboam, 40
Religion
    in Chalcolithic period, 7–8
    for Cro-Magnon man, 4
    in Egypt, 25, 28–29
    Etruscan, 143–144
    in Greece, 77–78
    Hebrew, 41
    Hellenistic, 136
    Hittite, 37
    Mycenaean, 54
    Persian, 48
    Roman, 146, 154–155, 163, 195,
        224–225
    Sumerian, 14, 17
Remedies of Love (Ovid), 197
Republic (Plato), 116
Rhaetia, 195
Rhetoric, 114
Rhodes, 126, 131, 132, 160
Roman Empire, 233. *See also* Roman
        Republic; Rome
    agriculture in, 215–216

Roman Empire (*cont'd*)
anarchy in, 201–202, 220
art in, 198, 214, 224, 238
chaos in, 223
Christianity in, 233–234
under Commodus, 219
under Constantine the Great, 232–233
under Diocletian, 229–231
fall of, 236
under five good emperors, 206–211
Flavian emperors in, 202–204
historical writings in, 213
industry in, 215
interregnum, 231
under Julian, 235
Julio-Claudian emperiors in, 196,
198–201
literature in, 197–198, 212–214, 238
Pax Romana in, 193–196
philosophy in, 212, 224
provinces of, 195–196
religion in, 224–225
social life in, 215
under sons of Constantine, 234
under Theodosius I, 236
under the Severans, 220–223
under Valentinians, 235
Roman Republic. *See also* Roman
Empire; Rome
art of, 163, 190
ascendancy of populares, 171–172
under Caesar, 180–181, 184, 186–187
Catilinarian plot in, 181
under Cicero, 178–179
civil war in, 185–186
conflict between Pompey and Caesar,
184
conquests of, 147, 150–151, 159–161
under Crassus, 178
culture of, 162–163, 189–190
destruction of Veii, 149
end of, 187–189
establishment of, 146–147
estates in, 166–167
under first triumvirate, 182–184
foreign entanglements of, 167–168
Gallic invasions, 149–150, 170
Gracchi reforms, 168–170
laws in, 154
literature of, 162–163
in North Africa, 171
Patricians and Plebeians in, 154, 167
philosophy of, 163
political life in early, 151–155
under Pompey, 177–178, 180
provinces of, 161–162
and Punic Wars, 155–159
religion in, 154–155, 163
second triumvirate in, 188

Roman Republic (*cont'd*)
social war in, 172–173
under Sulla, 173–175
and third Mithridatic War, 179
Rome. *See also* Roman Empire; Roman
Republic
kingdom of, 145–146
political life in, 146
religion in, 146
settlement of, 144–145
social life in, 145
Romulus, 144
Roxane, 123, 125
Rubicon River, 185

S

Sabina, Poppaea, 200, 202
Saguntum, 158
Sahara Desert, 22
St. Augustine, 238
St. Jerome, 238
St. Paul, 225
Saite Kingdom of Egypt, 45
Sakkarah, 30
Salamis, battle of (480 B.C.), 86
Samaria, 42
Samnite Wars, 150
Samos, 65, 76
Samuel, 40
Sardinia, 141, 157
Sardis, 44–45, 47, 83
Sargon I, 16
Sargon II, 16, 42
Sarmizegethusa, 208
Satires (Juvenal), 213
Saturnalia (Macrobius), 238
Saturnian verse, 162
Saturninus, Lucius Apuleius, 172
Satyricon (Arbiter), 213
Saul (Hebrew), 40
Schliemann, Heinrich, 55
Science
in Greece, 102
Hellenistic, 134–135
Roman, 213–214
Sumerian, 18
Scipio (Africanus), 159
Scipio, Publius Cornelius, 158
Scopas, 118
Scribonia, 196
Sculpture. *See also* Art
in Greece, 79, 103–104, 118
Hellenistic, 137
Roman, 190, 198, 214
Scyros, 88, 108
Scythians, 46, 83
Second Triumvirate, 188
Sejanus, 199

Seleucia, 129, 137
Seleucid Kingdom, 128, 129
government in, 129
height and decline of the, 129
Seleucus, 125, 126, 129
Seleucus II, 129
Senate, in Roman Republic, 152–153
Seneca, Lucius Annaeus, 200, 212
Sennacherib, 42
Senusert (Sesostris) III, 27
Serapis, 224
Sertorius, Quintus, 177, 178
Servian reforms, 153
Sesklo, 51
Set, 29
Seti I, 35
Severan emperors, 220–223
Severus, Alexander, 222–223
Severus, Septimius, 220, 221–222
Sextiae, Aquae, 170
Shalmaneser III, 42
Shapur (Sapor) I, 223
Shapur (Sapor) II, 234
Shulgi, 17
Sicans, 62
Sicels, 62
Sicily, 141
Siculus, Diodorus, 133
Sicyon, 65
Silius, Gaius, 200
Simnites, 62
Simon, 88
Sinope, 62
Siphnos, 56
Skepticism, 136
Snefru, 26
Socrates, 102–103
Solomon, 38, 40
Solon, 68–69
Sophists, 98–99, 114
Sophocles, 99, 100
Sparta
and battle of Marathon, 84
under Cleomenes, 70
colonies of, 62, 65
early history, 71–72
in Hellenistic period, 131
Messenian revolt in, 72–73
and Peloponnesian League, 93, 94,
96, 98
tyranny of, 107–109
Spartacus, 178
Sphacteria, 95
Stoicism, 135–136, 163, 210
Suetonius, 201, 213
Suevian, 236
Sulla, Lucius Cornelius, 131, 172,
173–175, 186, 194
Sumer, 11

Sumerians, 12
  art in, 18
  city-state government in, 14–15
  cultural development, 15–16
  dominance of Lagash in, 16
  height of, 17–18
  kings in, 15
  literature of, 18
  religion in, 14, 17
  science in, 18
  social and economic life, 13, 15
  writing in, 13
Superbus, Tarquinius, 147
Suppiluliumas, 35, 37
Susa, 48
Symmachus, 238
Syracuse, 62, 87, 90, 97, 110–111
Syria, 34, 203

T

Tacitus, 166, 201, 213
Tanagra, battle at (457 B.C.), 89
Taras, 62, 72
Tarentines, 151
Tarentum, 150
Tarraconensis, 201
Taurus Mountains, 11
Taxiles, 123
Telepinu, 37
Tell Halaf, 41
Terentius, Publius, 163
Terramarans, 142
Teshub, 37
Tetricus, 223
Teutones, 172
Thales, 76
Thapsus, 186
Thebaid (Lucan), 213
Thebans, 89
Thebes, 27, 65, 95, 107, 108, 112, 121
Themistocles, 83, 86, 88
Theocritus of Syracuse, 133
Theodosius I, 236
Theognis of Megara, 75
Theogony (Hesiod), 74
Theophrastus, 134
Thera, 56
Theramenes, 97
Thermistocles, 84–85
Thermopylae, battle of (480 B.C.), 85–86
Theseus, 53, 65
Thespis, 75
Thessaly, 109, 111, 112
Thirty Years' Peace, 89, 92, 94
Thrace, 83, 90, 111, 112, 200
Thrax, Maximinus, 222

Thucydides, 101–102, 115
Thurii, 90, 151
Thuriians, 151
Thutmose I, 32
Thutmose III, 34
Tiberius, 196, 198–199
Tiber River, 141
Tbullus, 197
Tigellinus, 200
Tiglath-Pileser, 42
Tigranes, 179, 180
Tigris River, 11, 18,
Tikulti-Ninurta I, 42
Timoleon, 111
Tinia, 143
Tiryns, 54
Titus, 202, 203
Toleration, Edict of, 232
Trajan (Marcus Ulpius Trajanus), 206, 208
Transalpine Gaul, 182
Trapezus, 62
Trebia, 158
Tribal Assemblies, in Roman Republic, 153
Triballi, 121
Trimalchio, 213
Troezen, 86
Trojans, 55–56
Trojan Women (Euripides), 100
Troy, 55
True History (Lucian), 213
Trytaeus, 75
Tullius, Servius, 146, 149, 153
Tuscany, 141
Tutankhaton, 35
Twelve Caesars (Suetonius), 213
Twelve Tables, 154, 216
Tyche, 136
Tyre, 38, 61, 123, 155

U

Al-Ubaid, 7
Ugarit, 38
Umbria, 141
Umma, 16
Uni, 143
Universal History (Diodorus Siculus), 133
Upper Egypt, 22, 35–36
Ur, 13, 14, 17
Urartu, 42
Ur-Nammu, 17
Uruk, 13, 14
Urukagina, 16

V

Valerian, 223
Vandals, 236
Varro, Marcus Terentius, 190
Varus, 195
Veii, destruction of, 149
Ventris, Michael, 54
Vercingetorix, 184
Vergil (Publius Vergilius Maro), 197
Verres, Gaius, 179
Verus, Lucius, 210, 211
Vespasian, 202–203
Vesta, 146
Vesuvius, 203
Vetranio, 234
Villanovans, 142
Viminal, 144
Vindex, 201, 202
Visigoths, 223, 236
Vitellius, 202
Vologeses, 208
Vologeses I, 201
Vologeses III, 210
Vologeses IV, 221
Volsci, 147, 149

W

Women, in Sparta, 73
Works and Days (Hesiod), 74, 75
Writing
  Etruscan, 143
  of Sumerians, 13

X

Xenophanes of Colophon, 76
Xenophon, 73, 108, 115
Xerxes, 85, 86, 88

Y

Yahweh, 41

Z

Zagros Mountains, 11, 46, 48
Zama, battle of (202 B.C.), 159
Zela, 185
Zenobia, 223
Zeno of Citium, 135–136
Zeus, 54, 77, 163
Zeuxis, 117
Zoroaster, 48